No More Tiaras

No More Tiaras

(A Memoir of Eight Decades)

Solange Batsell Herter

To order additional copies of this book, contact:
Xlibris Corporation
1-888-795-4274
www.Xlibris.com
Orders@Xlibris.com
71528

For my children and grandchildren, without apologies.

CONTENTS

PREFACE

I never dreamed that writing one's memoir was such an eye-opening way to figure out who you are, and even more surprising, learn how you got to be who you are. The following account (written mainly for my children and grandchildren to read) started out to simply chronicle the colorful mix of our ancestry. I guess I am now the matriarch. You can take that as a qualified statement that I am just getting around to admitting that I am becoming perhaps a tiny bit older and that it's about time I write all this down.

I shall be writing as truthfully as good taste and common sense allow, but I will remind the reader of Winston Churchill's admonition to his readers: "I care not one whit for accuracy. Praise is good enough for me." My feelings exactly.

CHAPTER 1

Family History

Opening lines are hard to come by. My favorite ones are from Mark Twain's "A Dog's Tale":

> My Father was a Saint Bernard
> My mother was a Collie
> But I am a Presbyterian.

I often think of them when I speak of my own pedigree and the response it evokes in others.

> My mother came from Paris, France.
> My father came from Paris, Missouri.

My mother was born in Geneva, Switzerland, and she was taken to France when she was just a few months old. Her father was a British subject born in France, her mother a French citizen who automatically lost her French citizenship when she married an Englishman. Nevertheless, my grandmother always carried a French passport, and so did my mother, although neither of them had a right to do so. In fact, Mummy had an automatic right to Swiss citizenship, but she never chose that option.

My mother always delighted in being a quasi-outlaw rebel. So I'm positive she derived great satisfaction in flashing her brazenly illicit passport as she crossed most of the world's borders. But she wasn't entirely fearless. One time during the war, she and I were on a train trip from New York to California. J. Edgar Hoover, the paranoid director of the FBI, was also on board. My mother was really taken aback at being so close to this contentious martinet of the law. But since we were confined to the train for a full two-and-a-half days, she decided to make the best of it. Never shy with strangers, on the second day aboard, she swept by Hoover's bodyguards and struck up a conversation with him. He did a double take and said, "Did anyone ever tell you that you look like Dorothy Lamour?"

Though probably shaking in her boots, my mother had the sangfroid to shoot right back, "No. But of course, I always thought Dorothy Lamour looked a lot like *me,*" which I guess shook Hoover up.

As a matter of fact, my mother *did* look a little like the sarong-wearing seductress of the blockbuster Bob Hope and Bing Crosby "Road" movies. And apparently, Hoover, though a not-so-secret transvestite, was entranced with Lamour. Who knows how far that love story ever went? Well, while Dorothy Lamour never admitted that such an affair ever took place, she never denied it either.

My mother on the train
when she met J. Edgar Hoover.
1941.

God knows what else my mother and J. Edgar talked about as the train ate up the miles. But I saw them getting along famously and I'm sure she left America's top sleuth dazzled. I know he always kept in touch. In fact, he arranged once for my mother and Dorothy Lamour to meet and, evidently, they hit it off beautifully!

My parents met in Paris, France, in 1925 when my father was director of the Service d'Affaires Internationales and editor of the monthly review *"European Economic and Political Survey."*

They were introduced at a party given by Colonel Olds, America's then undersecretary of state. My mother had a job at the American Library, and my father's work often brought him there. It seems he would ask her to locate some books or documents on the top bookshelves so he could glimpse at her legs as she climbed up and down the ladder. She did have great legs, and I don't know if that's what led to their engagement; but they were married in Paris on July 11, 1927, at the Mairie de L'Elysée.

But I'm moving much too fast. Let me start at the beginning.

My father was born on January 11, 1902, in Paris, Missouri, and was baptized Russell Walter Batsell. He was the son of George Washington Batsell and Ida Ragsdale Batsell. Paris, Missouri, was a nice town then and remains so today. It's the county seat of Monroe County and sits on the middle fork of the Salt River, smack in the heart of the vast Mississippi Valley. That area was mainly settled by Virginians and Kentuckians, who brought their Southern traditions with them. My Scottish forebears sailed to America in the very early 1800s and chose Kentucky as their initial American home. My great-great-grandfather, Harrison P. Batsell, moved to Paris, Missouri, from *another* Paris, in Kentucky. (He later became a judge.) His was the first brick house built in town.

They named their new town "Paris" in 1831. There's a record of Judge Batsell importing a minute California Redwood tree and planting it in 1832. Today, that tree soars one hundred fifty feet tall and still flourishes.

Paris, Missouri, has a quaint history:

In 1831, the County Court appropriated $3000 for a new courthouse and $100 for a new jail. Both burned down in 1835 but were rebuilt in 1912 and are still in use. In that fire, all the records of births and deaths were destroyed so the only family history we have are my grandfather's notes, painstakingly written out in his own hand. The paper, *The Monroe Appeal*, started as *The Missouri Sentinel* in 1849. In the late 1800s, a log church, the first store, and an opera house were built. In 1880, the town bought several hundred feet of garden hose for fire protection. Then they bought a horse-drawn engine and hose cart. Every night, all twelve streetlights were lit. The Female Seminary and the Male Academy were built in 1850. The high school was the third public school in all Missouri. There were two cigar factories and one hoop pool factory. By 1888, Paris had two thousand five hundred citizens, two banks, a public school, four churches, four hotels, a flourmill, a woolen mill, three shoe stores, a saddlery, and a racket store. (A "racket store" stocked harnesses, reins, lace, boots, lemon juice for freckles, wash pans for panning gold, and, as you've seen in so many western movies, peppermint sticks.) In 1896, ten thousand people poured into Paris to celebrate the Fourth of July. And for a hundred years, the tradition has been kept up on the twenty-two-acre fairgrounds.

Some feisty Irish blood was brought to our gene pool by our ancestor, John Moore, and his wife, Elizabeth. During their fruitful union, they produced ten more Moores, namely Caldwallander, William, George, John, Ruben, Albert, Matilda, Eliza, Angela, and last but not least, Amanda Moore (Batsell), my great-great-grandmother. On the other side of the family, my grandmother, Ida Ragsdale, was the daughter of Thomas W. Ragsdale and Elizabeth K. Smith Ragsdale. She was born on a farm north of Paris, Missouri.

The Batsell family tree got even branchier when the Batsells moved from Virginia to Kentucky and gave us:

Tom Batsell
Bob Batsell
Jack Batsell
Nat Batsell
Smith Batsell
Sallie Batsell (Taylor)
Susan Batsell (Wall)
Betsy Batsell (Summers)

That's a lot of Batsells. There were black Batsells too. That's because in olden times, slaves often took up the surname, or even the first name, of their master. So there was a black George Washington Batsell, a black Walter Batsell, a black Raymond Batsell . . . and so on. To my surprise, there was even a black Solange Batsell. I never met her, but I commiserated with her. With all the troubles I had with people struggling to pronounce my name, what must *she* have gone through?

Back in the mid-30s, Paris, Missouri, counted only one Jew amongst the populace. I never knew his name, because he was always referred to simply as "the Jew." I don't think back then that was pejorative but simply a convenient tag. And I mention it because I think it is of historic interest. I wonder what got him there and what he did. I remember hearing he had no family to speak of. It must have been a very lonely existence for him.

My paternal great-great-grandmother was born Anne Sidener. According to family legend, all Sideners from Germany are related. Her father, Jacob, was a farmer. He married Polly Lydick, also from good old Lutheran German stock. They emigrated, first to Bourbon then to Fayette County, Kentucky. Jacob was an enthusiastic stockbreeder and delighted in his purebred herds. He was a devout member of a sect called "The Disciples." Although he was poorly educated and reported to be "very nervous," he had a good head for business. His two children were smart and were sent on to college. One to become a teacher, the other, a preacher. Along with his brains, Jacob also passed on to them his broad forehead, black eyes, and a shock of unruly hair. He was not only wealthy for those days but noted for being generous to a fault.

The old Batsell homestead was about five miles out of town. When he was a boy, my father trudged those five miles at dawn to reach his one-room schoolhouse then hurried five miles back home to do his farm chores before daylight failed.

The Batsells owned huge tracts of rich farmland back then. In his obituary, my grandfather was described as a "well-to-do gentleman farmer from an old renowned family." My father sold off his share of that land when he went to the University of Missouri. Then in 1988, I sold the share my grandfather left me to a cousin, Donald Poore, so the land would stay in the family. It was appraised at $89,000, and the terms were 20 percent down, 9 percent interest over ten years. I still feel a little sad about selling it, but I was tired of coping with sorghum deficiency payments, commodity certificates, and endless letters from the State of Missouri pestering me regarding inlets for underground outlets, demands from the Quincy Soybean Company, and bills for Stauffer feed and, besides, I was glad to get the cash. (For sentimental reasons, I held on to one acre. My tax on that little acre has soared to a staggering $8.81 for 2009!) I gladly pay that tax because that acre is still fertile and produces a crop of soybeans and corn. It also gives me a warm feeling to know that if worse came to worst, there's a safe tiny corner of the world I could retreat to where I can take care of the soil, or the soil care for me, in peace as it did for my forefathers. But the original homestead remains in the family of my first cousin, Harold Batsell.

In those long-ago days, no family was complete without a copy of the Good Book. As it passed down through the generations, it became an irreplaceable document of family history. I inherited my father's Bible. Unfortunately, none of the family births, marriages, or deaths are recorded in it. The venerable tome was presented to my grandfather in 1869 by his teacher, who misspelled his favorite student's name. He inscribed it to George Washington Batsel, with just one lonely "l." Nevertheless, it is an

The Batsell homestead
Paris, Missouri.
Circa 1930.

important document in our family. It is also the only family Bible extant. Why it was passed to my father, the youngest son, I have no idea. By tradition, it goes to the oldest son with children. That would have been my Uncle Raymond, then down from him to his oldest son, Raymond, Jr.

I wasn't thinking about all this when I turned over our Bible to my son, Marc, a few years ago. As my only son, I thought of Marc as the head of the family, but of course he is not the head of the Batsell family; and I hope that, in turn, he will give it back to the head of the Batsell family where it belongs.

After my father's oldest brother, Uncle Roger, died his wife, my wonderful Aunt Grace, was sequestered in a nursing home. I went to see her and brought Marc with me, which was no fun (poor old people sitting in front of blank TV screens, etc.) To change the somber tone of that visit, I took Marc on to the Winston Churchill Memorial and Library at Fulton, Missouri. This was the site of Churchill's world-altering "Iron Curtain" speech. An English friend of mine, Joe Studholme, had had the Holbein portraits of the court of Henry VIII (from the Royal Collection at Windsor Castle) reproduced in very special *à-la-poupée* portfolios and had asked me to be the sole representative for them in the United States and Canada. I had arranged for them to be exhibited at the Winston Churchill Library in Fulton, Missouri, on the grounds of Westminster College.

We got there in time for the cutting of the ribbon, and it was very exciting. Thirty percent of the sale price was tax deductible, and that encouraged buyers. The library made a lot of money, and so did I. I sold quite a few of the portfolios to acquaintances and friends, one of whom was William Polk Carey, who decorated his offices entirely around the thirty-six engravings he hanged on his walls at Rockefeller Center, which was and is still quite an impressive sight. Nelson Rockefeller also bought a set.

What made a lot more money for the Memorial was when, ten years or so later, my friend, Edwina Sandys, Winston Churchill's granddaughter, installed sections of the Berlin Wall on the grounds of Westminster College in memory of her grandfather. It was a ceremony I also attended.

The one hundred fifty-five-kilometer-long Berlin Wall came down on November 9, 1989. The East Berlin government offered the four-foot wide sections of the wall for between $60,000 and $200.000 a piece. Edwina met with the powers that be in East Berlin and persuaded them to donate eight sections to the Winston Churchill Memorial and Library in Fulton. They did, after she reminded them that the French government had "given" the Statue of Liberty to the United States—so why wouldn't they give the United States eight pieces of concrete? Speaking of the Statue of Liberty, it's strange to think that it was built in 1885 by the sculptor, Bartholdi, rue de Chazelles, in Paris, just one block away from my apartment, rue Georges Berger (see photo).

The Statue of Liberty in Paris studio of sculptor Bartholdi.

The sections she selected were originally located in an area frequented by artists near the Brandenburg gate. And so it was that on November 9, 1990, near a statue of Churchill, "Breakthrough" was unveiled by ex-President Reagan. Edwina had the silhouettes of two human abstract human figures cut into the eight-inch-thick concrete "to show there was freedom to pass through." Visitors can use the cutouts as passageways through the sculpture, which is thirty-two feet long and weighs sixteen tons.

Mark Twain,
me, and Aunt Grace.
Hannibal, Missouri.

With cousin Harold Batsell on the farm in
Paris, Missouri.
Circa 1970.

It had divided Berlin for almost three decades and has been called the most important monument to be constructed on American soil.

A little bit of history: Near the end of World War II but before the election that everyone knew must follow V.E. Day, Churchill had fallen out of favor, and *The Times* of London suggested he resign his post as Prime Minister. He didn't resign but lost the election of 1945. Clementine Churchill, trying to think of something to say that might console her husband, looked at the returns and concluded that it might well be a blessing in disguise. Evidently, the old lion turned to his wife and said, "At the moment, it seems quite effectively disguised!"

His spirits must have soared when President Truman invited him to Fulton, Missouri, to give a talk at Westminster College. It was there on March 5, 1946, that he coined the phrase "The Iron Curtain," in his speech, which was titled "The Sinews of Peace":

> "From Stettin in the Baltic to Trieste in the Adriatic, an iron
> curtain has descended across the continent . . ."

The reaction the speech provoked was anything but peaceful. Newspapers on both sides of the Atlantic rushed to brand its author a warmonger. Harry Truman knew better, and the people of Missouri were highly pleased with Churchill's visit.

I also took my daughter, Mary, to Paris, Missouri, and a strange thing happened. We were taken by my cousin Harold's wife, Wanda, and shown the family tombs. What really shook us up was what she told us happened at the grave of her baby, Mary June, who died at birth. On what would have been Mary June's sixteenth birthday, Wanda baked a cake for her and sat there with it under the tree that shaded the tomb. She lit sixteen candles, made a wish, blew out the candles, and then ate the cake all by herself. Pretty poignant!

Edwina Sandys, Churchill's granddaughter

Berlin Wall segment

At the Holbein exhibit in Fulton, Mo.

Henry VIII

Daily News Article by Aileen Mehle known as Suzy
SUZY
Pasts and presents, great and small

HAVE YOU HEARD about art connoisseur Solange (Mrs. Frederic) Herter's fascinating new project? The lovely lady is marketing a stunning portfolio of 36 colored engravings of the Holbein portraits of Henry VIII and his family and friends, the originals are in Windsor Castle in the royal collection.

The portfolio was first published during the time of the Prince Regent in 1812, and then the copper plates were lost, only to be rediscovered hidden under a press in a London printing office. After the new hand colored edition, limited to 175 impressions, is published, the portfolio will be returned to the British Museum.

Solange has the colored engravings hanging in her spacious apartment at the Dakota for private viewing by friends, but in late January there will be a charity exhibit at a leading New York gallery before Henry VIII and friends move on for a showing at the Winston Churchill Memorial and Library in Fulton, Mo., and finally to Calgary, Alberta, the new all capital of the West.

Among those who are already proud owners of the engravings are Mrs. Calvin Plimpton, Guggenheim heir Michael Wettaeh and movie director Peter Yates. It's so nice to have a little Holbein around the house.

I had let my driver's license expire. So I had to ask Mary to use her license to rent a car at the St. Louis airport. I think that's the first time I ever asked a favor from one of my children, and Mary seemed very pleased by my request and proud as a peacock to show her *New York Times* ID.

We drank deliciously of the pure icy waters from the well on Uncle Roger's place. This water was refreshing; it's easy to see why they still draw it from the well. In my grandparents' day, there was no running water inside the house. I can remember lugging those arm-stretching pails from the well up to the house when I stayed with them. The last time I stayed with aunt Grace in her house she took out of the dining room side board three beautiful soup spoons and told me she wanted me to have them because they were part of our family history - they had been made from melted   Kentucky coin silver and had Paris, Kentucky stamped on them. I asked her to please keep them but she insisted I take them. It broke my heart - It was such an abnegation of everything.

My maternal grandfather was Lewis-Clair Panzera. He was born in Antibes, France on February 3, 1867. He died there, very young . . . only 44.

His wife, my grandmother, Jeanne Elise Dawint, was born in Dunkerque, France, on May 11, 1869. She died an extremely long lifetime later, in 1963, in Beaugé (Seine et Marne). Her parents had really impressive names: Emma Elise Noppe Dawint and Julien Symphorien Cornil Dawint. When she was sixteen, my grandmother was sent to Geneva to live with her maternal aunt, Madame Ernans, at the Hotel de Russie, 4 quai du Mont Blanc. Madame Ernans owned the hotel, then the grandest one in Geneva. While studying the piano at Geneva's Conservatoire de Musique, it became time for my grandmother to have her "coming out" and be presented to society. And it was during that glamorous event that she met the young man who became my grandfather. He owned hotels himself, including the Hôtel Suisse in Geneva and the Hotel des Isles d'or in Hyères on the Cap d'Antibes, where my grandparents eventually settled down. (But the Hotel de Russie obviously had a special attraction to my grandmother because she returned there for the birth of her three children.)

My grandfather was very handsome, with languorous, brown eyes; and he must have been very romantic. He certainly had flair. Who else would have had loaded a horse-drawn wagon with thousands and thousands of mimosa blossoms (my grandmother's favorite flower) and sent them across the whole length of France, from Antibes to Dunkerque, to decorate the church for their wedding? The church, l'église St. Eloi, dates back to the fifteenth century, and my grandmother's ancestor, Jean Bart, was buried in the churchyard in 1702.

After turning the church yellow with mimosa, on an icily cold January day, the whole cortège marched a good distance to the town square and liberally festooned Jean Bart's memorial statue with the surplus mimosa blossoms. The statue was magnificently sculpted by the well-known David d'Ange and erected in 1847. It still commands the square, standing tall and proud, surviving World War II, even as every surrounding building was bombed to smithereens.

To me, Jean Bart (or Jan Baert, as his Dutch birth certificate spells his name), is our most fabulous and irresistible ancestor. He was born in Dunkerque in October 21, 1651, the son of a simple fisherman. In his early teens, he joined the Dutch navy under Admiral de Ruyter. But in 1672, when war broke out between Louis XIV and the United Provinces, he switched to the French navy, enlisting as one of the Dunkerque Privateers. Because of his low birth, he didn't at first have a true command in the navy. Instead, he held an irregular sort of commission. Whatever his title, he won great distinction; and his successes won him rapid promotion to lieutenant then captain and finally admiral. And he seemed undefeatable. His historic battles were won during the War of the Grand Alliance. The Grand Alliance was a coalition of England, the Holy Roman Empire, Portugal, Spain, Sweden—most of Europe, in fact. Fed up with the absolutist rule of Louis XIV, they joined to fight a nine-year war against France.

In 1689, as that long war began, Jean Bart and Claude de Forbin, his first mate, were captured by the English and taken to Plymouth. Only three days later, they escaped in a rowboat loaded with twenty other sailors. He soon got himself another boat and got back into the thick of the fighting. He slipped through the Dunkerque blockage and terrorized the Grand Alliance merchant fleet.

So to the French, Jean Bart was a heroic corsair. But to the British, he was a despised and feared pirate. His fast-moving, hard-hitting, and always outnumbered fleet used clever seamanship to outmaneuver the more heavily armed but lumbering English ships. Time and again, he sailed home in triumph, with enemy ships in tow, loaded with priceless plunder of cacao, timber, coal, beans, and wine.

Jean Bart's greatest victory was the Battle of Dogger Bank (1696) when he captured one hundred fifty Dutch ships in a single raging sea fight. This cargo of Baltic grain saved Paris from starvation and guaranteed Jean Bart's immortality. It also prompted Louis XIV to invite him to a royal audience in Versailles. My ancestor left Dunkerque, proudly donned his best togs, and marched into the court, plumes flying, and threw himself into the arms of the astonished monarch. The courtiers were flabbergasted, fearful that the king would have him drawn and quartered for daring to touch His Majesty. Far from it. The "Sun King" embraced him right back, and, on the spot, promoted him to Admiral of the Navy, instantly turning Jean Bart into the First Marine Officer of France. So much for protocol.

But our dashing forefather obviously didn't spend *all* his time at sea. He first married a sixteen-year-old girl, Nicole Gontier from Dunkerque, and quickly sired four children. François Cornil Bart, Anne-Nicole, Jeanne-Nicole, the fourth child, died in childbirth and was never given a name. When Nicole died at age 22, he married Jacoba Tugghe, and *that* union produced ten offsprings: Jeanne-Marie, Antoine, Marie-Françoise, Marie, Magdeleine, Jean-Louis, Paul, Nicoise-Francoise, and Magdeleine-Marie. The tenth and last child also died in childbirth and was never named. And speaking of names, for the past two hundred years, there have been twenty-seven combat ships in the French navy christened with the name Jean Bart. The most recent is an anti-aircraft frigate, which is still in service today.

Jean Bart's first son with Nicole Gontier, François Cornil Bart, became a marine guard at age fourteen, and, like-father, like-son, rose in the ranks and was ultimately dubbed a Rear Admiral by Louis XIV. He was my maternal grandmother's great-great-great-grandfather. (And I can remember my grandmother proudly explaining that Francois was *her* mother's great-*great*

Bust of my ancestor,
Admiral Jean Bart.

Le Capitaine Jean Baert de Dunquerque
La terreur des flottes ennemies sur L'Océan
Paris, Chez Bonny, Bonnart, rue St Jacques, au Coq, avec privil.

Jean Bart
21 October 1651 - 27 April 1702

Portrait by Mathieu Elias

Jean Bart in court attire

grandfather and that his middle name was Cornil, just like her father, who was Julien-Symphonien *Cornil* Dawint.

But let's go back to my grandmother's wedding in Dunkerque. The groom's mother, Madame Louis Panzera, attended it, undertaking the arduous journey from far-off Cannes. So did the bride's maternal grandmother, Madame Noppe, but she had only a few yards to walk to the church from her house. After the ceremony, the bride and groom went home to Hyères, near Antibes, entering into a very comfortable, lavish, lifestyle. But thirteen years later, all this changed almost overnight when my grandfather suddenly died. His hotels were sold, and my grandmother moved to Paris, with three children in tow. They were aged twelve, ten, and eight. She was short of money but long on courage and faith. Uncomplaining, she educated her children properly, sending them to good private schools both in France and England. She somehow managed by working at a woman's exchange called "Chez Pérette," on the rue de Miromesnil, not far from where she lived. This was a place where women of society who had fallen on hard times could bring their needlework or knitting and discretely sell them. My grandmother handled all the arrangements for the ladies. By doing this, she never considered herself "in trade," which would not have been respectable in her book. It was more like charity work, though that word was never used either.

My grandfather may have had a short life, but he had a grandiose and romantic past. The Panzera family was from Naples, Italy, where they lived in the Palazzo Calabretto (de Calabretto is another family name). The impressive palace still stands today on the Posillipo. As a chilling note that brings the past to life, my great-grandmother told my mother how, from her bedroom, she could watch the restive Vesuvius volcano rumbling and sending forth its warning smoke signals. An Englishman, Lord Roseboro, bought it in the late 1800s and renamed it Palazzo Roseboro. Louis Panzera's sister, Augusta Albertina, married Count Giovanni Tarantini and lived in the nearby Palazzo Tarantini, which has also passed on to other hands.

I can trace the European side of our family back to 1766, the year Antonio Panzera was born. Antonio married Mary Ffrench, who came from Ross Common, Ireland. (That's not a typo, the extra "F" tacked onto "French" is a sign of Irish nobility.) At the time, there was much naval traffic and commerce between England and Italy. Wealthy English citizens maintained grand domiciles in Italy where the weather was balmier and more dependable than England's and there were many intermarriages between the two countries as a result.

Antonio and Mary's son, Joseph Panzera, was born in 1795 in Bath, England. He became a British citizen and married a French-Italian noblewoman named Eleonore d'Orazio, who, in 1824, bore them a son, Louis-Jean. Louis-Jean married a French girl, Virginie Gaillard from the Commune du Petit-Bornand in Savoie. They had a son, Lewis-Clair Panzera, my grandfather.

My grandfather was very close to his first cousin, Lieutenant-Colonel Francis W. Panzera, CMG, who became quite famous. He was named Resident Commissioner for the entire Bechuanaland Protectorate in South Africa in 1902 when he was still only a major. The Protectorate was enormous, over seven hundred thousand square kilometers. It had about one hundred twenty-five thousand citizens, out of which only one thousand seven hundred were black. Colonel Panzera settled several boundary disputes in South Africa, fought in the South African War, and survived the endless siege of Mafekeige. But more important than all those details was his partnership with Colonel Baden-Powell in creating a "nice new cannon" to celebrate Majuba day! It could hurl a twenty-five-pound shell crammed with TNT, which inflicted horrible damage. "We baptized it this evening during the Mafekeige battle," they boasted. "'The Wolf' behaved splendidly." The weapon became known as the Panzera cannon, not the Baden-Powell cannon. But Colonel Baden-Powell ensured the continuance of his family name by founding the Boy Scouts, while his wife, not to be outdone, founded the Girl Scouts.

After he left South Africa, Francis Panzera became Commandant of the Alien (or Prisoner-of-War) Detention Camp in Knockaloe on the Isle of Man. With only two thousand four hundred fifty troops, he was in charge of twenty-three thousand prisoners. He ruled fairly and wisely for years and died there; but he was most remembered for his brilliant participation in the Boer War (1899-1902). My mother was fascinated by the Boer War maybe because of him and knew, step by step, how it had been fought. It was quite embarrassing to me that when I applied to Cornell University, she and the Dean of Admissions refought the whole bloody war (supporting the different sides). It's a wonder I was ever accepted or maybe why I was (but I never went).

Strangely enough, my mother kept up a correspondence with the daughters of Francis Panzera: Mary and Augusta. She even traveled to Bath to visit them. They were two prim, proper old maids who sincerely advised my mother to get married as soon as possible to rid herself of the Panzera name. Both these spinsters wished they themselves had taken husbands. "Panzera" was simply too Italian-sounding to the WASP-y society they lived in, I guess.

I got a surprise one day recently when going past Hunter College in New York, I spied in their new art gallery a sign with the name Anthony Panzera. I walked right in and learned that he was the head of the Art Department and taught classes there. When I met him, it was like finding myself face-to-face with my uncle Charles Panzera!

We became friends, and he gave me some photos he had taken in Italy of a bust of Antonio Panzera, a Piazzetta Panzera in Lucce, and a Via Panzera in the town of Goldone in the Provence of Molise, outside the capital, Campo Besso. There's also a World War II monument there, inscribed with many Panzeras, all listed as fallen heroes. I was delighted to learn that Anthony had installed some stained glass windows in St. Mary's Convent in Greenwich, New York, three miles from my house in Battenville. The windows commemorate the Visitation and his wife, Marie Panzera, is the model for the kneeling St. Elizabeth. Just imagine! A kneeling Panzera saint depicted right there in Washington County.

Bust of Antonio Panzera
in Naples, Italy.
1776

Anthony Panzera
in Piazzeta Antonio Panzera.
Naples, Italy
2006

Lieutenant-Colonel
Francis W. Panzera
and his bride.

Lieutenant-Colonel Panzera's
spinster daughter, Mary.

My grandmother,
Jeanne Dawint Panzera.

My grandfather,
Lewis Clair Panzera.

"Les Iles d'or"
in Hyères

My grandfather smoking a water pipe.

My grandmother.

My grandfather with
two musical friends.

My mother
at Hyéres.

My Aunt Jessie,
Uncle Charlie,
and my mother
at Hyéres.

My mother and her Saint Bernard
on the grounds of
"Les Iles d'Or."

The Panzera family and nanny
at the Lavandou beach.

My mother, her sister,
and brother in front
of the gates of
"Les Iles d'or."

A "bilboquet" contest at the school my mother
attended at Hyéres.

She is in the third row on the right,
second from the right.

My grandmother followed by two friends
at foot of the Matterhorn.

Me at the Matterhorn with a member of
the French Olympic Team.

Anthony also does wonderful drawings. In fact, he attends life classes at the Century Association in New York City with my husband, Fred Herter. (Of course, he and Fred are serious about painting . . . not like the old codgers who go there just to ogle the naked models. Oh no . . . not he and Fred.)

Here's something I have never understood: Shortly after he entered college, my father changed his name. He was christened Russell Walter Batsell and suddenly inverted his name into Walter Russell Batsell. In 1921, he began writing as W. Russell Batsell. His loose-leaf binder cover is stamped W. Russell. But on the same cover, written in his bold hand, is Walter Russell Batsell. His Phi Beta Kappa key is stamped Walter R. Batsell, Missouri (December 5, 1923.)

The first two papers he wrote under his new name were: "The Franco-Soviet Negotiations" and "The Treaty of Washington." There is a letter from a Swarthmore professor, Robert C. Brooks, dated October 24, 1923, and addressed to Professor W.R. Batsell at the University of Missouri. The letter asks his advice on a paper by Raymond Buell of Harvard titled "The Mandatory System: An Antidote to Imperialism."

He laid out his advice to Dr. Brooks then composed his own essay, also titled "The Mandatory System," soon published as a book.

During this period, Russell Walter (or Walter Russell) attended both winter and summer sessions, picking up two degrees in only three years instead of the usual four. He graduated with honors and won the very first Louis Beer Prize for his ponderously named but highly readable book "The Mandatory System: Its Historical Background and Relation to the New Imperialism." The Beer Prize, a very regarded award, was given to the author of a new work on European international history.

Come to think of it, maybe my father deserved to call himself two different names because he was accomplishing as much as two ordinary men.

CHAPTER 2

From Missouri to Russia

Then in 1926, he turned out a special report for the *Bulletin of International News* under still another moniker, this time signing himself as "Europa." It was called "The Soviet Slavish Agreement," a lengthy treatise that won great reviews. About this time, my father won a scholarship to Harvard.

There he met Archibald Coolidge. (Dr. Coolidge was the Director of the Widener Library at Harvard. During a dedication ceremony in 1918, it was he who presented the library with the only extant John Harvard book to survive the terrible library fire, which happened on the third Tuesday of July, 1766, ten years before the United States was born. John Harvard's private collection of four hundred books was the foundation of the Harvard Library, which has grown to six hundred fifty thousand, plus the one that Archibald Coolidge turned over that day.)

Professor Coolidge became my father's mentor and encouraged him to write his PhD thesis on Soviet rule in Russia. It was turned into a book by Macmillan and published in 1929. My mother took me to the Library of Congress in Washington DC once and proudly showed me the bookshelf where his book was kept. My father's spoken Russian was extremely fluent, and his use of it, so colloquial that people there usually thought he just came from a different province, not another country. This skill came in handy as he traveled through Russia to do his research.

It seemed he even flummoxed the Ukrainians (whose Russian is spoken with a different accent than in Moscow—the hard "g" becomes a soft Ukrainian "h," and there is a euphonious Ukrainian lilt).

In 1927, he wrote "The Debt Settlements and the Future." In it, he untangles some knotty contractions between the debt funding agreements and the reparation payments. He brings to life the clash of national policies and the cynical play for economic and political advantages (euphemistically called justice, morality, and humanity.) It contrasts the present indebtedness and its awful relationship to war profits measured against the impossibility of ever fulfilling the debt agreements. This muddled financial patch becomes crystal-clear in my father's vivid writing and enlightening details.

His continuous travels in Russia and total mastery of its complex tongues made him an unequaled expert on Russian affairs. He wrote entertainingly, in great detail, of his journeys and took myriads of photographs, many of which were military maps. But these maps never appeared in his thesis. So there was clearly another side to my short-lived father.

Russell Walter Batsell in ROTC uniform.
Paris, Missouri.

Roger Batsell
Raymond Batsell
Russell Batsell

My father on the left and his two brothers.
Paris, Missouri.
(A haberdasher's dream)

Walter Russell Batsell,
University of Missouri.

My father in
a "city" suit on the farm.

My father in his Moscow office.

My father and Ashley Chanler
traveling as "mujiks"
in Russia.

Throughout her life, my mother seemed to be effortlessly and serendipitously in the right place, at the right time.

In 1927, she found herself right in the middle of the awestruck crowd at Le Bourget airfield when Lindberg and his plane "The Spirit of St. Louis" landed. It was nighttime, and there were no electric lights on the field. So everybody held up candles to guide the tiny plane to the ground. She recalled that the "Spirit of St. Louis" was almost smothered by the crowd that fell on the newly nicknamed "Lone Eagle" as he climbed out of the cockpit onto the tarmac and into history and international fame.

Another time she was in an opportune place was when she met Alexander Calder. When my father was working on his PhD at Harvard, she was invited to a tea party given by Henry Wadsworth Longfellow's daughter in Cambridge, Massachusetts, and there she met Alexander Calder and his wife-to-be. Across the room, my mother spied a charmingly unkempt young man. Aside from being rumpled, there was nothing all that special about him except that he was embroidering a giant red "C" on a white bath towel. Nothing ventured, nothing gained, so my mother marched right up and asked him what he was doing. "I'm getting married next week," he said. "And this is my contribution to my bride's trousseau." (Louisa, his bride-to-be, was the niece of Henry James.)

Mummy and Sandy and Louisa Calder soon became fast friends. My father was never that close to the Calders. I guess he was too busy with world affairs to be concerned with mere "artistry." After my father died, the Calders kept in touch with Mummy, both in France and in the United States, during World War II and after. She and I spent many weekends at the Calder place in Roxbury, Connecticut. I never liked staying there. It was too primitive and too rustic. Mary and Sandra, the two Calder daughters, and I slept on the floor on sheepskins. And not only that, none of the doorknobs worked very well. (No wonder! Instead of the usual hardware, each one was a little mobile crafted by Sandy.) Sandy also made all the kitchen utensils in the house because he claimed he couldn't afford to buy them in the local hardware store. I guess there wasn't that much money floating around. I quickly decided the Bohemian life was not for me. Let me be tucked cozily between nicely laundered sheets in a proper bedroom with real knobs on the doors. (Oh, how little I understood.)

When I married for the first time, Sandy gave me a beautiful silver, mobile-like necklace. Unfortunately, he didn't make a habit of it for my ensuing marriages.

To celebrate Calder's seventy-fifth birthday, I was asked to pull together a vast collection of Calder works to tour six countries in South America. Braniff sent me on a veritable red-carpet tour, and I spent six glorious months and God knows how many dollars organizing the shipping of major Calder pieces to various sites, setting up exhibits in museums, galleries, public parks, and private houses.

Working on Calder exhibits
in South America.

One memorable layover was in Machu Picchu. The day before I was scheduled for yet another TV interview, the hairstylist suggested that he darken my hair for better contrast on camera. So I let him give me a rinse. Well, the gods of Machu Picchu clearly did not approve because the next day, it *rained* cats and dogs. Rained buckets. Rained torrents on the just and the unjust alike. And I stood there, drenched, viewing the ruins through a mist of henna dissolving off my head. (To this day, I always think of Machu Picchu wrapped in the dark brown haze of Clairol's "Frivolous Fawn.")

Sadly, after all the plans, after all the anticipation, after working out all the crating and shipping entanglements, the whole project abruptly came to a halt. Sandy Calder died in 1976 just before his enormous birthday celebration could take place. The whole spectacular undertaking was cancelled. Everyone was inconsolable, except for Louisa Calder. She never explained why she didn't like the idea, at least not to me. All these years later, I can still see Sandy Calder bubbling over with excitement, manipulating the model Braniff planes, as pleased as a little boy playing with a new toy.

While I was deeply immersed in the endless intricacies of Calder's South American tour, I was dealing daily with Braniff Airlines, which was footing the bill, and its president, the bristling Harding Lawrence whose wife, Mary Welles, was president of her own ad agency, Welles, Rich, Greene, which handled the Braniff account. I remember one embarrassing time when our paths clashed. Fred Herter and I were living in a duplex at One East End Avenue, and the Harding Lawrences were ensconced in the penthouse just above us. The Lawrences and I had never seen each other outside the workplace. Until one very warm summer's day.

It was one of those rare weekends when we decided to stay in town. So of course, Manhattan turned horribly hot and hopelessly humid. Marc came around for lunch, and we decided to have a makeshift picnic on the roof. I asked the elevator man on the way up if the Lawrences were in town. He assured me they were not. While I was unpacking our lunch on the public part of the roof, I looked over at the Lawrences' terrace, and their space looked much more enticing. So we hopped over the little fence and settled down on the Lawrences' comfortable lawn furniture. Our lunch was delicious, life seemed good, and our little dog, Schouette, decided to take a leisurely leak. At precisely that moment, the penthouse door opened, and out stepped a very-frowning Harding. He glanced at me, glowered at my husband, glared at my son, scowled at the dog, and then stormed back inside. Before we could collect our wits, we were confronted by Mary Lawrence, followed by her maid. Without even a "Hello," Mary whirled on her heels and spoke to the maid, who informed us that we were on private property and must leave *immediately*. Mustering our dignity, we beat a retreat. Marc was mortified, but at least we'd had a good time. Especially Schouette.

It wasn't long after this that my great friend Pat Cavendish O'Neill came to visit us. (You'll read a lot more about Pat later.) Harding and Mary Lawrence had just bought her mother's fabulous house, "La Fiorentina," on Cap Ferrat in the south of France. Well, before Pat had even settled herself in at our apartment, the doorbell rang; and huge baskets of flowers arrived for her from "Harding and Mary." I took that as a sign of truce and invited them to come for a party we were giving for Pat. But they never acknowledged the invitation or came to the party. Pat couldn't have cared less. She didn't like the Lawrences. She found them terribly "*nouveau*" and thought the changes they'd made to the Fiorentina were execrably "middle-class." They had hired the decorator Billy Baldwin to redecorate "La Fiorentina," and he had chintzed up the house to a fare-thee-well. Chintz was the last material that should have graced a Palladian villa, and it, along with the other Baldwin touches, wrecked the simple, elegant decor with which Rory Cameron, Lady Kenmare's son, had enhanced the place. He had given it a superbly traditional and understated look that was admired worldwide, including Sisal carpets, which had never been seen before. I guess Harding and Mary simply didn't "get it." But decorator David Hicks did. He picked up on the idea of Sisal rugs and made them fashionably popular. Anyway, that was the last I saw of the Lawrences. and I didn't mind either.

CHAPTER 3

Early Years in France

My father was not with us when I was born on September 8, 1928. My grandmother was ecstatic because September 8 was the date the Virgin Mary, allegedly, was born (there I go, dropping names again). So I was born a year before the Great Depression and, as it so happened, exactly one hundred years after the death of Franz Schubert. Raymond Poincaré was the president of France, and Herbert Hoover, the president of the United States, which, then, had only forty-eight states.

My father's parents were a little bit less ecstatic about my arrival. When they got the announcement telegram, they wired one back that simply said, "Well, I guess she'll never be President of the United States." (I don't know if they meant because I was born in France . . . or maybe because I was a mere girl.)

My French grandmother moved quickly to take advantage of my father's absence and whisked me off to be baptized in the Catholic Church. Daddy had always made it clear that his child shouldn't be introduced to any faith before knowing what religion was all about. My grandmother, who was more Catholic than the Pope, disagreed. When my father got back from Russia, he was really upset. He quickly hauled me around Paris, getting me baptized in one church after another. Maybe that's why my approach to religion has always had so many facets. Throughout my life, I've happily oscillated between Catholicism, Quakerism, Episcopalianism, Methodism, and the Baptists.

Meanwhile, my mother couldn't make up her mind on a name for me. She was so positive I would be a boy; she had chosen only masculine names. Alain was her favorite. After much pondering, she named me Solange after George Sand's daughter. (Sand was her favorite author.) Then she added

Marie after her old nurse and tacked on Nicole as a nod to an old school chum, Nicole de Montera. So there I was! Solange Marie-Nicole . . . very, very French.

I have only a few, hence all the more treasured, recollections of my father. I certainly remember how *tall* he was. (A towering six feet, five inches.) And I remember that I loved it when he chanted a favorite ball-bouncing rhyme with me:

> "One-two-three O'Leary,
> My first name is Mary,
> My second name is Anna,
> That's how you spell banana."

After each line, he'd swing his right leg high over the ball and so high over my head it looked to me like his foot reached the ceiling. Writing this, I can still recall the thrill I got when he would put me on top of one of the steamer trunks. Partly, I guess, to get me out of the way. But also, I think so we could see eye to eye.

There were always trunks around because my parents were forever traveling. I can still see my mother knitting little booties from my perch on one of those trunks. That didn't register in my young mind, and it wasn't until much, much later that she told me she had miscarried the baby she was knitting those booties for. Actually, she revealed this to me shortly after I was married and lost a child myself. I'm sure she wanted to console me for my loss; but typical of her reticence about relating too personal or unpleasant facts, she never brought up the story of her lost baby again—nor did I, for that matter.

Another memory also involves our trunks. It was the time when I was included on a trip to England. I couldn't have been more than five or six. For some reason, I was left by myself in our hotel suite one night. When I realized I was alone, I was so scared that I hid in one of those steamer trunks. When my parents came back, they couldn't find me. And after a frantic search, someone had the bright idea of looking into the trunk; and there I was, cozily ensconced, sound asleep, and quite happy.

Another terrifying memory, but again with a happy ending, was during Christmas in our flat on the Rue Albert-Samain. In those long-ago days, trees were decorated with real candles, and they were lit only on Christmas Eve. Because my father was delayed for several days getting home for Yuletide, our tree had dried out. And when we lit the candles, the tree exploded and was engulfed in flames. As we all stared dumbstruck, my father grabbed a blanket and smothered the flames. Even through my tears and fears, my father was my hero. I can still recall the piney scent of that tree burning. I also remember that all my toys were saved. And so was Christmas.

Even though the Depression was leaving many financial institutions shaky, my father's business held its own. It was named Batsell & Company and offered clients financial investment expertise. His office in Paris was at 52 Avenue des Champs Elysées. Whenever he took me there, he let me step into the glass-encased cubicles, where the clattering ticker-tape machines spewed forth their endless ribbons of financial news. Batsell & Company expanded with offices in London and New York City. When my father died, his seat on the *New York* Stock Exchange sold for $100,000. (Those same seats until recently sold for $3,500,000.)

There are only two presents I remember getting directly from my father. I had just learned to tell time and was feeling really pleased at my accomplishment. But not as pleased as when he handed me a prettily wrapped box. Inside was the most delicate rectangular watch with a fine pigskin band. I treasured it for years, delighting in my new sense of punctuality. Another gift my father brought back from London was a pair of dark mahogany brown shoes—but the wrong size. My feet had to grow for two long years before I could wear the shoes. By then he had died and how I wished he could have seen how much I loved those shoes. Here's a peculiar memory: One day, for a treat, my father took me to the famous Coquelin Patisserie in Paris. A reward for winning some good grades that week. It was a charming tearoom my grandmother also used to take me to, again for getting high marks. (Since I worked hard to keep my grades high and had a sweet tooth, I got to know the Patisserie pretty well.) Anyway, on this visit, my father asked what I wanted. I chose my favorite, a dish of vanilla ice cream. Imagine my shock when he dumped my ice cream into a glass of carbonated water.

"There!" he said. "In America, that's called an ice cream soda." I thought it was a shame to spoil perfectly good ice cream, but I bravely gulped it down. I could see that the waitress who knew me well was sorry for me. But that didn't bother my father. No more than he cared about the disapproving looks he got when ordering a glass of milk at dinner in even the most elegant restaurants. He also would have corn on the cob sent from the U.S. to Paris, which shocked the French because only cows ate corn in France then.

My mother
just before she was married.

My father.
Paris, France.

Me in Beaugé 1928.

Beaugé   1928

In my mother's arms
in Beaugé.

On
my grandmother's lap
in Beaugé.

My mother and me
in Paris.

Me at Chateau de
Razac, 1931.

On our Paris balcony
Rue Albert Samain,
1932.

With Fraulein Hilda.

Me having a jealous fit
in Square Albert, Samain.

My mother on our Paris balcony
showing off her new bathing suit.

My father in Paris looking very happy circa 1934
(about the bathing suit?).

My father in the
Bois de Boulogne, Paris.

My mother in
The Bois de Boulogne.

My father in the Bois de Boulogne.

My mother in the Bois de Boulogne
(Jardin d' Acclimatation).

My father in the Parc Monceau,
Paris.

In my Uncle Charlie's
garden in St. Cloud.

CHAPTER 4

My Father's Death

Obituary from Paris, Mo. newspaper,
The Monroe Appeal

Russell Batsell Dead

Russell Batsell, aged 32, youngest son of George Batsell and wife of Paris and known throughout the scholastic world as a brilliant and able scholar, died of heart failure in New York, supposedly on Friday of last week. The remains were cremated and will be taken to Paris, France, where he married and where he has lived for some ten or twelve years with his French wife and little daughter, now six years old. Batsell, who has been working for one of the large American research foundations since he left Harvard, had returned to New York this winter, where he had important work to do. His wife came with him, but left the child in France with her parents on account of its illness. She was called back home several weeks ago by the continued illness of the child and was on board ship, returning to the United States last week when she received the cablegram, announcing the death of her husband. She immediately forwarded it to his father and mother here and Mrs. Batsell and her other two sons, Ray and Roger, left immediately for New York. Nothing more will be known until their return.

Russell graduated with honors from the Paris High School in 1919 and then attended Missouri University, where he again captured the highest academic honors, going from there to Harvard and winning a scholarship at that institution. He chose law for his profession but on being offered a position with a large educational foundation, abandoned the law and went to Europe, where his duties compelled him to live. For most of the time he has made his home in Paris. During the time of his residence there, he has traveled all over Europe, even going into Russia during the troublesome early days of the Soviet regime, to gather desired information. In addition to his regular work he has written two widely read treatises on the European situation, both from the political and economic standpoint. He was unusual even as a boy and his unfortunate death at so early an age is to be regretted. Friends at home mourn with the bereaved family, which bears one of the oldest and most honored names, both in Monroe county and Kentucky.

Age 6, just before my father died.

One of my favorite childhood things to do was to climb into my grandmother's bed at night. It was a warm and comfy and *safe* feeling. But my father did not approve. Come to think of it, about the only times I can remember my father scolding me was whenever he caught me sharing my grandmother's bed. I can also remember once walking down the street with him and reaching up for his hand. He shook my hand off, held his straight down, and admonished me to hold mine straight up. That way our hands touched but were not entwined. It enduringly hurt my six-year-old's feelings. I can only guess that holding hands must have offended his conviction that affection should never be displayed publicly. (Apparently, not even the innocent handclasp with one's own child.)

My mother and I were in Paris when she learned of my father's sudden death, on March 11, 1935. Actually, my grandmother was the first to learn about the awful news. She opened the telegram from New York and, after absorbing the shocking message, called my uncle and sent him to the hairdresser, where my mother was having her hair done. When he blurted out the news, my mother apparently gathered up her things and wordlessly walked out, her hair still sopping wet. Within days, she sailed off to America while I stayed home with my grandmother. Although I was told nothing, I knew something dreadful was afoot. I wrote him a letter on March 19, obviously still unaware of his death. My grandmother started dressing herself in traditional mourning outfits: black dresses, long black veils, black shoes and stockings, black gloves, even black jewelry! Before my father died, she had always worn light and lively colors. I was kept in the dark about the tragic news until that autumn, when my mother returned to Paris and took me for a walk. She sat me on a bench on the Boulevard de Courcelles near our new apartment, Rue Georges Berger. But instead of coming right out and telling me that my father had died, she created a complicated story about his going on a long, long trip and never coming back. She camouflaged the facts so much that I could neither grasp nor accept any part of her story. I only vaguely got the idea that he was missing and kept asking her, "But where is he? Where is his head, where are his legs?" Finally, I understood that he had died.

Death was an enigmatic concept for a little girl to comprehend. I guess my grandmother finally realized I was having a hard time understanding the loss, and she sent me to see a priest at the Sacré Coeur, the wedding cake basilica in Monmartre, to talk about it. He and I sat on the front steps of the church, overlooking Paris. The solemn priest, scary enough in himself with his stale breath and snowfall of dandruff on his cassock, started to talk to me about . . . eternity! The concept of eternity is even more complicated than death for a child of seven to swallow. I think it was then that I started having a recurrent nightmare. In it, I am walking down some dank wooden steps leading down, down into a murky cellar with dripping stone walls on either side and then emerging into stark white fields, slogging through a ground cover thick as semolina, each step dragging heavier than the last. I hopelessly struggle to reach the edge of the fields, but never do. This vivid nightmare bedeviled me all through my adolescence. Even today, when I'm not up to par, I have the same dream, just as hopeless and unresolved as ever.

Not long after my father died, my French grandmother gathered all his silk shirts from Sulka and had them cut up and turned into dresses for me. I hated those dresses. They had Peter Pan collars with a thin ribbon to tie them closed. Consciously or subconsciously, I must have sensed where they came from. It was a happy day when I outgrew them. I have always been afraid of death. Why, I don't know, for after the disappearance of my father, I wasn't really exposed to it except once when my mother took me to see an old friend of hers, Madame Franklin, who had just died. It made a terrible impression on me, with the kerchief holding her jaw up and all—particularly since I remembered Madame Franklin, who must have been in her eighties, as quite lively and chasing her ninety-year-old boyfriend, Monsieur Gérard, down the street to find out where he was going. She had strong suspicions of his having a girlfriend around the corner. He died shortly afterward, and I was sort of glad. He was a lawyer, and I had overheard him advising my mother to send me off to boarding school rather than be burdened by me. Obviously, I had been frightened to death that she might listen to him.

Madame Franklin lived in an apartment in the sixteenth arrondissement. It had a long, long corridor separating the kitchen and servants' quarters from the masters' living space. We would often go there for lunch and, after lunch, when the grown-ups were having coffee, I would slip down the dim corridor, at the end of which, strangely enough, was a wonderful grand piano, away from everything; and I would bang on it to my heart's content, pretending I was playing proper things. But I was really playing anything that went through my head—sheer bliss!

CHAPTER 5

The Normandie Crossing

My mother went back to New York to settle my father's estate and sent for me a few months later. I was to make the ocean voyage alone at age seven. For the trip, I was outfitted in a sailor suit with a pleated skirt and a jaunty hat printed with the logo of the superliner, Normandie. And for a first-time crossing, the Normandie was certainly the way to go. The ship was a grandly appointed luxury liner with every indulgent amenity. She had made her maiden voyage on May 12, 1935, sailing from Le Havre to New York only four short months before I made mine.

My grandmother and my aunt Madeleine Panzera took me to Le Havre by train and introduced me to the ship's captain, Commandant Pugnet, who was an old friend of my Uncle Charles Panzera. They knew each other through the musical world, and I was put in his charge. He told them that they shouldn't worry about me and that I would be "la Reine du Normandie" (Queen of the Normandie) for the Crossing.

Uncle Charles was a celebrated baritone, a great favorite with operatic audiences. He was the first to sing the title role in Debussy's opera, "Pelléas." Debussy was so moved by my Uncle Charles's performance, he dedicated the opera to him. My uncle was also the first performer of many works by Milhaud, Honegger, Dutilleux, Fauré, and Duparc. He sang at both the Opéra and the Opéra Comique and also performed in concert halls like the Salle Pleyel and the Salle Gaveau. He was noted particularly for his definitive performances of German leider. The only reason he didn't have a great career in America was his maniacally possessive wife. She was a pianist who insisted on being his only accompanist, and she was adamantly opposed to the idea of his touring on his own. At the Paris Conservatoire, where he taught, he had won first prize in 1919, a signal honor. When he finally "escaped" to New York, he performed at various venues, culminating with a concert at Carnegie Hall, and also taught at the Julliard School of Music. My mother, whose artistic circle included the world of music, arranged a concert tour that would have taken him across America, adding to his fame; but his wife insisted he return to Europe, thus thwarting his American career. But she was a superb pianist, and they were both acclaimed performers in Europe.

The Normandie's captain was an accomplished organist; indeed, he had had installed a fine organ in his cabin—an impressively large one on which he played every day before lunch, which I was included in, along with his officers. Dinners I always had in the children's dining room, which was decorated by Jean de Brunhoff, the artist who had created Babar, the Elephant, Queen Celeste, and their entourage. I can still see them, all cavorting around the walls.

I quickly became a sort of ship's mascot, partly because of my saucy sailor outfit, I guess. I had been given a life-size doll which was almost as tall as me. She was dressed in the same sailor suit with the same Normandie logo sewn on her hat. I named her Solangette and carried her around everywhere. How I loved that doll and her flawless celluloid complexion. She was my constant companion. Many photographs were taken of me and Solangette, and there were numerous newspaper articles written about the seven-year-old orphan traveling all by herself. The Normandie's décor was the essence of the Art Deco Streamline Moderne style. The vast first-class dining room had seven hundred passengers at each sitting. The towering Lalique crystal columns kept things bright. The swimming pool, with different depths, even had a sandy "beach" for the children.

I had tea and ices daily with a fellow passenger, a friend of my mother's who happened to be on board. I don't remember his name, but I do recall how formally he asked the captain for permission to take me to tea. A nurse had been appointed to tuck me in bed each night and help me get dressed in the morning. Oh, yes, life at sea was pretty tough.

This said, the shipboard nights were sad for me, and I felt very much alone in my little cabin. But even at that age, just as I have throughout my life, when I was stuck with lemons, I simply made lemonade. I quickly discovered that I could order anything that took my fancy. The ship's chefs, who couldn't be stumped by the most demanding gourmet, were hardly flummoxed at filling my childish requests. And for the first time, I could toss down *oceans* of tomato juice. (Tomato juice was rationed at home because my grandmother thought it was too acidic.) And there were chocolate desserts galore . . . more than even I could eat . . . and *gallons* of my perennial favorite—vanilla ice cream.

To say nothing of movies and storybooks . . . even comic books! When we got to New York, I recall a memorable visit to FAO Schwartz, the dream-come-true toy store on Fifth Avenue. I was presented with five tiny dolls, all five of them tucked into one bed. They were replicas of the Dionne Quintuplets, the human litter whose recent birth had electrified the world. Each diminutive doll wore a dainty gold bracelet inscribed with her name: Cécile, Marie, Yvonne, Annette, and Emilie. The girls gained fame and fortune as the first quintuplets ever to survive birth. Their country, Canada, became known thereafter as Fertility Land.

On a more serious note, during our New York stay, I was taken along to the courtroom with my mother and her squadron of lawyers. The court case was all about my father's contested estate. He had left behind two very large insurance policies on his life; and the insurance companies, like all insurance companies, were fighting to keep from paying them off. They suggested that my father had committed suicide, which would have voided the policy. When my father had come back from Russia with his friend Ashley Chanler, they had stayed at New York's Berkley Hotel. (Ashley's father, William Astor Chanler, who was a backer of my father's brokerage firm, had asked my father to take Ashley with him to Russia. I guess he hoped to get his son interested in making a career of his own. But Ashley didn't have it in him to do much of anything.)

My father had tinkered for a long time with a process to make invisible ink, most likely to disguise the confidential government reports he was writing from Russia. One of the chemicals that showed promise was a harmless-looking clear liquid, but it was actually deadly poisonous. As another security procedure, he was developing his own films. Dangerous chemicals were also involved in that process. One theory was that when he got up during the night for some water, he mistook the drinking glass for one with a chemical residue in it.

His death was silent and swift and a complete shock to Ashley, who found his body in the bathroom the next morning. Ashley was perplexed because when they had dinner the night before, my father was in good spirits, neither depressed nor discouraged. There was a third party at that dinner, who had gone up to my father's and Chanler's suite for a nightcap. That person also testified in court that he was cheery that evening. Speaking of meetings he was looking forward going to the next day, etc. The last person to see my father alive had nothing more than that to say, and the lawyers never took it any further. And that was that.

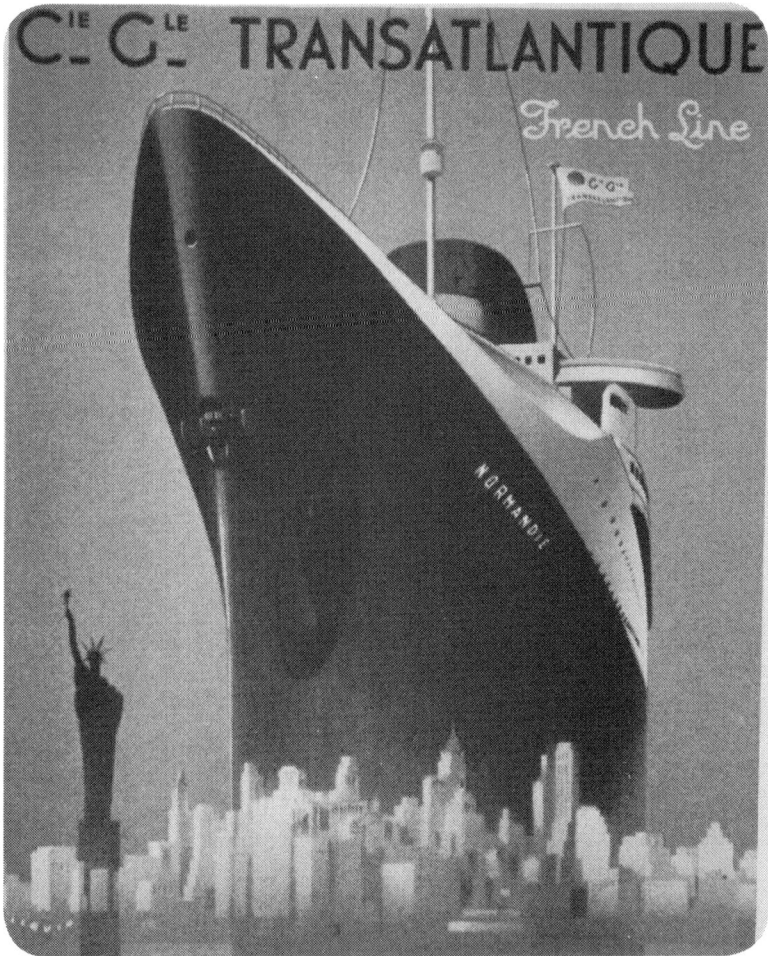

The Normandie on which I crossed for my first trip
across the pond in 1935.

One Paris newspaper declared the Normandie "a city on the
scale of a great ship."

I was introduced into the courtroom by my mother's lawyers to demonstrate my father's happy home life complete with a nice little girl and a beautiful, though heartbroken, wife. The unspoken question was: "How could a man with a family like this possibly contemplate ending his life?" I remember not being sad but rather being terribly aware that something awful was going on, and I hugged my mother a lot and was glad to be with her during her travails. The insurance companies protested that the very fact that he had taken out such large policies only a couple of years before his death certainly raised suspicions. The words "foul play" were bandied about quite a lot. I asked what they meant but was never given an answer. The next time I was to hear those words, years later, it was from the lips of the Prince of Denmark himself, and it sent shivers down my spine.

("All is not well. I doubt some foul play. Would the night were come! Till then, sit still, my soul, foul deeds will rise, though all the earth o'erwhelm them to men's eyes.") Poor Hamlet; somehow, I related to him.

Their spurious objections were swept aside when a clear-headed judge dismissed such arguments, threw their case out of court, and ordered them to pay the insurance policies in full. It was a significant sum but was grievously diminished after the lawyers took their huge bite out of it.

I think my mother always hated lawyers after that. And just as she had no use for lawyers, she was wary of doctors too. (Which may be why she didn't exactly shout "Hurrah!" when my husbands included two doctors and a lawyer.) She thought they were all money-grabbers; and whenever she would go to a doctor's or a lawyer's office, she would turn around the large sapphire ring she wore on her left hand so they wouldn't think she was rich!

Eighty-five years later, all hell broke loose in the enigmatic world of Soviet espionage.

We have to go back a bit . . . to the height of the "Red Scare" that threatened to upset both British and American national elections. At that uneasy time, there was inflammatory evidence called the "Zinoviev Letter" purportedly written by Grigori Zinoviev, President of the Communist International in Moscow. The letter instructed the British Communist Party to set up cells in the country and let the public know that the communists were supporting the Labor Party. The ensuing scandal brought down the Labor government and sent it into disgrace for ten years.

While my father was touring Russia as a Harvard Sovietologist, he acquired photonegatives of the Zinoviev Letter and mysteriously stashed them in the back vault of the Harvard Law School Library. He had strong connections in Poland, where the letter was originally passed on to the British and probably got them there. The photonegatives were only recently found.

The letter that directly influenced the British elections of 1924 could have changed the direction of the American election that year, which put Coolidge in the White House. But last month, new evidence cropped up that proved that the notorious letter was a forgery, perpetrated by a British intelligence agent, Captain Sydney Reilly, known to the inner circle as "the spy who never makes a mistake." In 1998, Foreign Secretary Robin Cook launched an official historical review of the Zinoviev letter. And to this day, many questions remain unanswered.

Contemporary scholarship on the so-called "Zinoviev letter" dates to a 1967 monograph published by three British journalists working for *The Sunday Times*. The trio—Lewis Chester, Steven Fay, and Hugo Young—asserted that two members of a Russian monarchist organization called the Brotherhood of St. George composed the document in question in Berlin. The widow of one of the two men said to have authored the document, Irina Bellegarde, provided the authors with direct testimony that she had witnessed the forgery as it was performed.

So was it Reilly or Irina Bellegarde's husband who had committed the forgery? The evidence shows that Reilly was in contact with my father and other influential inner-circle members but does not mention his knowing Bellegarde.

Was my father's inexplicable and sudden death arranged by forces who wished to silence the unbendingly and brave patriotic man?

For me, these new and totally unexpected revelations are a godsend, and I'm going to take great satisfaction in exploring the American angles to the Zinoviev Letter and discovering just where Walter R. Batsell figures in this intriguing development. If I don't succeed, maybe one of my descendants will take the matter up and solve it once and for all.

My mother's lifelong involvement with artists and performers was a natural consequence of her antipathies for the establishment. Hers was a different world and certainly a more amusing one. She believed—and so do I—that the love of art—poetry, painting, sculpture, music.—and those who create it enables people to transcend any of the barriers to mutual understanding that man has yet devised. And God knows there are barriers! Her connections in that world led her to buy interesting art at reasonable prices; and little by little, she built up a superb collection, which I have had the good fortune to inherit.

My mother was so busy settling my father's estate that she couldn't really take care of me. So I was sent off to a camp in New Jersey called Eagle Nest Farm. I was by far the youngest girl there and felt pretty lost. Yet though I spoke very little English, I made the best of a difficult situation.

I pressed flowers into books, took long walks, canoed, and, as always, I blissfully read the days away. When my father's estate was finally settled, my mother and I sailed back to France on board the USS Bremen.

I can recall every infinitesimal detail of my trip *to* America on the Normandie . . . exploring every deck . . . befriending the crew . . . the captain's organ concerts . . . different outfits I wore . . . even little souvenirs I collected. They're still part of my past. But memories of the voyage back are blank. It's as if my mind went into a ten-day blackout. I don't remember the excitement of leaving the dock, I can't recall the bustle of disembarking or the details of anything happening in between. I think this selective amnesia is the first example of what turned into a lifelong habit of my mind. I seem to utterly block out specific episodes that are probably too mournful or too depressing. It's never a purposeful effort on my part, and I apparently go through the motions appropriate to the occasion. I usually have to think twice when asked by doctors or anyone else on which side I had a mastectomy. I often say left instead of right. And that is despite the fact that I am only too aware every day of my life of the physical damage done to me some thirty years ago on that right side.

And while I'm confessing things, here's another of my idiosyncrasies. For as long as I can remember, I've been a contradictory blend of self-assurance . . . and a sense of inadequacy. Often at the same time! Is it possible for a single psyche to swing from a disdainful superiority complex to a debilitating inferiority complex in an instant? Well, I vacillate between these two poles all the time. And it's baffling. But who knows? Maybe this helps me to keep bumbling along.

We returned to France carrying my father's ashes. Why my mother didn't have him buried in Paris, Missouri, I don't know. Maybe she wished the two of them to eventually be together in France. So he was buried in the Panzera family plot in Antibes. It's a pretty place, overlooking the port of Antibes and surrounded by lovely trees. My grandfather and my grandmother and my mother are also buried there, and it is where I shall be buried too. There's plenty of room for any other candidates, if candidates there be. One of my foresighted ancestors saw to *that* when he bought a very large plot and built a huge mausoleum on it. One time, when my mother visited the cemetery, she couldn't find the mausoleum and was told it had been destroyed and that the coffins of our family had been moved to graves in a newer part of the cemetery. No one asked permission; no one informed us. So Mummy sued them and won a handsome sum for the desecration. Still, the handsome eighteenth century mausoleum was gone.

In Paris, life took on a more normal tempo. I somehow felt more secure and at home with my grandmother. Mummy was in and out, back and forth, hither and yon as was her want, but I stayed settled and content. I went to a public school around the corner: the Lycée Carnot. It was a scary place, and maybe that's why I was late every morning. I hated those ponderous wooden doors that banged shut on my tardy nose; and I often had to stay after school as punishment for being late. But somehow, I lived through it along with my fellow alumni, a boy named François Chirac, who became a President of France, Couve de Murville, who became a Prime Minister, and Bernard Buffet, the artist! On my most recent trip to Paris in the fall of 2009, I strolled back to the Lycée Carnot's entrance. And there it almost *wasn't!* They were demolishing the whole side on the Avenue de Villiers. Of course, those dreaded green heavy wooden doors were still standing . . . no doubt to terrify a new generation of children. But now the inner courtyard—which had been such a shut-in spot where pupils screamed and shoved and still-remembered bullies ruled—was finally open and naked to the eye, which somehow cleansed some disturbing memories.

The next year, I transferred to the Cours Hattmer, a private girls' school and ever so much nicer. You went to class and just listened. There was no give and take. I can tell you none of us would have dared ask a question or make a statement. After a few hours of passive listening, you'd grab your books and go home to do a lot of homework. Most of the other students had governesses who brought them to classes and stayed for the lessons. For some reason, most of these governesses were enormously fat. We students sat around an oval table that was covered with a red felt table cloth with a yellow fringe that touched the floor. The governesses sat behind us, most of them lumpen and sloven. Since I didn't have a governess, there was always an empty chair behind me. And, thank goodness, I didn't have a governess's fat legs that didn't close properly to worry about.

I didn't have a governess, but I had Joseph, who was employed by my grandmother. He was a nice, kindly man. Mamame called him a chauffeur. (*Chauffage* is French for heating, and Joseph *did* tend the stove.) We didn't have a car for him to drive, but he did haul up the coal up from our basement. In order to use the elevator, Joseph had to put the coal in a briefcase and pretend to be a businessman or a doctor or a lawyer or *someone* bearing documents so people wouldn't object and so he wouldn't have to lug that load five flights up the spiral back stairs.

Joseph would also take me to school each morning; and I hate to admit it, but I was ashamed of him. He always looked so bedraggled. I would make him drop me off a block from school so my classmates wouldn't see me with him. He was always unshaven. But kindly old Joseph didn't mind my turning him loose even one little bit because it gave him a little extra time for his favorite pastime: gambling. So once he dropped me off, he'd hot-foot it to the nearest bar that also had a PMU (an OTB.) While he downed a couple of eye-openers, he'd handicap the horses, decide on his picks, and make his bets. I knew all this because Joseph unfailingly shared all his exploits with me when he picked me up each afternoon. Always, of course, on that same allotted spot, a block away from my school, so I learned a bit about horse racing and betting early on in life. Once safely home, I'd share a wonderful "gouter" with my grandmother. She was always there, waiting for me when I got home. After we talked over the events of our day, she'd help me with all that homework.

Since my mother was away so much at this time, my grandmother became a tremendous influence on my life. She was devoutly Catholic, not only attending mass every Sunday but often on weekdays. Seeing her get dressed for church was as impressive as watching the priest donning his vestments to say the mass. With a little lace cape over her shoulders, she would arrange her chignon, sticking long hair-pins into it, and slowly put on her hat, her crystal pendant earrings, her veil, her scarf, her gloves. Then she'd walk to L'église Saint Charles de Monceau with me in tow. Not rain or sleet or hail or snow could deter her. On the way home, hand in hand, we always stopped at a *patisserie* to get a delectable cake for lunch, but only on Sundays.

She was a great woman, my French grandmother. One of the last of the Victorians. And though very kind, she was also very severe. Her posture was superb—always sitting straight enough for two and walking, head high, with a ramrod bearing. She never ventured outside unless perfectly groomed and dressed right down to the immaculate and properly matching gloves. As she strode (never strolled) the avenue, she'd wave those gloved hands to her friends or acquaintances, looking ever so much like Queen Mary acknowledging her subjects. In fact, this modern-day Victorian woman was often called "La Reine Mère" by her admiring friends. (Queen Mary, of course, was the Queen Mother.)

During World War One ("La Grande Guerre," the French called it), she worked as a volunteer for the Red Cross at the Hotel Rothschild in Paris for long, long hours. She certainly never smoked and didn't indulge in spirits. But late in life, she'd religiously imbibe an *apéritif* before dinner. A Cinzano, I still remember, or a Quinquina. One night, she asked for an unheard-of second glass. Her son, who was there, was scandalized and asked if she didn't think she might be overdoing the drinking. I can still see the steely glare she turned on him, staring him down, and then she announced that she was merely following her doctor's strict orders. Unspoken, but heard, was her warning that he mind his own business.

"Mamame," as I called her, was a striking figure and had obviously been a beautiful young woman. I picked up through the grapevine that when she and my grandfather lived in Antibes, her children's tutor had a mad crush on her. And then as the children grew, he was mad for my mother. And eventually, when I was old enough, he transferred his hormonal drive toward me. At least he was consistent. This romantic's name was Raoul Mattei, and he started the first rent-a-car operation in the world in Marseille. His rent-a-car company was unique and very successful. He had a sumptuous house on the Cannebière, (the Fifth Avenue of Marseille) overlooking the sea. After his wife died, he had built a smaller replica of the Taj Mahal in the woods on the property in her memory. I often went there to play with his young daughter, Linette. After her mother's death, her dressing room was kept just as it had been in her life. We would sneak in and play with all the gold brushes and hand mirrors that were still displayed on her *table de toilette*. And of course, the fun was spiced up because we weren't supposed to go in there. Actually, it was really quite spooky.

Until my grandfather died, Mamame was attended by a platoon of servants. But by the time I lived with her, she was reduced to only one. And that was our long-suffering maid, la Vieille Marie, who did *every* thing. She cooked and served and cleaned and laundered and ironed and, to show her appreciation, my grandmother treated her like a slave. But the gallant Marie, who loved my grandmother, took it all in stride, never got upset, and was always cheerful. In addition, I have never known anyone who prepared a *roti de veau aux carottes* as delectable as hers. I can still remember the smell of it filling the apartment every Thursday night—menus were strictly organized for the week. Gates Helms, my beau at the time, never failed to show up for those Thursday dinners.

I had met Gates and his brother Dick when they were at Williams and I, at Bennington. Later, I often ran into Dick in Washington when he was

Director of the CIA. I could tell people were rather surprised when, at parties, the very secretive man who hardly ever spoke to anybody would drag me off into a corner and talk endlessly. God knows what they thought. He, obviously, didn't care; nor did I, for that matter! Reminiscing is an interesting thing to do.

Mrs. J.K. Haynes,
head of Red Cross unit,
where my grandmother worked
from 1915 to 1916
(in same uniform).

For me, the days at rue Georges Berger stand out in memory as a nice and orderly life. I had a very regular, steady schedule. There was no getting around it, and sleeping late was simply not in the book. My grandmother would call "Solange" from the kitchen window up to my little room promptly at seven in the morning. I practiced the piano for an hour every morning before leaving for school. Mamame sat near me, listening for mistakes. She always had peeled apple slices for me, waiting on the top of the piano, for encouragement. I spent most of my free time in my little room at the top of the stairs. This was my private domain. The Claude Marot (famous designer of the times) blue and white curtains on my window were of a material that looked like fluffy clouds. I can still recall the way they rippled in the breeze and gave intermittent views of the Paris rooftops.

In the summer of 1939, I was sent to Camp MacJannet on the Lac d'Annecy. It was an American camp for American children living in France. They didn't teach us anything. It seemed we spent most of our time sitting on a roof, playing the triangle—a lyre-shaped metal scale we struck with a wand. Brilliant character-building activity!

Once again, I was about the youngest child there. Like all children everywhere, we played doctor and nurse. In lieu of thermometers to take temperatures, we used toothbrush handles. Guess whose temperature got taken a lot? It was on that same Lac d'Annecy that the Deschamps family had their country house and where, many years later, I got married to Henri Deschamps.

From there, I went to stay with the Johnsons at their house, "Ombremont," in Savoie on the Lac du Bourget. That's where Lamartine wrote his great ode *"O temps suspends ton vol."* ("Oh time, suspend your flight!") I stayed there until late August. Then, just like that, war was upon us. My mother sent a telegram from America, pleading with my grandmother to come to the States posthaste and bring me with her.

But for my second trip across the pond, I was again on my own. My tradition-bound grandmother couldn't bear to leave France (or even her beloved Paris). Her other daughter, my Aunt Jessie, lived in Marseille in the unoccupied part of France, and my grandmother could have gone to stay with her; but this was the third German war she had been around for, and she was terrified the Huns would break into our apartment and steal everything. So she stayed behind in her beloved Paris.

Once again, she took me to Le Havre by train on August 31, and I waved her a forlorn farewell. Then, wiping my eyes and facing my future, I trudged up the gangplank of the SS Manhattan, the largest luxury liner ever built in America and the last boat to leave Europe before the actual declaration of war. Among the passengers was a friend of my mother, a Mrs. Hyde. She was a member of the Oxford Group. I remember hearing something about The Group, and even at my age, I was amazed that such semifascist organizations really existed.

CHAPTER 6

Outbreak of World War II

War was officially declared on September 1, 1939. Our ship, the *Manhattan,* was scheduled to stop in Southampton late on August 31 then go on to Cobh, Ireland, the next day. (I can remember writing out the tags for my luggage and spelling Manhattan as two words. I had never heard of the Isle of Manhattan and thought it was named after a man named Hattan.) While we were docked in Southampton, I noticed that the reading and smoking lounges were being outfitted with sleeping cots, enough for a hundred new passengers. On top of that, by the time we reached Cobh, they had even drained the ship's swimming pool, where they added still more cots and passengers, which crushed me as I had been so looking forward to the sensation of swimming yet again in a pool while sailing over the ocean.

During the day, while walking the decks, we often saw German submarines. At night, we had to close the curtains over the portholes because those lights made us a perfect target, though the boat was equipped with enormous projector lighting her side sides to show huge American flags as the U.S. was still neutral. Strangely enough, my future husband, Jean de la Bruyère, sailed from Genoa to New York later that same year on the same boat with the same lit American flags on its sides. I wasn't old enough to be scared or even to have an inkling of what it was all about. But I knew excitement was in the air, and I liked the feeling. Another passenger on board was Gene Autry. He clumped around in his western boots, wearing a huge ten-gallon hat. Everybody talked about this celebrity, but I had never heard of him or his horse, Champion, who was also on board, taking up the place of at least three passengers! (Long after the war, I watched all his movies and loved every one of them.)

When we steamed into New York Harbor, under Lady Liberty's torch, on my birthday, September 8, you could almost feel the entire ship breathe a sigh of relief . . . and thanks. We were the privileged first—and unconsciously heroic—group to cross the Atlantic under wartime conditions.

My mother was waiting and waving from the pier as the ship docked, and she quickly collected me, bag and baggage. (I didn't have much baggage because my grandmother had just shipped me off with a few summer clothes. She was convinced that the World War about to engulf the entire planet was nothing but a silly rumor and couldn't last long enough for me to need my *winter* clothes.) Anyway, we drove directly from the pier to the World's Fair. This was the perfectly named "World of the Future" with its landmark Trylon and Perisphere.

The smoking room on the SS Manhattan, transformed into a
ladies' dormitory for last-minute passengers fleeing Europe.
September 1939.

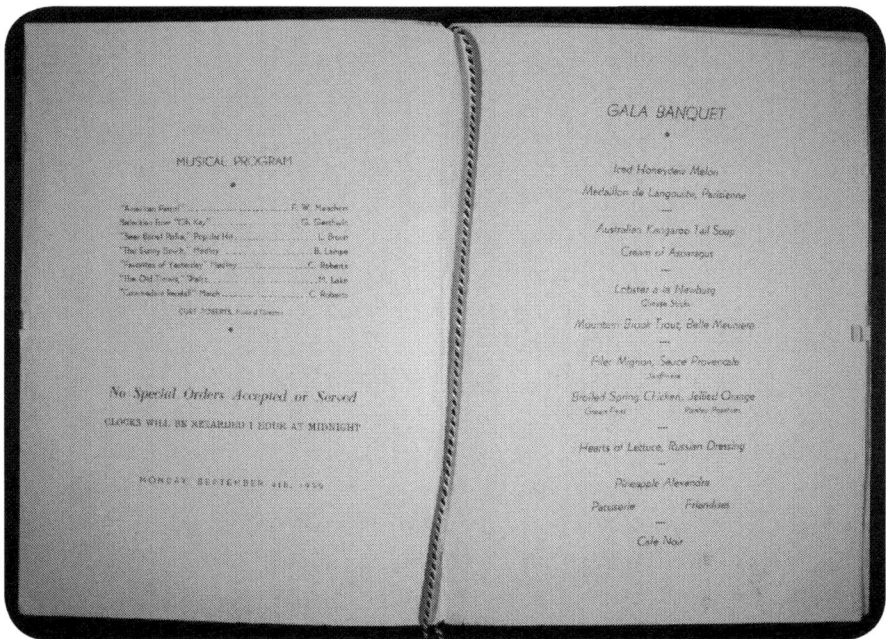

SS Manhattan menu the day after war was declared.

It was more fabulous than any dream. I still remember the rides and the futuristic exhibits and the *crowds!* But isn't it strange that I remember most of all out of all these wonders a *restaurant?* Well, it wasn't just a restaurant. It was "Le Pavillon," which the iconic chef, Henri Soulé, had created as his masterpiece. This restaurant so exceeded the bounds of excellence that the memory of it remains the gold standard for ambitious restaurants throughout the world. The operation kept fifteen master chefs bustling and dozens of cooks hustling. No wonder the prices were so astronomical. Lobster in a Shell Fish Sauce? $1.80! *Filet of Sole, au Beurre?* 75 cents! And *Dom Pérignon Champagne?* $6.50 a *bottle!* (When the World's Fair closed, Henri Soulé brought "Le Pavillon" to Manhattan, where it became an oasis of pleasure in the midst of New York's then mediocre dining spots. Soulé's big secret? He kept many, many New Yorkers clamoring to get in by keeping many, many New Yorkers out.)

Almost all the world's nations had exhibits at the Fair, and we trekked to (and were amazed by) most of them. We even went to the German Pavilion. Isn't it eerie to think that it stayed open even while Germany was starting its murderous rampage, invading by the horrendous *blitzkrieg* one innocent European country after another?

Finally sated with the fantasies of Flushing Meadow, we went back to the New Weston Hotel in midtown Manhattan. I was agape at its splendor. The Vassar Club was on its top floor, and my mother quickly got to know some of its members. This meant that when she had other things to do, she could park me there, where I could stare at the arriving members, and write on the richly embossed Vassar Club stationery. They also had bowls of the most wonderful peppermints, free for the taking, to suck on till your tongue was afire. I spent many happy hours at the Vassar Club reeking of peppermint and developing my lifelong habit of entertaining myself.

I was giddy with vertigo each time the elevator man *whooshed* us up the fifteen floors to our cozy room. Do you know I still have a wooden dress hanger with the New Weston name and address printed on it? 34 East 50th Street. And I treasure it, though by now, it has many splinters.

To me, living there was like living in the clouds, with all of Manhattan at my feet. There was a secret ledge outside our window where I could stash the Wrigley's chewing gum my Uncle Roger sent me monthly from Paris, Missouri. My mother wouldn't tolerate it in the room, and I wouldn't dream of chewing gum in front of her. Instead, I'd lock myself in the bathroom and chew away to my heart's content.

During those days, I worried constantly about my grandmother, who had been left behind in France. I wrote numerous letters (on official-looking Vassar Club stationery) to Franklin Delano Roosevelt, whom I had heard was the President of the United States, and asked him to take a minute or two out of his busy day to declare war on Nazi Germany so the American Army could march into Paris and rescue my poor grandmother from the Germans. But that Mr. Roosevelt didn't answer a single letter, and I hated him. I knew he had other things on his mind but not to answer even *one* of my letters! (My mother consoled me by revealing that my devotedly Republican father would have applauded my miffed-ness because he also hated Roosevelt and all his liberal ways . . . as did all bankers).

The New Weston Hotel.

But I lived in constant fear that the bundle might fall off the ledge, gaining lethal speed as it fell fifteen floors, braining a passerby. I imagined the *Daily News* headline:

"INNOCENT PEDESTRIAN KILLED BY PIANO PRODIGY'S CHEWING GUM."

What a way to go!

CHAPTER 7

Life in Paris, Missouri

When my Batsell grandparents moved out of the old homestead in Paris, Missouri, they turned the place over to their second son, Raymond, my Uncle Ray. My grandparents were much happier living in town in their old age (their seventies) and were quite comfortable in their very pretty townhouse on Seminary Street. My grandmother's widowed sister, Mrs. Curtright, lived in a house immediately adjacent to hers and the two ladies spent a great part of every day together. Mrs. Curtright's daughter and son-in-law lived with her. His name was Paul Gerster and he had a very impressive title of Post Master General of Moberley County, and that fact was a boon for me because he would take care of my mail free of charge. Every Sunday, just before supper time, he would ceremoniously cross the lawn that separated the two houses and come to pick up the letters I religiously wrote to my mother and grandmother everyday of the week—sort of daily little journals which took quite a few stamps to send to New York City and Paris, France. I know my French grandmother treasured these missives. In fact, so much so, she sort of wallpapered her bathroom walls with them. But to go back to Paul Gerster, I was very grateful to him and always asked him if he would stay for supper, but he never did. I think he was shy and in awe of my grandparents and didn't want to intrude.

I still recall the flutter my mother and I created when we showed up in Paris, Missouri, in 1939. Everyone knew about my father's success, and they were proud that their local boy had made good. But his exotically foreign widow was quite another matter. God knows what image they'd conjured up in their mind of a typical French girl. Probably one who was over-rouged, under-dressed, addicted to *mascara,* and perpetually kicking up her heels in a wanton Can-Can. It fact, one morning my Uncle Roger (obviously a master of tact), discreetly took my mother aside and pleaded with her that whenever she was driven to smoke or drink, to do so in solitude behind the barn like any other dissolute. So she wouldn't shock anyone.

But everybody soon caught on to what a remarkable person Mummy was, and they developed a respect for her that I watched turn into outright admiration.

I, on the other hand, was treated like a princess from the beginning, I guess because I was the first Batsell girl born in four generations. And not only *that*, I think they took pity on me because I was fatherless.

My mother stayed in Missouri for about a week then left for New York leaving me to live with my grandparents. They sent me to the local public school, the one and only school in town. My English was timid and limited, and of course, my classmates didn't speak a word of French. I reacted to my loneliness by taking up the flute. I guess I figured that if I couldn't communicate with them in my broken English, well maybe they'd understand my flute-playing. It worked. A little. I practiced my flute a lot and became pretty good at it. I even won a prize! Which was a flute, and I didn't anymore have to use the communal one which was the school's. Pretty disgusting when you think about it, sharing a flute!

But I didn't neglect my first love, the piano. Three times a week, I got to use the piano at Helen MacKamey's house directly across the street. Miss MacKamey was a well-to-do spinster who had been madly in love with my father and had been crushed to hear he'd married a foreigner! Despite her broken heart, she was ever so attentive to me, plying me with cookies and candies and cakes. But she always made me uncomfortable, endlessly talking about my father, recollecting the walks they'd take, as he held her hand. (My father? Who wouldn't' even hold his little daughter's hand? Really.) But the piano had a fine tone to it, and I played the pieces I could remember by heart because she had no sheet music and my meager allowance was not enough to buy even a little book of scales.

Soon after I got to Missouri, it was Halloween (a holiday I'd never heard of before). My grandmother got me all dressed up as a ghost. It was a very elaborate costume, which required poking three holes in a sheet for the eyes and the mouth. (This spooked me a lot. I simply could not imagine my fastidious French grandmother raiding her super neat linen closet, where she kept her color-coded ribbon-tied sets of sheets and cutting holes in them.) Then they sent me off to a Halloween party, trick-or-treating with some of the neighborhood children. Talk about culture shock!

In somebody's house, we all sat in a circle blindfolded and passed around some grisly handfuls of the body parts of what we were told was a dead cat: raw oysters for the eyes, cooked spaghetti for the guts, earmuffs for the ears. We all shrieked and shuddered and shivered. I almost drowned bobbing for apples in a deep tub of water.

Then we played pin the tail on the Donkey, which I thought sounded like a pretty cruel game. That Halloween party scared me nearly to death, and I couldn't help wondering what kind of people I had fallen in with.

But anyway, back at school, everything was fine and dandy. I had my flute. And I had a brand new friend, whom I nicknamed "Fancypants." I can't think why I called him that . . . except maybe his pants were really fancy. Or maybe because I had just learned the English word "fancy." Anyway, Fancypants became a self-appointed bodyguard and really watched over me.

A more socially impressive personage was my handsome younger cousin, Kenneth Batsell. He manned the popcorn machine at the movie house on Saturday nights. The movie was the big social event of the week. Everybody went, but I had eyes only for him. He piled my carton with a ton more popcorn than the other envious children got.

So Fancy Pants and Kenneth were my first Paris, Missouri, heroes. My third hero was the ancient organist who made beautiful music during the movies' intermissions. (Most movie houses still had the organs that had added pathos or excitement to the otherwise silent movies. I think my movie organist's renditions reminded me of those little recitals by the captain of the Normandie.) Unfortunately, my cute little cousin Kenneth was killed in a car accident while still in his teens. His older brother, Harold, was my age. The three of us always got together on Sundays whenever they came over to our grandparents' house. This weekly feast was always topped off with ice cream, which was homemade. It was the best ice cream you ever tasted. Even better than that of the Patisserie Coquelin in Paris. But oh, the job of making it was like being sentenced to hard labor. It took hours of cranking the cream-filled cylinder surrounded by salted ice. The cranking only got tougher and tougher as the cream thickened and as we kept adding chopped up strawberries or peaches. But it was a sacred and enviable and rewarding chore. We experimented with every kind of flavor, but for me, nothing beat my all time favorite—plain classic vanilla, which I had a monopoly on (it was also the easiest to make).

There was a lush and fecund vegetable garden behind the house that seemed to stretch to the horizon. My green-thumbed grandfather grew red and yellow potatoes, yams, squash, melons, peas, beets, beans, parsnips, garlic, and cabbages, all lined up in disciplined rows. I remember walking through tall vines bending with plump tomatoes and always swiping a couple to eat right on the spot. They were messy to eat but delicious as only forbidden fruits can be. But then one day, my grandfather caught me at it and gave me a silently accusing look. He never uttered a word; but I still felt ashamed for helping myself to something that wasn't mine and never did it again. While he was looking.

On Sundays, my grandmother would take me to the Methodist church, which had all sorts of social activities. Once, in the church basement, I was asked to sing the French national anthem. I knew the tune, all right, but only a few of the words. I remembered "Courage, courage, *aux bons Français*" being one of my made-up lines. But I was nonchalant about it because I was quite aware nobody there understood French anyway . . . let alone the "Marseillaise." My grandmother didn't know the difference either and was really proud of me; and I didn't disillusion her and let her ply me with lots of cupcakes afterward. I think my grandfather was a Baptist, but I never knew him to go to church. And only once did I hear him mention God.

It was at the dinner table when I announced that when I grew up, I would like to have four children, two boys and two girls. My grandfather told me to hush up . . . that those decisions were made only by God . . . and never by mere mortals. No one uttered another word. Planned parenthood had not yet been invented! My grandfather never felt the need to speak much anyway, not even to ask for anything at the dinner table. Instead, he would gently rap his fork against the plate, a signal that he was still hungry.

My grandmother, never having had daughters or granddaughters around, didn't really know how to cope with a little girl, but she did the best she could. And every morning, she would put my underwear to warm up on the pot-bellied stove in the living room. I guess that was her way of telling me she cared. She also sent me a St. Valentine's Day card religiously until she died

All those days, I missed my mother terribly and finally decided that I'd had enough. I had a girlfriend, who had let me try her shiny new roller skates. I had no idea how to use them, and I was not sure whether I planned what inevitably happened next. But I do know I managed to take a pratfall under the persimmon tree, which grew right in front of my grandparent's house. I actually banged my head pretty badly and quickly decided to play it for all it was worth. I acted extra dazed and even pretended I couldn't walk. In a panic, they called the family doctor, a cousin, Dr. Ragsdale. I think he saw right through my charade, but just to be on the safe side, he suggested that I be taken to the nearby Moberly Hospital, where I malingered. When neither my walking (nor my honesty), improved, Aunt Grace and Uncle Roger drove me all the way to the Children's Hospital in St. Louis. (I must have had some pangs of guilt because I sent a pathetic little telegram to my mother saying I was doing fine except for some really bad headaches.)

Of course, just as I hoped, my mother left New York and came rushing to my bedside. She stayed with me at the hospital where I carried on with my act, weak and helpless. I was so happy holding my beautiful mother captive. She stayed with me, talked to me, read to me. The readings were from the hospital's books. I think we read all of Mark Twain. Whenever she got her hopes up that I'd fallen asleep, she'd test me by repeating the same sentence a few times then adding, "And they ran and they ran and they ran . . ."

But I'd sit bolt upright and complain, "I'm not sleeping! And please finish the story." And Tom Sawyer would be reduced to a walk.

I managed to stretch my frailty fraud out for a month with doctors abetting me until I got bored and began my new campaign. I had to convince my mother of how unhappy I was being away from her. I kept it up until she relented and took me back to New York with her, which is what I had in mind all along. My walking improved immediately!

"The Adventures of Huckleberry Finn" came with us. And Mark Twain remains a lifelong companion. I've always been fascinated that my mother, with her almost totally French background, delighted in Twain's great books and understood the blend of disparate speech sounds: the Negro dialect, the backwoods Southwestern dialect, the everyday Pike County dialect. Not to mention all the modified varieties of this last. It's shocking to think that when "Huckleberry Finn" was published in 1855, a member of the Concord, Massachusetts, Library Board called it "the veriest trash" and banned it. Just as shocking is that in 2008, Alaska's Governor Sarah Palin, Republican candidate for Vice President of the United States, banned the book from the state's school libraries. Probably because Aunt Polly, the gentlest woman in American literature, used the word "nigger." Even though her use of it exposed racism in a way no other work has done. This is the book that Hemingway said of: "All American literature comes from a book by Mark Twain called 'Huckleberry Finn.' Nothing like it had appeared before; nothing as good has been written since.'" So my mother was in pretty good company in her affection for the works of Samuel Clemens.

CHAPTER 8

Rose Haven School for Girls

I was blissfully happy to be back in New York and near my mother even though I was immediately sent off to a boarding school called Rose Haven School for Girls in Englewood, New Jersey. Our school for girls was no picnic. The school uniform was torture. We wore blouses starched stiff as a board, with collars rubbing our necks raw. Each morning, we lined up like troopers. That's when the school nurse, Miss Carlson, would come along and thrust a long straight-pin to close our collars right under our chins. She'd always stab one or two of us, I was convinced, intentionally. Whatever her purpose, our posture was straight, proud, and painful. Miss Van Strum, the formidable corseted headmistress, saw to *that*. Only once a week were we allowed to wash our hair. And we could never dry it with towels because that would result in far too many wet towels. We had to dry our hair by swinging it to and fro over the bathtub until we couldn't see straight. We were stark naked when we performed this exercise, which is horrible when you think about it. To this day, whenever I dry my hair with a towel, I feel very privileged, which is pretty pathetic.

There was a triangular driveway leading up to the front of Rose Haven. It had two purposes: One was for cars to drive around. The second was more memorable, at least for me. Rose Haven positively abounded in rules. They had rules for *everything*. And for every rule broken, there was a demerit issued. For every demerit, you had to "walk the triangle," as they called it, twenty times. In good weather and bad. I must have worn out many shoes on that gravel. The infraction I got the most demerits for was bed-wetting. Try as I would to hide the evidence, I always got caught and would turn crimson with shame. I was clearly a nervous (and damp) child; but nobody seemed to think it was a good idea to address that problem in a different way. Today, you would be sent straight to a psychiatrist.

Those were unhappy days at Rose Haven. Some of the girls ridiculed me because I was French. Some made fun of my name. They pretended they couldn't pronounce it. They'd mangle it as "So Long" or "So-Lan-Jee" or even worse. (That's when I first changed my name to Marie.) They also laughed about the war in Europe. I remember that one of the girls complained that her wooden ruler was missing. And another suggested that I'd taken it and sent it to the French soldiers so they could burn it to warm themselves. Luckily, there was a nice girl, Mary Malone, a year older than me. She befriended me and even protected me. There must be a special spot in heaven for her kind soul.

There was only one other girl who spoke French. Her name was Michele Farmer, and we became friends. Michele's mother was Gloria Swanson, a Hollywood superstar ("Sunset Boulevard," etc.) She had a boyfriend named Joseph P. Kennedy, the father of then future president, John F. Kennedy.

On Sundays, parents would come to visit their children. On the weekends when my mother couldn't make it, Michele would invite me along to have lunch with her mother and Mr. Kennedy. They would pick us up in a long black limousine, which had not one but two chauffeurs who were in wine-colored livery and wore puttees. I can still remember Swanson's feathery boas and just as vividly, Joe Kennedy's stylish spats. Unlike most men's drab gray spats, Kennedy's were two-toned—beige on top, black on the bottom. We would be swept into their car, treated to a wonderful lunch at Miss Swanson's house in Englewood, and then swept back to school, with both chauffeurs endlessly opening and closing doors for us.

My life at Rose Haven School seemed dreary and dull as life can seem only to a teenage girl. The only task I remember starring at was turning the music pages for the father of one of the girls, a concert pianist, who would come to perform once in a while for students and their parents. I would sit next to him on the piano bench, sharing in the glory.

The memory of schooldays at Rose Haven and the visits by Gloria Swanson and Joe Kennedy served me well years later, in 1954, when I was staying with the Kennedys in Palm Beach. The house, called "Lagrend," had six bedrooms, a huge living room, a sparkling pool, and a manicured lawn that sloped down to the Atlantic. Jack and Jackie's corner bedroom had been on the ground floor, with French doors opening onto the tennis courts. But after Jack had his second back surgery, they moved him to a room with a hospital bed, technical equipment, and a live-in nurse. So Jackie and I shared their old bedroom by the pool. One morning, as Jackie walked out one door to see Jack, Joe Kennedy burst through the other and pounced on me. I guess he had figured out Jackie's schedule so he could plan his lascivious move. Stunned, I fled through the French doors onto the patio and plunged into the safety of the pool.

When I told Jackie about it, she shrugged it off. "Oh, he pulled the same trick last week on Lee" (her sister). And she explained his behaviour like this:

> "But don't you see? He's already had his way with all those Hollywood 'bad' girls. So now he wants to try his hand (or something) with some 'good' girls."

At dinner that night, there was a rare lull in the table talk. I looked at old man Kennedy right in the eye and said sweetly, "Oh, Mr. Kennedy. I remember years ago when you'd visit the Rose Haven School for Girls, and you would take Michele Farmer and me out for Sunday lunches." The old goat turned pale and squirmed. Luckily for him, Rose Kennedy at that moment asked for the cottage cheese to be passed, and he was saved by the bell. Or at least by the cottage cheese.

At this same swimming pool, Joe Kennedy had his "bull pen," a wooden enclosure with benches where, I heard, he sunbathed in the nude, slathered in cocoa butter, wearing only a broad-brimmed hat. There he held financial sway, swigging beer and barking out buy-and-sell orders over the phone to Wall Street lackeys who did his financial bidding. At the poolside, I got a kick out of hearing the way this tycoon would so casually sell short twenty thousand shares of Standard Oil here or buy long ten thousand shares of IBM there.

The cuisine served at the Kennedy compound was at best mediocre. But resourceful Jackie kept a cache of goodies like caviar and pâté hidden in the back of the icebox, which we raided in secret. It took her a long time in her own house to substitute peanut butter and jelly sandwiches for *oeufs en gelée*. Jack complained loud and long about Jackie's "improvements." But he gradually got used to them. This is the same Kennedy kitchen that had a revealing note scotch-taped on the refrigerator door addressed to the staff:

IF THE FAMILY IS SERVED STEAK, THE HELP WILL EAT
HAMBURGER.
IF THE FAMILY IS SERVED HAMBURGER, THE HELP
WILL EAT HOTDOGS.

I hate to think what the staff ate when the family was served hotdogs. This was just another reminder of a trait I've noticed so often in the very rich. Blessed with more money than they could ever spend, they usually have streaks of shocking stinginess. I remember a Christmastime, when I was visiting Jackie at "Merrywood," her stepfather Hugh Auchincloss' house, in MacLean, Virginia. (The house was Henry Jamesian, sort of a throwback to the one James described in "Washington Square.") Anyway, during this visit, I noticed several boxes stacked in an outside porch, which I thought were Christmas presents.

"Are you kidding?" Jackie said. "That's just my stepfather's way of economizing. He shuts off the freezers every winter and stores all the frozen food outside." Another tightwad award should have gone to the world's richest man, John D. Rockefeller. My godfather Welles Bosworth, told me that while pouring over receipts, John D. discovered that his kingly "Kykuit" estate on the Hudson (which Uncle Welles had put together for him) was burning eight hundred fifty tons of coal a year! He issued this command: "All thermostats must be lowered each night and raised later each morning." He added, "If one can save anything with today's high price of coal, it is criminal not to do so." (Actually and ecologically, he was way ahead of his time.)

Actually, when we arrived at "Merrywood" Jackie, Lee and I, Mrs. Auchincloss, Jackie and Lee's mother, had greeted us at the door and warmly greeted us by saying "Don't expect any meals, girls, the staff is too busy." Furthermore, she said she was very upset because the pyjamas she had ordered for Michael Canfield for Christmas had not arrived and I remember distinctly her saying "ah, well, it doesn't matter, he can sleep without pyjamas on Christmas night." Warm, she wasn't.

Jackie always invited my children and me for her Christmas party in New York. I remember one time, when at one of these parties, Mrs. Auchincloss rushed up to Marc who was six at the time and said "Now, you be a good boy, John-John." Marc was rather taken aback and so were the other people who witnessed the scene, though it's true that Marc & John looked rather alike . . . still . . . She became more and more vague in her later years and Jackie was wonderful about taking care of her, enlisting the help of her step-brother, Yushe. He was a saint to be so good about it, as she had not been particularly nice to him, ever. Her vagueness turned into Alzeimer's disease and she had to be watched like a hawk. At the reception following her daughter Janet's funeral, she disappeared. Searching parties were sent out to find her and finally tracked her down, hours later, wandering happily on Madison Avenue, some twenty blocks away from the Colony Club, from which she had jauntily set out.

CHAPTER 9

Hollywood

And then, a blessed day! My mother decided we should move to California. Her friends back East prompted her to move to Hollywood, painting a life that was happier and snappier, sunnier and funnier compared to dull, gray New York City. They even hinted at a glamorous life for me, where I would master surfing, tennis, water skiing, and maybe even find a career in the movies! (I'm glad that finally came true but only two generations later. Today, my twenty-year-old granddaughter, Melissa, is being seen in hit TV series like "Lost," "Cold Case," and "Law & Order." She's also getting major roles in movies like "Temple Grandin" and "Moth Diaries.") In a twinkling, our move to Hollywood drove away memories of my dreary, doleful year at Rose Haven. In glorious living color! The foliage! The houses! The celebrities! My mother certainly knew her share of actors: John Barrymore, Charles Boyer, Claudette Colbert, Walter Brennan, Mary Pickford, Cary Grant, and other out-of-this-world shining stars. Her inner circle was made up of serious artists and painters like Marcel Duchamp, Man Ray, Eugene Berman, and architects like Neff and Soriano, all of whom had moved to that magical land during the war.

We settled into a place called the Villa Carlotta at 5959 Franklin Avenue.

In 1941, *The New Yorker* described our neighborhood like this:

> *Franklin Avenue, skimming past the mouths of Hollywood's eastern canyon, at the disappearing edge of city maps, forms a half-hearted high street for the apartment dwellers clustered on its banks. Public life happens in the Mayfair grocery store, and in a*

block-long stretch of cafes and used-book stores. The apartment
buildings are old, and in some cases beautiful, like the Villa Carlotta,
a late-nineteen-twenties Mediterranean-style structure designed by
Arthur Harvey, where the architect Wallace Neff lived for many years.
Across from the Villa Carlotta is the avenue's defining anomaly: a
monumental turreted castle, also designed by Harvey, on a three-acre
site, with formal gardens, a bubbling stream, the famous tennis courts,
and a pair of rubber trees that are over one hundred years old. Seven
stories tall, the castle is like an overgrown folly the color of farm cream,
surrounded by swaying longneck palms that seem to graze its roofs.
Throughout the thirties and forties, the chateau was a Hollywood
hangout. A framed menu from 1937 quotes the price: (Creamed
Turnips, Gooseberry Cobbler, Filet Mignon Dinner, $1.50.) This
was in the primo eating-place in town, is the dining room where
Humphrey Bogart probably dined with Lauren Bacall.

The Carlotta had a private and treasured courtyard with a reflecting pool and a little stream surrounded by lovely trees and luxuriant flowers. I loved to watch the waters ripple and hear them gurgle. It added a magical bonus to living there.

I remember every glittering party my mother threw at the Villa Carlotta. They were unforgettable fun. Our ground floor apartment had a large living room with French doors that opened onto the courtyard and only one tiny bedroom. That was no problem for my inventive mother. She'd simply borrow, or rent, the apartment across the way for a single day and then have ample room for guests to stack their hats and coats and have space for extra guests to spill over into.

I had never heard of a Murphy bed; but now I had one and mine was in our living room and I couldn't believe what I was seeing the first time I watched it being pulled out of the wall and transformed into a bed. It was tidily made up and ready to jump into. An actress named Marguerite d' Alvarez lived in our building. She was Spanish and played as many Spanish parts as Katie Jurado did in later movies. She and my mother became great friends. Marguerite would often invite us up to her apartment for dinner, and we never refused. She was a superb cook. Her place smelled wonderfully of garlic and tomato sauces and herbs and spices.

These marvelous meals were doubly deeply appreciated because my mother didn't cook very much at all. She loved good food but had no interest in being in the kitchen. For example, she didn't exactly labor over my school lunch. Invariably, it was a slice of bread, a whole bar of Philadelphia Cream Cheese with another slice of bread slapped on top. If the spirit moved her and she was bursting with ambition, she'd pull out all the stops and create her dinner specialty: a grapefruit cut in half, a quick squirt of honey on top then on the grill for a minute or two. Serving it, she'd beam as if she'd roasted a whole ox on a spit.

The Villa Carlotta supplied us with Filipino servants who came in every day to make the beds and tidy up. They glided gracefully about, leaving a scent of Lysol trailing behind them.

In 2009, I went back for a visit to Franklin Avenue. The tennis courts at the Château Elysée have been turned into basketball courts, but the gardens were still blooming and well-kept. The Scientology Institute now owns the place and has turned it into their idea of a grand hotel. It's very glitzy, without a trace of tradition. I also revisited my beloved Ville Carlotta, and I'm happy to report that it hasn't changed one iota. There's the same grand piano in the same dark front hall, surrounded by the same red-velvet-covered Spanish chairs matching the red satin on the walls. The patio still has the bubbling little stream, and each bubble made me a little more nostalgic. Out of nostalgia, I put my name on the rental waiting list. And strangely enough, I had a call just the other day from the manager! He proudly announced that he had a short-term rental available. Oh, how I hated to turn that down. It would have been such fun to have a few Proustian moments there, a *La Recherche du Temps Perdu* sort of thing.

At the Château Elysée, the greatest tennis player of that time, Big Bill Tilden, reigned supreme. Before I went to school every morning, I took a lesson with him, volleying for a frenetic forty-five minutes. He always had the best-looking ball boys. I was very interested in these handsome dudes, but alas, Bill Tilden was even more interested in them. And that predilection proved his undoing. This great world champion later went to prison for unseemly approaches to seemly ball boys. But in those younger, better days, Tilden set the style. In tennis and in fashion. He wore wonderful long cream-colored flannel pants and was so distinguished-looking and handsome. He absolutely dominated every court he played on. And as brilliant as he was competitive, he was also unmatched as a teacher. He had created an extraordinary teaching technique. He would mark off his side of the court with squares and number them 1 to 20. When he'd return a ball to you, he'd yell out "Fourteen!" or "Seven!" or "Five" or whatever, and then you had to hit the ball back to that called-out square. His method forced you to developed terrific control so you became very precise at placing the ball.

The Adonis-like John Barrymore often dropped in for dinner. At that time, he was idolized and lionized by New York stage audiences and millions of movie fans the world over. This high-living, fast-moving paragon was a charismatic presence who entered a room about thirty seconds before he arrived. But "arrive" is the wrong word. Barrymore made a show-stopping *entrance*. He would swoop in, his faithful valet a precise three feet behind him, mostly to steady The Great Profile's course, I'm certain. After doffing his enormous feather-bedecked hat, he'd fling it across the room toward the bed where the coats were, and I, panting with adoration, would race over to catch it. He always talked a blue streak, performing all the while so it hardly mattered what he said. Effortlessly, he transformed everyone into an audience, his orchestra of a voice making his every utterance something to be treasured. Barrymore lived life and loved life. Once, when asked to explain his insouciance about drinking, I distinctly heard him quoting Mark Twain on the subject:

> "You can't drown yourself in drink. I've tried. You float." And Barrymore did a lot of floating.

Another movie star actor living near us was the unpolished-seeming Walter Brennan. He parlayed a gangling shuffle, a querulous voice, and an invincibly lifelike style that delighted movie and TV audiences decade after decade. But very few audiences were aware that the characters he portrayed in Hollywood's epic World War I and II movies were matched by his real-life performance as a soldier. His daughter attended Immaculate Heart High School, where she and I became friends.

Arnold Genthe, the great German-born photographer, was an admirer of my mother and took endless photographs of her. (He did the same with Greta Garbo and is credited with first discovering her matchless beauty. Indeed Genthe's camera revealed Garbo's incredible photographic magic. Hollywood producers didn't see much promise in the great star until they saw Genthe's photos.) He also had me pose for him, and I hated the results. But since Isadora Duncan, Mary Pickford, Theodore Roosevelt, John Barrymore, Toscanini, Paderewski, and Woodrow Wilson also sat for him, I guess I was in fairly good company and didn't realize it. He was living in San Francisco during the great earthquake and lost his studio, his archives, his equipment. But undaunted, he borrowed a camera from a passerby and took three iconic photos of the still-blazing city, the only ones in existence. One of them is of such superb quality you'll see it reproduced in every major collection.

The painter Eugene Berman also lived at Villa Carlotta. I would sit for him after school. He made me feel special, and the modeling pocket money came in handy. Berman often asked me to let my hair hang down over my bowed head. He was essentially drawing my wild, unruly hair, not my face, thank you very much. I kept my hair really long in those days, and I could hide my schoolbooks underneath and do my homework. I still have some of Berman's sketches of me (and my hair). His drawings became increasingly well-known. His subjects were mainly theater personages. He created a lot of Diaghilev's ballet sets. People said Berman was a closet gay. I didn't know what that meant; years and years later, he was murdered in Central Park in New York City. The rumor was that his death came about because of some homosexual activities in the park.

Two of America's bigger-than-life movie stars, Charles Boyer and Claudette Colbert, were frequent dinner guests of my mother. Boyer usually showed up without his toupee but *with* his mother, Madame Rossignol. Boyer's forceful parent was obsessed with her plan for her son to marry Claudette. Her dream was that these two brightest of French stars would be a magical (box-office) team. The only fly in the ointment was that Claudette loathed Charles, and Charles disliked Claudette even more strongly.

And neither ever tried to disguise their feelings, which made for some very chilly dinner parties. It took all my mother's considerable conversational skills to keep things on an even keel even as Boyer's mother kept beating those marital drums, which, for some reason, I was quite aware of.

When I was in Barbados during the early 1990s, I was taken for lunch at Claudette Cobert's charming house overlooking the ocean. Though ninety years old, she was faultlessly groomed and garbed, looking just about the same as in those fast-paced films of her MGM days. I asked if she remembered those long-ago evenings at the Villa Carlotta. She immediately made the connection, and we reminisced together over those nights, even laughing again about the marital plotting of Boyer's ever-hopeful mother. Later on, Claudette played some Edith Piaf records for me, and the Little Sparrow's mournful melodies had her crying and crying on my shoulder. It was a touching and memorable moment. (Marred only by the fact that at age ninety, Claudette had false teeth that didn't fit all that well, and I was terrified they'd fall out onto my sympathetic shoulder.)

Arnold Genthe
photos.

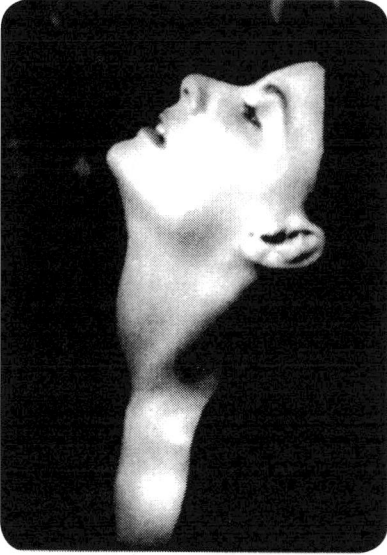

Greta Garbo.

My Mother.

My Mother

Marie Batsell (Me as Barbara in a 1941
Hollywood play of the same name)

The Villa Carlotta
in Hollywood.

Entrance hallway.

Courtyard.

Each morning I'd walk the ten blocks or so from the Villa Carlotta up Franklin Avenue to Immaculate Heart High School. This was the school where all the Catholic movie stars sent their daughters. The nuns who taught us wore floor-length habits with starched wimples and clicking rosary beads. We had to greet them in Latin. "Ave!" for "Hello," "Vale!" for "Good-bye." I spoke Latin with a very strong French accent and saw no reason to copy my peers, who pronounced their Latin with an *American* accent you could cut with a knife. And *they* made fun of *my* pronunciation?

Ah, but Immaculate Heart was a wonderful school, and I loved it. I had a schoolgirl crush on Sister Victoria and harbored dreams of becoming a nun myself. She was so beautiful and ever cheerful. She shared my love for tennis and played a mean game of it—long habit, veil, clunky shoes, and all. We had a lot of classes on religious education and said our prayers daily (lots and lots of prayers) always in Latin. My image of nuns up to that time was of shamefully restricted women with shaven heads, dressed in medieval costumes and under the belittling thumb of men. From the Pope, right on down to the littlest priest like that still-remembered one who had discussed "Eternity" to seven-year-old me on the steps of the Sacré Coeur in Monmartre.

I didn't think of them as individual humans able to laugh or cry or feel *any* emotion except maybe an unfocused piety. But now I got to know them as spirited women who, when they weren't frightening their charges into submission, were thoughtful, inquisitive, and obviously longing for friendship and laughter.

An exception to this was the Mother Superior, who left me paralyzed when, in front of the class, she told me that since my mother and my father had not been married in a Catholic church, *I was a child of sin!* That was certainly hitting below the belt; but on second thought, it made me sound kind of different and special, and life went on. Every morning after my tennis lesson and before classes started, I practiced on the piano in one of the tiny music cubicles on the third floor, which were very foreboding.

(We didn't have a piano at home, and my mother was determined not to let my previous music training fade away.) There were no apple slices on top of the piano, and that made me miss my grandmother even more.

The school had an exceptional music and dance department. For one production, I was cast as a Russian soldier in Tchaikovsky's Nutcracker Suite, in which I performed, boot-slapping and all (which I still could do until last year when my over-Cossacked knees gave out.) I also took dance lessons with the famous modern dance instructor, Lester Horton, who made us dance African dances in bare feet and was the first one to introduce the genre in the U.S.

My mother had a persistent admirer from the movie industry. He was some kind of Hollywood mogul, and I simply couldn't stand him. Somehow I discovered he was Jewish, and I figured out my plan. At Immaculate High, as at other Catholic schools and as a reward for good grades, the nuns handed out religious pictures (or "holy cards," as they were dubbed.) My good marks helped me amass a thick stack of St. Josephs, baby Jesuses, St. Francises St. Annes, Virgin Marys, etc. So whenever this man came for dinner, I would substitute his place card with a holy and haloed Catholic saint. And I could tell it really got under his skin. Although she was a stickler for good manners, I don't think my mother ever scolded me for it. She didn't particularly appreciate going with me when I was invited to my classmate's houses, but I managed to drag her to them once in a while. I remember one that she really hated. At dinner, the father always sat at the head of the table. Once the serving dishes were placed in front of him, from the other end of the table, his wife would shout, "Dish it out, Roland!" That was certainly not my mother's style (but the expression stayed as a code between us to indicate hopeless boorishness).

Speaking of dinner tables, to this day, I feel guilty if I don't finish everything on my plate, as I remember my mother admonishing me if I didn't eat "until I saw the bunny on the plate" and telling me about the thousands-*thousands*-of poor little Chinese children on the other side of the globe who were starving and who would be so grateful to have even just half of what was left on my plate. I once suggested we could always send my left-over string beans to those thousands of poor, hungry, little Chinese children; but that didn't go over too well. I had no idea where China was except that I had repeatedly been told when digging a hole in the sand on the beach that if I dug far enough, I would get to China- and I thought that would be a pretty direct route to send the string beans.

At some point, my mother grew disenchanted with the school's Catholic imprinting on me. She certainly took a dim view of my plans for becoming a nun. So she abruptly switched me to Hollywood High. I only stayed there for one year, but what a year! It meant a new freedom to me, and besides, where else would you get to sit next to Elizabeth Taylor in your typing class?

At age fifteen, Elizabeth Taylor was already impossibly gorgeous and glamorous. She wore fake fingernails and taught me how to put them on my fingers. The nails were so long that sometimes the glue would fail and a nail would fall between the keys of our typewriters. Luckily, in typing class, we switched seats every day, so nobody could figure out who was wrecking the machines. Not even the hapless repairman who was going crazy fixing the typewriters.

Elizabeth Taylor's father owned a gallery at the Beverly Hills Hotel, and he and my mother were friends, though Mummy didn't think the artworks he showed were quite up to snuff. I often went there with Liz. Then came the day she quit school to star in "National Velvet," her first step toward superstardom. But it's a small world, and our paths would cross again.

Mummy and I went to the Beverly Hills Hotel a lot. She often played tennis there with Katharine Hepburn. The two of them were matched closely enough athletically to keep the game interesting. I remember how shocked I was the first time Mummy took me along to watch them play. Hepburn was turned out in these white sharkskin shorts. They were all the rage back then. They were glossy and kind of sheer. And Kate, the Great wore no underwear. You could see everything! I was a prim and proper convent miss in those days, and I made my feelings known. I told my mother that Hepburn's outfits were simply disgraceful and that the nuns certainly wouldn't approve. She shook her head and told me not to be such a little prude. But I noticed that Mummy continued to wear underwear under *her* sharkskin shorts.

For me, the best thing about the Beverly Hills Hotel was the enormous swimming pool. Renowned sun worshippers lounged all around it. Talk about the Beautiful People. There, in person (and in the flesh) were stars and starlets, male and female, their bodies as perfect as their faces. The women with their hair piled up into pompadours or stiffly sprayed into complicated hairdos. I'd see Betty Grable, Hollywood's highest-paid star, Ida Lupino, the most talented, and Victor Mature flexing his oily biceps. One standout was the artist Salvador Dali, as surreal as his paintings, with his signature waxed moustache pointing heavenward. Dali never put his head under water. His mustache would have flopped down. I remember that he showed me his watch, which had live ants walking around inside the dial. He was a consummate showman, easily attracting more attention than the showbiz showoffs. Somehow he discovered that I had sailed on the Normandie in 1935, and that impressed him. He carried on and on about how he'd made a Normandie crossing himself in 1936. He seemed a lot more excited about it than I ever was. I got to know the Dalis better years later, and they invited me to their house in Cadaquez, Spain, for the funeral of one of their beloved Andalusian stallions. Now this was what I'd call a genuinely surrealist burial. Young girls, almost naked, their long hair flying in the breeze, rode bareback on equally long-maned Andalusians and jumped across the Dalis' horse's open grave over and over again, accompanied by wild Castillian music. This was followed by an even wilder luncheon. Dali had just illustrated a cookbook called "Gala's Dinners," and every course came out of that book. I remember "Casanova Cookies," "Aphrodite's Purée," "Pierced Heart," "Green, White, and Red Lobster," and for dessert, "Queen of Sheba Sherbet." Gala and Salvador Dali were light years beyond eccentric. In New York, they lived at the St. Regis Hotel and loped across Fifty-second Street almost every day for lunch at the Côte Basqve, where Bernard Lamotte had his beautiful murals. Nothing out of the way there, except that along with his cloak and hat, Dali would check his full-grown, diamond-collared cheetah. The hat-check ladies were expected to care for the beast. That cheetah scared many of the customers (and many of the hat-check girls) away.

Around the Beverly Hills Hotel pool, I could always pick up an autograph or two for my burgeoning collection. But the best place by far for getting signatures was at Grauman's Chinese Theater at Hollywood and Vine. It's still there and still a great tourist attraction to this day. I'd faithfully join the fans to watch while the latest anointed stars added their hands and footprints to the famed sidewalk. Then I'd stick my autograph book under their perfect noses and get them to sign, sometimes getting them to add a little personal message.

Our beach was nothing special. It was only perhaps the most majestic in California: Malibu! It was even fun to say. My mother had friends there who would pick us up and drive us out to the beach in a nifty convertible with a rumble seat. To my mind, there's never been anything as exciting as a rumble seat. There was a rubber footpad on the rear fender. You stepped up on that then down into the rumble seat. It was really cozy. What was less—or was it more?—exciting was one day when I shared that rumble seat with this very attractive older man. He was probably pushing thirty or maybe even thirty-one. This dinosaur started flirting with me. I couldn't quite figure out what was going on. At some point, he grabbed me and tried to kiss me. That was the first time anyone tried to kiss me. A stolen kiss from an older man is pretty torrid stuff, especially when you're all of fifteen and in a rumble seat, to boot.

My practical mother never liked to spend money uselessly. For example, if we went to the beach on our own, she wouldn't dream of getting a bathhouse for us to change in. Instead, we switched into our bathing suits while hiding behind a parked car. One time, while I was in the middle of my fast change, the car pulled away. There I was, in the middle of the parking lot, naked as a jaybird. Mummy thought it was very funny. I didn't.

One summer, we rented a house in Benedict Canyon. That was the summer Fifi Johnson stayed with us. (Her father, James Wood Johnson of

Johnson & Johnson fame, had been one of my father's backers and advised Mummy about different financial things after my father died.) The same Johnsons who had me stay with them in France before the war so I guess she felt we had to reciprocate. Fifi had a blasé attitude about money. One time, she borrowed twenty dollars from one of the staff, who told on her when she didn't return the loan. Fifi then lied and swore that *I* was the borrower. Finally, to my endless relief, her mother and father came back from Hawaii, collected Fifi and took her away; but our paths crossed again in New York; and we became friends and even shared some beaus. One of them, Ron Caffrey, just called me out of the blue the other day to find out how she and I were. (So he could improve his "bucket list"!) Life turned out very badly for poor Fifi. She eloped with a man called W.C. Klenk. Apparently, they got caught making out bad checks in South America and ended up in jail. James Johnson had to bail them out. She finally divorced W.C. and checked into a psychiatric hospital. That's where she married a fellow inmate, who had been lobotomized. Spiraling downward, she slipped into a suicidal depression and killed herself. Hers was a sad, very sad life. She was my second childhood friend to die, and it made a lasting impression on me. The first friend I lost was a girl at Friends Academy who hanged herself from the shower. I was the one who found her, and in the strange manner of young people, somehow felt I was responsible. For not getting there in time to save her, I guess.

Back again to Benedict Canyon. I concentrated on my other great passion, horseback riding. The stables were a good half-hour walk from our house, but walk it I did every day. The stables were run by a Mr. Skinner, who was young, handsome, and tall in the saddle. I remember something else about those stables. To control the flies, they had these electric machines that would attract them then electrocute them. I can still hear the ghastly sizzle when the flies met their end. I spent a lot of time on horseback, there and at the Bel Air Hotel stables. The latter were very grand. And it was there that I fell in love with a dreamboat—who also rode very well—Alan Keith. I was dazzled by Alan and his Australian family. They lived in a beautiful house in Bel Air. Greer Garson who had won an Oscar in 1942 for "Mrs. Miniver" lived next door. He'd come around to see me at Margaret Camp's, where I was staying at the time. I was mad about Alan. One day, he and I were sitting in her living room with the lights down low. Without warning, Margaret came storming in, turned the lights all the way up, and yelled, "Now, listen! You children must learn how to behave!" We were behaving pretty well, I thought, and we turned the lights low again as soon as she left.

Whenever my mother had to leave town, she would leave me with Margaret Camp. Mrs. Camp was the head of the Red Cross in California and the widow of the legendary football coach Walter Camp, Jr., for whom the football stadium at Yale is named. She lived in a pretty little house in Westwood, which had a professional croquet court in the back. Margaret sort of introduced me to the facts of life. My mother certainly never thought of broaching the subject. She hadn't even explained to me that with girls, a certain thing happened every month. Well, when that natural and normal situation happened to me, I thought I was dying. I remember some of my classmates had to tell me very vaguely and a bit inaccurately what it was all about. Margaret, on the other hand, was very explicit. In fact, she carried on about it quite a bit. She revealed that once when she and Mr. Camp were hiking up a mountain, she reached back to take his hand and instead felt something hard in his pants. She wondered why he was carrying a rock in his pocket and only later figured it out all by herself. The story didn't make much sense to me . . . but it somehow remained vaguely in my mind until much later when I finally guessed what was what. You must understand, there were no men around when I was growing up; we were a totally matriarchal clan—my grandmother, my mother, and me. It wasn't until I was fourteen that I saw a naked man. I mean, I had seen some statues in museums. But letting my imagination go astray, I thought that the reason men wore long trousers was to conceal whatever they had to hide in those long trousers and that whatever it was that they had to hide went down their pants all the way to the floor and that they would use that long thing to lasso girls' waists with. So when I saw the real thing, it was a bit of a disappointment. I was staying with the Johnsons in a house they had rented for the summer in South Norwalk, Connecticut and I was madly in love with my friend, Fifi Johnson's older brother, Francis and was crushed that he paid absolutely no attention to me no matter how hard I tried to impress him. He and his college friend, Frank Warren, would invite tons of twenty-year-old girls to parties, and naturally, Fifi and I were not included in their festivities, which infuriated us, so, one day, we decided we would get even and go spy on them. They had all just come in from swimming and had gone to change in the guest bedrooms upstairs, and I persuaded Fifi to walk along the gutters of the first floor hanging onto the window sills above so we could peek into the windows. Well, from the first window we reached, we saw Frank Warren standing in the middle of the room quite naked; and it was a horrible sight and a terrible shock. Not only did he have a lot of hair on his chest but all over the place too, and all I could think about was how Darwin, whom I just read about, was right and that we were indeed descendants of the apes. He spotted us and told on us, which we didn't think was a very nice thing for that gorilla to do. We also spied on the butler and the cook and caught them "at it" in the servants' quarters, looking through a *vas ist das* window on top of a door, which we had hoisted ourselves up to on a shaky ladder. I guess we were quite athletic, determined girls. They also caught us and came after us with brooms and fly-swatters. We really got into trouble for that and were forbidden the beach for a week so instead of moping inside, we spent that time we lost at the beach cutting the flowers from the cutting garden, setting up a stand on the Old Boston Post Road, and making quite a lot of money selling them. Our prices weren't very high, and one day, a neighbor congratulated the Johnsons on our entrepreneurship and shrewdness at selling their flowers at below the market prices. That cost us, and we were put to work in the pantry washing dishes for a whole week (the help was delighted!).

Every Sunday, Margaret Camp invited people to come for a huge buffet supper, and they all played her cutthroat brand of croquet afterwards. She had a boyfriend named Mr. Borden, who lived in the house next door. Sometimes, out of the blue, Margaret would rush me out of the house to run a trumped up errand; and by the time I got back, there would be Mr. Borden, grinning sheepishly. In those innocent days, I didn't know anything. I didn't even suspect anything. I just thought Mr. Borden didn't like to do errands.

From Margaret, I picked up some secrets for setting beautiful tables. I watched once as she laid out huge red poinsettias on her dining room table. No vases, no water, just plunk! Right on the tablecloth. A milky substance seeped out of them, and I was appalled. I pointed it out to Margaret.

"Those flowers will ruin your tablecloth."

Margaret shrugged and told me the effect was artistic.

"When you're seeking beauty, Solange, you should never be too practical." And I have always followed that advice.

During one of her longer absences, Mummy left me with Margaret Camp for a whole four months. I had to transfer to the Beverly Hills High School from Hollywood High. My mother was traveling all over California, Arizona, and New Mexico with Hazel Guggenheim McKinley. Hazel's father was Benjamin Guggenheim, who went down with the Titanic. He had two daughters. Hazel and Peggy. Peggy was also Mother's friend, the famous (and infamous) Peggy Guggenheim, a collector with an incredible eye, whose art-filled palazzo in Venice was a Mecca for artists and writers. When she died, Peggy left her extraordinary palazzo and collection worth many, many millions, to the Republic of Venice. She had no children left, and nothing at all went to any of her grandchildren. Anyway, Hazel was a little crazy. And no mother ever had a greater reason to be. I find it almost impossible to describe her tragedy, but here it is: Hazel was staying in the penthouse of the Plaza Hotel. One day, she was out on her terrace with her two children. She was carrying the infant baby girl while her two-year-old son was playing at her feet. When the boy suddenly ventured too close to the edge, Hazel made a grab for him. When she did, the baby fell out of her arms and over the railing, hurtling to the ground far below. In the confusion, she lost her frantic grip on the other child, who also tumbled to his death. It was an inconceivable, unacceptable, and still almost unmentionable trauma from which Hazel never recovered.

Years later, she married a much younger man who was the nephew of President McKinley. Eventually, Hazel divorced young McKinley, whose only other claim to fame was being a pilot and an erratic one at that.

Hazel was always attracted to younger men. I remember when I married Fred Herter, she kept calling him on the phone. Nothing in particular to talk about, she just loved Fred's young—sounding voice. One generation off or not, I kept her at bay.

Margaret Camp had given me not one but *two* tennis racquets. I was so proud of them that I hung them, crisscrossed above my bed. I thought they looked very artistic. But I caught hell from her just because I'd pounded two nails into her guest room wall. It suited my idea of decorating, and, after all, she hadn't minded those poinsettia stains. Anyway, the racquets had to stay to cover the nail holes, so I was happy.

Margaret always wore a wig, and whenever she got mad or excited, it would shift all over her head. My reaction was a mixture of hilarity . . . or guilt . . . if I had caused her anger.

I knew a boy named Joe who was dull as ditchwater. But he'd invite me to dances, and we'd take the bus to get to wherever the dance bands were playing. The first dance I went to, I wore rubber soles and soon found out you simply can't dance smoothly wearing rubber soles. So I saved up my allowance and bought myself a nice pair of black patent leather party shoes, which I loved. They were very shiny and had a lovely strap, which went over the top of the foot and buttoned on the side. One night, Joe and I were walking home after one of the dances. I spied a couple of tires. They were just sitting there, on a front lawn, and since tires were so scarce during the war, I got Joe to help me wheel them back to Margaret Camp's house. I was sure she'd be tickled pink at this serendipitous windfall. Well, she was far from grateful; she was *furious*. She not only made me roll the tires back but made me apologize to the owner. That was my first experience proving that no good deed goes unpunished. Gallant Joe blamed it all on me so I quickly dumped the spineless vertebrate and found other boys to take me to dances.

That same summer, I also had a crush on the boy who worked at the local drugstore on Franklin Avenue. His name was Tommy, and he performed his art behind the soda fountain. I was mesmerized by his mastery of the ice cream scoop. I found myself going there a lot and must have gulped an ocean of ice cream sodas and sundaes. But he wasn't just a soda jerk. In a pinch, he also filled in at the prescription counter. Mummy didn't share my fixation on this drugstore cowboy. She tried to nip our romance in the bud by sending me to the drug store to buy the most awful things, like Kotex and suppositories, and I would get very flustered and embarrassed when I had to approach the counter and ask my ideal for these unseemly products. Ah well, my crush didn't even last the summer. I guess I was more interested in playing tennis and admiring Bill Tilden's ball boys. I think I was what they call "boy crazy."

In Hollywood, my mother became naturalized, and she brought me with her for the ceremony. I was mortified. The very thought of having a foreign mother was demeaning. But I dutifully tagged along, and was I *glad!* The minute we walked in, there he *was!* America's idol. No. The world's idol. Cary Grant! All I could see was my mother and Cary, both raising their hands at the same time. The two of them becoming America's newest citizens along with a dozen others. That made the whole day okay. Even better than okay because after that, Cary Grant often came for dinner at the Villa Carlotta. Of course, it was convenient for him because he lived right across from us at the Château Elysée. And best of all, Cary Grant in real life was just as charming and captivating as he was in the movies, except that off-screen, he often reverted to his strong Cockney, accent which was a bit off-putting. He was born Archibald Alexander Leach in 1904, which made him six years younger than my mother, but it didn't stop him from being an admirer. This quintessential Hollywood superstar died in lackluster Iowa while on a cross-country tour, still young, and it made me terribly sad.

When we moved away from Hollywood and back to New York, it meant leaving Alan Keith. My heart was broken as only a fifteen-year-old's heart can break. Actually, I had already heard on the teen grapevine that the minute I left, Alan took up with a girlfriend of mine. Soon after we moved to 33 Sutton Place South, he came to New York and dropped in to see me. I was all atwitter even though I knew he'd been "unfaithful." He arrived at Sutton Place and hugged me, and I asked if he could stay for dinner. Actually, since I had no "dinner" planned, I was hoping he'd ask me out to a restaurant, but he blithely said, "Oh, no. I have a date with a girl, and I can't renege because she's grilling a steak for me." So she grilled his steak and cooked his goose at the same time.

Au revoir, Alan Keith. Or so I thought. But years later, I actually saw him again, at good old Bel Air. He looked pretty spry at age eighty-two, but he didn't seem to remember much about me from only sixty years ago at the alluring age of fifteen! Talk about fickle!

I was soon enrolled at Friends Academy in Locust Valley, Long Island. The school was chosen because an old friend of my father, Welles Bosworth, lived near the school on Piping Rock Road, in a beautiful house called "Old Trees." His daughters, Françoise and Audrey, also went to Friends as day students. They were so francophile that whenever anyone said anything against Napoleon, Louis XIV or XV or XVI or XVII or XVIII or XVIIII or *any* French subject, they would burst into tears, making a mawkish scene. Their mother was very anti-Vichy, and my mother was not particularly Gaullist; in fact, she was a great friend of the ambassador from Vichy, Henri Haye, and was a frequent visitor to the embassy in Washington, which people like the Bosworths didn't approve of. But strangely enough, my Mother met de Gaulle after the war and became quite friendly with 'Le Grand Charles' and 'Tante Yvonne' and I remember one time when she took me with her to Colombey. Madame de Gaulle was furious about having to receive the German Chancellor Konrad Adenauer in her house, "La Boisserie" for lunch—I couldn't believe it when I saw all the chipped plates and platters, the miserable kitchen silver and the mis-assorted glasses that had been put on the table which was usually quite well laid-out. It was her way of showing her displeasure at having to have a "Bôche" under her roof. When he arrived, Adenauer immediately understood the situation and, without skipping a beat, thanked her for receiving him as if he were a member of the family.

But, to get back to Ambassador Haye during the war he periodically went back to France. While there, he'd visit my grandmother, bringing presents and letters from my mother. He was really a good sport to do this because he had to climb up and down five flights of the service stairs at rue Georges Berger. My grandmother's elevator, like most elevators in Paris, didn't work at all during the war. She herself climbed those stairs four times a day: In the morning, when she went to work, then home for lunch, back to work in the afternoon, and finally one more trip when she came home at night. She was in her late seventies, stiff with arthritis and lame with rheumatism. I recently installed a mechanical stair chair just to go up and down *one little flight in our New York apartment* and often think of how my grandmother was more valiant than I.

Uncle Welles faithfully showed up at our school theater for plays or concerts. He always flaunted a big black opera cape which flared when he walked, exposing its red silk lining and he flourished a gold-knobbed stick. His hair, what little he had, crisscrossed his skull. It looked like railroad tracks gone awry. I was always very embarrassed when he made an appearance. But I realized later what an interesting man he was. Thanks to John D. Rockefeller, Jr., Uncle Welles was appointed *Secrétaire General du Comité pour la Restoration de Versailles, Fontainebleau et la Cathédrale de Reims*, and he earned vast commissions from the post. These, of course, on top of the huge amounts of money he got from the Rockefeller family for planning and executing the fabulous gardens at the Rockefeller estate on the Hudson River, "Kykuit." He completed the costly landscaping with the encouragement of John D. Junior over the strong objections by John D. Senior, who thought Welles Bosworth was much too extravagant and expensive. The billionaire didn't go for Uncle Welles's idea of the great "Benefits of the Unnecessary!" (It was John Junior, who, after France fell and the Nazi storm troopers commandeered the Bosworths' house outside Paris, helped the Bosworth's find refuge in Long Island.)

I was invited to "Kikuyit" quite often by Nelson Rockefeller and one day while we were having lunch, all these helicopters started circling the front lawns, making luncheon conversation quite impossible. I asked Nelson why they were doing this and he told me that he had found it more economical to move his outdoor sculptures (Henry Moores, Calders, Brancusis, David Smiths, etc.) by helicopter than by ropes and pulleys. Bosworth's house, near Versailles, was called "Marietta"; and the French, being French, thought it was named after an old girlfriend. But the real story was much less romantic: Uncle Welles came from Marietta, Ohio, though you'd never guess it. And I don't think he ever told the French.

After the war, John D. Rockefeller gave Uncle Welles a million dollars, (like $20 million today) to make improvements to the Château de Versailles. The French hoped he'd use the windfall to do things like regilding the entrance gates or other glamorous things. But instead, extremely practical Uncle Welles used up all the money to insert thousands of little triangles in the walls to stabilize the stonework by creating aeration. Maybe it wasn't artistic, and the

French derided him, but curators later acclaimed his work and confirmed that those little metal triangles are the only reason Versailles is still standing.

Whenever Uncle Welles took us to tour Versailles, he'd endlessly point them out. They weren't particularly thrilling to us, but they made him pleased as punch. And rightly so.

I loved my time at Friends Academy and studied very hard. I graduated in 1945 summa cum laude. There is still a brass plaque of the cum laude Society there which bears my name. Marie Batsell . . . not Solange. Like my father, I often changed my name. When I proudly took Fred Herter to see that plaque, he had the nerve to question whether that girl named "Marie" was actually me!

CHAPTER 10

The Return to France after the War

My Mother and I took the very first "Liberty" boat going to France in 1945. The so-called Liberty boats were luxury liners that had been stripped down to bare minimum to transport troops during World War II; and when the war ended, stripped as they were, they were temporarily used to carry paying passengers across the pond: six bunks to a cabin, a very, very small cabin, a very Spartan bathroom down the hall, a pretty basic mess hall, that sort of thing. But we didn't mind; we were so happy to be amongst the first expatriates to go back. Actually, in our cabin, we were seven. A rather large German lady by the name of Mrs. Taub, one of our bunkmates, the first night out announced that she was travelling with Mr. Taub; but he was incognito. She told us she had had to smuggle him aboard because the powers that be had wanted her to pay for his passage even though he had been reduced to ashes! All very jolly except that I slept in the bunk under Mr. and Mrs. Taub (she had also told us he never left her side), and it made me rather uneasy during the whole journey.

When I came back to America that summer of 1945, I spent a year with my mother in New York at 33 Sutton Place South. I attended the Lycée Francais, where I got my baccalaureate. The Lycée was at Seventy-second Street between Madison and

"Marietta," Uncle Welles Bosworth's house near Versailles.

Excerpt from Friends Academy year book
C L A S S   O F   1 9 4 5

SOLANGE MARIE BATSELL
Marie
PROVERB: "Music is said to be the speech of angels."
BORN: September 8, 1928, Paris, France
ADDRESS: 33 Sutton Place South, New York City
DATE ENTERED: September, 1943
COLLEGE: Cornell or St. Lawrence University

ACTIVITIES: President of Girls' Athletic Association, President of Press Club, President of Latin Club, "Red and Black" Staff, Student Council, Vice-President of Class, Cheer Leader, "Madness in Triple Time", Orchestra, Debate Club, Executive Board, Junior Varsity Basketball, Varsity Basketball, Varsity Lacrosse, Archery Squad, Student Teacher, Cum Laude and Scarab Society.

PREFERENCES: France, "Valentines", rhumbas, "Smoke Gets in Your Eyes", dancing, skiing, Bill Prince, snow, motorcycle rides, Chopin and "Globules."
DISLIKES: Bratty little boys, 7 a.m., Math., bugs, soup lappers, and squeaky sopranos.
AMBITION: A dancing journalist.

Year book photograph.

Fifth Avenue. A very grand building which now belongs to the Emir of Bahrain. To my dismay, there were absolutely no sports taught or played there. I missed them terribly, being spoiled by all the wonderful green playing fields in Long Island and the swimming and tennis and eternal sunshine of California. All we had at the Lycée was one measly, rusty, bent, basketball hoop in a miserable stone courtyard that measured about the size of three small cars. We were also allowed one hour twice a week to *walk* in Central Park. And that comprised our entire exercise regimen.

Our railroad flat was on Sutton Place South, part of what was called the Phipps Estates. Henry Phipps, one of Andrew Carnegie's partners, bought a row of tenement houses back in the 1920s. They were in terrible shape, and in 1922, Phipps gave Dorothy Draper, New York's stellar interior decorator, a free hand in transforming them. And she did. Ours was one of a dozen charming little brick houses painted black with handsome white fire escapes and balconies and bright red doors. Draper created a magical row of memorable houses. They were enviably nice. They overlooked the East River, and there was a huge garden, which everybody shared that sloped right down to the riverside. This was during World War II. We had a German superintendent, Mr. Boom, whom I was convinced was a Nazi spy. Well, no wonder! Mr. Boom lived in the basement, which had windows just at the level of the lawn where he could easily keep track of all the East River boat traffic. I suspected he owned a high-powered spyglass to see everything and a short-wave radio to contact submarines and zeppelins or whatever a wicked spy did. To my great disappointment, and I spied on him a lot, Mr. Boom was never caught. In real life, Fred Boom turned out to be an exemplary (if unadventurous) American citizen.

To this day, I can still recall an old lady named Mrs. Ackerman, who lived across the hall from us. She kept a dozen or so scraggly cats that howled and yowled and smelled to high heaven. They were endlessly snarling or hissing at us from her windowsill. I blame those devil-cats for my lifelong aversion to their kind. Cats still make me shudder so, of course, no matter how many people are around, they always choose me to rub against. But there was a good side to Mrs. Ackerman. Every year, she hid eggs in the garden for all the neighborhood children to find, and the gates were flung open for them to come to our very private enclave Easter egg-hunting

Our railroad flat was quite a delight. You walked right in off Fifty-fifth Street and the Sutton Place South sidewalk into our living room, where I had my piano. (This was a Christmas present from my mother, who, when it didn't arrive on time for Christmas one year, charmingly announced its imminent presence by making a drawing of a piano and putting it under our beautiful little plastic snow-white tree.) Off the living room was the central corridor, which led you through the apartment. At its end was our kitchen, tucked behind louvered doors. To the left were some closets and then the bathroom. A large bedroom overlooked the garden, which overlooked the mighty East River. It was small but all in all a charmingly rustic spot amidst the hurly-burly of Manhattan. A New York Times article pretty well sums it up.

My mother infront of 33 Sutton Place South

Storied Brick Houses in Sutton Place to
Tumble Soon Under Wreckers' Hammer

Cannon Point houses, overlooking the East River at Sutton Place,
between Fifty-fifth and Fifty-sixth Streets.

By MEYER BERGER

*FOR more than a year the windows of the black-painted,
white-trim brick houses in Sutton Place on the East River between
Fifty-fifth and Fifty-sixth Streets have worn the wreckers' doom mark
— the whitewash cross. Scaffolding went up around the old dwellings
last week. Soon the row will be rubble. A nineteen-story and penthouse
cooperative to be called Cannon Point North, straddling Franklin D.
Roosevelt Drive, will soar from the old plot. It will be a companion
development to Cannon Point South, now under construction.*

*Indians speared and netted fish off rocky Cannon Point for
ages. They found it rich in oysters, too, and feasted on them at that
same spot. After the Britons took Manhattan from the Dutch in
mid-seventeenth century, Sir Edmund Andros granted sixty acres
there to David Du Fou, a native of Mons. The Du Fou family later
turned up in deeds as Du Fore and Devore. The original rental of
the sixty acres was "one bushel of good Winter wheat."*

*Capt. William Kidd the pirate came to own a farm a mile north
of Cannon Point, on the shore, in the eighteenth century. He got it
through marriage with Sarah Cox Oort, a lively lady who managed
in one lifetime to dispose of no less than five husbands including the
captain. As a matter of fact, his death by hanging left the title to the
farm "attainted," as they put it in those days.*

•

*The river acres off the mid-Fifties were lush and rich in fruit
trees and nut trees, especially walnuts. In 1782, the gentleman who
had the property up for sale described it in local journals as "that
most delightful and elegantly situate farm of Ruremont . . . within
four and three-fourths miles of the City."*

*Eighty years later, though, the whole aspect had altered. Grimy
coalyards, breweries and fat-rending plants made it untidy. Effingham*

Sutton, the drygoods merchant who built the row of houses on the bridge that sloped to the river, went broke on the venture.

The Sutton mansions, all brick and from three to four stories high, with sweeping river views, changed from one-family dwellings to blackened, untidy tenements. In the Nineteen Twenties, Mrs. William K. Vanderbilt, Lady Mendl and Miss Ann Morgan, J. P. Morgan's sister, led a sort of Drang Nach Osten from Fifth Avenue to Sutton Place to live in converted or newly built brick houses in Sutton Place. In 1928, however, a poor writer or artist could have an apartment in the river row for as little as $15 a month. The catch was that there were no utilities.

By that time the property had come into the hands of Henry Phipps, an Andrew Carnegie partner. He left the buildings just as he found them, but William L. Laurence, one of his $15 tenants, installed hot water, a hotwater heating system and a bathtub, and did a superior interior decorating job.

•

Dorothy Draper, a visitor at the Laurences, was inspired. She induced the Phippses to give her a free hand with the row, and they did. With black paint for the brick, white paint for the handsome fire escapes and balconies, formal back gardens and brightly colored doorways she transformed the dwellings.

The flats, all walk-ups with lovely river views, attracted new tenants, mostly affluent. The Bohemians who had enjoyed what they called "The Ark," were nudged out of it. Henry Huddleston Rogers Jr. was a new tenant. So was Bradley Martin, a grandson of Henry Phipps. McAdoos and Hartfords, Fred Gevaert, the film man, Clarence Francis of General Foods came to live there. So did a titled Briton who loved to take pot shots at river wild life from his back window. Young Rogers practiced marksmanship from his flat, too.

A genial concierge appropriately named Boom—Fred Boom of Cannon Point—kept the row tidy. James Flanagan, a handsome doorman, did all manner of chores for the tenants—hung out dress suits to air, shook out ladies' minks, helped at back lawn cocktail parties on summer evenings, rode herd on Dead End kids who liked to assemble in an old life-savers' shack just back of the row. They remember that a Mrs. Ackerman, one of the tenants, always hid eggs in the garden at Easter for children to find; that beery loafers were apt to sneak in there for a snooze in the sun.

*Now Cannon Point Row must die. The wreckers are to start
tearing it down this week.*

Some of my mother's friends were chronic worriers. One of them called
her every morning to make sure she was still alive. Another saw a burglar
or sex fiend behind every lamppost. They were all convinced that a woman
wasn't safe living by herself so dangerously on a ground floor. Mummy, on
the other hand, trusted everyone and had no time for paranoia. She kept a
lovely bronze Degas horse right on our front windowsill. One of her friends
told her she was crazy to leave the sculpture out like that. "Somebody could
just stroll by and walk away with it!"

"Nonsense," mother shot back. "There are bars on the window."

Her friend walked out of the house, stuck his hand between the bars,
grabbed the sculpture, brought it back in, and waved it under my mother's
nose. The Degas was swiftly assigned to a safer perch.

My unpredictable mother was a curious blend of sweetness and light
wedded to a somewhat mercurial temper. Once, after I'd done something
wrong, she grabbed a kitchen stool and hurled it at me, the entire length
of that corridor. My reflexes were fast, and I quickly ducked so it caught
me only a glancing blow. She must have been very aware of her temper. I
remember a postcard she wrote to me from New York when I was back in
Paris. I was having a problem with a tutor who was sick and couldn't teach
me any longer. My mother's postcard promised, "Maybe I'll have to come
over and tutor you myself. But with calm, with calm." Apparently, my protest
about her uncalm ways had registered.

My first New York beau was named Guion Case Morgan. He went
to Princeton and came into New York on weekends. We used to sit on a
three-seater blue couch underneath the barred window in the living room
and hold hands. If Mummy thought he was sitting too close, she had no
compunction about kicking him out. Indeed, she showed him the door quite
often. It's a wonder he ever came back. His grandfather was Frank Case, the
owner of the Algonquin Hotel. He often invited the two of us to sit at the
historic Round Table in the Oak Room, where luminaries like Ilka Chase,
Sinclair Lewis, Gertrude Stein, William Faulkner, James Thurber, Alexander
Wolcott, Robert Benchley, Dorothy Parker, New Yorker editor Harold Ross,
and Manhattan's greatest wits wittily held forth. But I was more impressed
by the wonderful food than by these so-called celebrities I'd only vaguely
heard of. And I was always hungry, particularly after enduring my mother's
half grapefruit stints in the kitchen.

Case was editor of *The Daily Princetonian* and gave me one of their official press cards. It was great because I could flash it at the door of museums, games, concerts, and all kinds of events, and miraculously get in for free or ahead of the line. The card had two large parallel red bands on the upper right side, which really caught the eye and made it look very official. The only date on it was 1876, the date of *the Daily Princetonian's* first issue so it never expired and flummoxed most gatekeepers. It was really an "Open Sesame" to almost any place. He gave one to my mother too. It's a toss-up as to which of us used the card more. She and I were both in the major leagues when it came to getting into places for free.

One winter, Case invited me down to Nassau to introduce me to his father, whose splendid name, believe it or not, was Morgan Morgan. Mr. Morgan was remarried to a skinny, bleak English woman with limbs like a tarantula, whose chilly nature was not redeemed by her having absolutely no sense of humor. Morgan Morgan, on the other hand, was outrageously funny and very down-to-earth. I remember a dinner where he explained that while it was always "perfectly acceptable to fall in love," (looking straight at his son), "it was just as easy to fall for a rich girl as with a girl who has *nothing!*" (looking straight at me.) That certainly built up my self-esteem.

Another bonus for living in Sutton Place was the Ripley tennis courts across the street. How wonderful to roll out of bed, run out, and play a set or two. And I played a lot. One time, when our flat was being repainted—the place was a wreck, books stacked all over the floor, and all the furniture on end—my mother gave me a hard time because I was across the street playing tennis instead of lending a hand. She didn't seem to realize the cosmic importance of a pick-up tennis match! Huge, unattractive modern buildings replaced the courts a few years later.

But all in all, we had a happy time there. It was a wondrous place to come home to once I started college. And even after I graduated and went on to law school in Paris, my mother kept the place so I always had a pad in New York.

I applied to four colleges: Radcliffe, Bennington, St. Lawrence, and Cornell and was accepted at all four (getting into college wasn't so difficult in those days). I chose Bennington and majored in the arts, but soon switched to a major in Political Economy. I was late coming back from France when I got to Bennington, and the college was already in session. Friendships had already formed and alliances declared by the time I was assigned my room in Swan House, and I felt a bit lost. I was already two weeks behind in my studies, and some instructors thought I was taking my tardiness much too lightly.

The only close friend I made that first semester was a terrific girl named Evangeline Hayes, nicknamed Vangie. She was at Bennington on a full scholarship and so was I, which was lucky because Bennington's tuition was then, and still is now, the most expensive in the country.

I had to work in the dining room, carrying trays and bringing water to hyper-thirsty students. Vangie worked in the candy store, and we always had an inexhaustible supply of Milky Ways, Snickers, jellybeans, and M&M's. Vangie and I had lots of other things in common. She was an only child too and was also mainly brought up by her grandmother. But there was a difference; she was born out of wedlock. Her father was a well-known sportswriter. She never spoke about him ever. But then one day, she excitedly told me that out of the blue, she had gotten an invitation to join him for her twenty-first birthday at Toots Shor's, his favorite New York restaurant. So on September 8 (my birthday too), she got dressed to the nines and took the train to New York, looking terrific. She slunk back that night, red-eyed and miserable. What happened was that when she walked into the restaurant and asked for her father, a big-mouthed, burly, boisterous Toots Shor led her to her father's table filled with his noisy friends, who were already in their cups. All through the lunch, they talked only about horse races, football, baseball, hockey—all of it going over her head and none of them paying her the least attention. After the dessert, her father bundled her into a taxi, wished her a happy birthday, ceremoniously presented her with a large white envelope, and bid her a curt "Good-bye." When she opened the envelope, she found twenty dollars and a note that said, "For the train." And that was that. I felt awful for her, and we never mentioned it again. Vangie had a brilliant career in advertising, working as a casting director for giant agencies like Foote Cone and Belding and J. Walter Thompson. She never married and died this year, just short of her eightieth birthday. She spent her last days in a nursing home, dispatched there by a "friend" who had been given the power of attorney after Vangie showed signs of Alzheimer's. She hated the place and one day decided to never eat again. I tried to intervene when she was first put in the home. I spoke to her lawyer, who claimed he was powerless to act. He was working for Vangie's "friend" with the power of attorney. It broke my heart.

There was another girl in my class I made friends with. She was Groucho Marx's daughter, adorable and funny like her father. Unfortunately, she also walked just like her father in that strange crouched way. People made fun of her, but she didn't seem to mind and taught me how to do walk that way too. We had a lot of laughs.

At Bennington, I had a superior piano teacher, Ernst Levy. He was a fine composer and an even finer pianist. He gave me an hour-long, private lesson every morning. His teaching was tough, his attitude was strict, and his discipline was absolute; but I liked him very much. So much so that I asked him to be my academic counselor. Playing the piano had always been important to me. Not just subtle interpretation but even the deadly scales, and tedious exercises. To this day, one thing that always makes me feel better about life in general is to sit down at the keyboard. While I play, worries melt away, and if my mood is black, I can always bang away the anger or the sadness. (It works better than lying on a psychiatrist's couch—which I've only done once and fell asleep—and what's more, it's free.)

I took an introductory course in Political Economy with the famous Peter Drucker. I was surprised to find that I loved the subject and swiftly decided to switch my major from music to Political Economy and wrote my thesis under Mr. Drucker's guidance with Mr. Levy's blessings.

Bennington was also deep into dance. Just think of it! The incomparable Martha Graham taught there; and when she left, her protégé Martha Hill took over. It was exhilarating. I loved how modern dance let the body respond to gravity's pull unlike ballet with its emphasis on being airborne. We often danced outside, feeling free as birds.

Bennington was noted for a superb art department. I'd never felt I had any graphic talent; but my teacher, Paul Feeley, told me I painted better than Helen Frankenthaler, who was in my class and went on to great fame. Which shows you how much *he* knew. Helen defined Bennington's art division with this bold declaration in the college magazine. "Exposure to people who are fully practicing their art gives the learning experience a certain aura of magic." And that's as true now as the day Helen wrote it.

After we had left Bennington, I once went down to Soho to see "Frankie," as I called her. I was shocked to find her living quite openly with Sam Greenberg, the art critic. Sam's reviews helped to launch her, though with her talent, I don't think she really needed "launching." But maybe she did. Maybe all artists need some kind of launching.

Those were free and easy days, and we were lucky enough to savor them. Mummy came up every once in a while from Manhattan. She took the train, and we'd spend the whole day, sometimes the entire weekend, together. I'd tell her all my news, and she'd tell me hers. The college wasn't exactly unstructured, but it was very casual. Fitting my style to a T. Sometimes, the teachers held classes in our dorms' living rooms while we sat on the floor, knitting things as complicated as Argylle socks. I got so good at knitting I could make those socks in the dark of a movie house! They came in handy as Christmas presents to various beaus.

Bennington sported an impressive roster of teachers. They took off during winter break to do their own thing—performing, painting, writing—and came back for the spring semester. This arrangement probably saved a lot on the fuel bill because mid-winter was cold as hell up there.

Paul Feeley, Simon Mocelsio, Kenneth Roland, and Jules Olitski all taught there. Together, these four and others made up a formidable cadre of "Color Field painters" who dominated the art scene during the 60s. Feeley organized several influential exhibitions starring work by the most significant artists of the day (including giants like Jackson Pollock, David Smith, Hans Hoffman, and Barnett Newman.)

Dancing as free as a bird under Martha Graham's
tutelage at Bennington College.

These stunning shows were a vital learning resource for Bennington students, providing them with hands-on exposure to the most groundbreaking art of the era. The group certainly opened our eyes to rule-breaking.

My own painting career had a short life. And here's why: I had always hated Georges Rouault and his black outlines. So can you imagine my horror when I looked at my own paintings. They looked just like Rouault's! Seriously, right down to those same horrible black outlines. Bernard Buffet painted somewhat that way too; and though I have owned a few Buffets, I also dislike his work intensely so I quit my dabbling. I figured there were already enough bad painters out there anyway.

I began work on my thesis in my third year at Bennington. Actually, my third year was also my senior year because of extra credits transferred from the French Lycée. My thesis, which was published in French, had the impressive title: *L'Assainissement du Franc, 1945-49*. A rough translation would be: "Re-evaluating the Franc, Between 1945-49. It was an esoteric subject, but I found the work fascinating. (I probably had a greater interest than most normal people in what happened to the franc during those years. Although in retrospect, God knows why I did!)

My advisors and I decided it would be ideal if I could complete my thesis in France, where I would have more access to the information I needed.

So it was back to Paris again, settling down at Rue Georges Berger with my grandmother and Mummy, attending both the Institut des Sciences Politiques and the Faculté de Droit, and working on my thesis all the while.

It wasn't at all easy doing this because the French method of teaching is very much more stringent than the American approach, particularly at that level. I can tell you there was no knitting of Argylle socks on the floor of the Faculté de Droit. Out of roughly one hundred students, there were only five girls in our class. The ratio wasn't entirely unwelcome, especially by us girls. But the work-load was never-ending, and one had little time for fun.

I remember a class I had with a Professor Laufenburger, an Alsatian with an accent you could cut with a knife. All his Vs came out as Fs and his Ds as Ts. This chauvinist didn't like having girls in his class, and he let us know it. He certainly jumped down my throat every time I spoke. As he put it, *"Matemoiselle, fous etes pete mais, fous etes cholie alors, continuez."* ("Matemoiselle, you are stupid but pretty so continue.") And that was that. Well, at least he gave me a little credit for *some*thing.

For some reason, most of the friends I made came from across the pond. Jacqueline Bouvier was one of them. She was spending her Vassar junior year abroad, taking classes at the Sorbonne. We were lucky that a few of the fellows we knew were well-heeled because neither Jackie nor I had a cent to call our own. For variety and convenience, we often shared our wardrobe. Jackie had clearly American clothes while my limited wardrobe was more sophisticated and French. Jackie loved my dresses, and I craved her more mundane American frocks. I owned a pink linen strapless gown studded with silver stars. It was actually a model's sample I had bought on sale at the end of a Balmain collection. Jackie borrowed it so often I finally gave it to her outright.

One of our favorite hangouts was a popular restaurant called "La Grenouille." Its owner, Roger, welcomed all the girls by asking for a kiss on his cheek. As they complied, he'd quickly twist his head, tricking us to plant one on our lips. Even if he didn't succeed, he was a good sport and always rewarded us with a little ceramic frog. You could always tell when we had eaten at "La Grenouille" because we reeked of the massive amounts of garlic the frog's legs were cooked in.

Jackie had entered a contest from *Vogue* Magazine called *Le Prix de Paris*. The entrant picked which persons in history she would like to have known. Jackie chose Baudelaire, Wilde, and Diaghilev. I remember she wrote that "Baudelaire and Wilde were both poets and idealists, able to depict sin with honesty, never stopping to believe in something nobler." She was convinced that Diaghilev possessed a talent that was even rarer than authentic genius: that was his ability to extract the very best from each artist, combining the result into a theatrical masterpiece. She also wrote, "If I could be an artist during the twentieth century, it would be these theories that I would apply." Jackie's essay won first prize; but her mother wouldn't let her accept it so Jackie's plans for a longer stay in Paris were sunk. When Jackie Kennedy and I were in school in Paris, she told me her stepbrother, Yusha Auchincloss, was coming to France that summer. She was dying for me to meet him. She was convinced that we'd really get along. Jackie was right. Yusha called me up; we met and immediately took a liking to each other. He was staying on the Left Bank at l'Hotel Cayre, didn't speak a word of French but was fascinated by the French people and longed to speak their language. He also took a liking to me, a little bit. I mean he must have . . . he asked me to marry him. Actually, to this day, he continues to claim that we *were* married . . . by the captain of a ship we took from Marseille to Corsica. Maybe so. But if it's true, it's just one more memory I've blocked out.

With my grandmother in Vichy.

Vichy.

Flying back to New York.

My mother in Capri.

Me in Capri in front of the Faraglionis.

On the balcony Georges Berger
with my grandmother.

My grandmother and me.

My grandmother and my mother.

Madame Franklin and my grandmother,
rue Georges Berger, *apéritif* time.

My mother rue Georges Berger.

My grandmother
and a nun at the Beaugé convent.

Getting out of Jean's Jaguar in Paris.

Yusha then went into the Marine Corps, and I continued my studies in Paris. The next year, his father invited me to the annual Yale-Harvard football game at the famous Walter Camp Jr. Stadium. He took me and Yusha and Michael Canfield, and what a thrill! My very first football game. After the game, we all went to dinner at a then-famous restaurant "La Crémaillere" and Mr. Auchincloss presented me with the biggest stuffed bulldog you ever cuddled up to. It lived comfortably with me for a dog's age.

Michael Canfield was married to Jackie's sister, Lee. He worked at the American Embassy in London with his fellow attaché, James Symington, the son of Democrat Senator Stuart Symington. Jimmy once gave a party attended by three couples:

Michael and Lee Canfield,
Prince Stanislas (Stash) Radziwill and his wife, Grace,
The Earl of Dudley and his wife, Laura,

Well! Within two years of that party, those couples had reconfigured like the partners in a Grande Gavotte. Talk about wife-swapping!

Michael divorced Lee and married Laura.
Stash divorced Grace and married Lee.
Dudley divorced Laura and married Grace.
Jimmy Symington later wondered what the chef served that night for dinner!

Meanwhile, Yusha and I were unofficially engaged. But then, while he was toughening himself up in the Marine Corps, I met Henri Deschamps in Paris, lost my heart to him; and very soon, we were married.

Another friend I made was Shirley Oakes, whose silver-mogul father, Sir Harry Oakes, had been murdered in Nassau a few years earlier, his body ignominiously mutilated with a blowtorch. His son-in-law, Alfred de Marigny, was suspected then arrested and tried for murder. That's when Nancy Oakes, Shirley's sister hired the flamboyant Sol Rosenblatt to defend him. After a lengthy and celebrated trial, Marigny was exonerated, but innocent or not, they extradited him from the Bahamas.

The Duke of Windsor was then the governor of the Bahamas, and he mishandled the whole scandal. To begin with, (instead of enlisting the nearby Florida police) he called in Scotland Yard, a full week's travel away, to do the investigation. That was the beginning of the comedy of errors that the homicide investigation turned into. The murderer was never caught although many gruesome theories abound all these generations later. Including one that blames a local black man avenging his wife who had been seduced by Sir Harry.

During her year abroad, Shirley Oakes was ensconced in style at the Hotel Lutetia on the Boulevard Saint Germain. It had a fabulous swimming pool that was almost never used. The whole place felt luxurious to me after the drab and grimy halls of the Faculté de Droit and of the Institut des Sciences Politiques, and I went swimming there a lot.

When Shirley was presented at the Court of St. James, her mother, Lady Oakes, gave a huge party at the Dorchester Hotel in London. She asked me to bring the *petits fours* for the party all the way over from Paris. So I set off for England, carrying a *thousand petits fours*. I somehow got through Customs without paying a penny in duties. It was a pastry-perfect performance on my part and an extraordinary party on Lady Oakes' part. (Lady Oakes didn't do *any*thing in a small way. That same year, she imported one hundred thousand earthworms to Nassau from God knows where to aerate the soil around her house and make a better lawn, which the worms did successfully. Another time, when we were traveling to Biarritz to celebrate Shirley's birthday, Lady Oakes overtipped the porters so much that Shirley kicked up a huge fuss, protesting that it was embarrassing and there we'd be robbed when the natives saw how rich her mother was.) Shirley's presentation dress was created by Christian Dior and cost a fortune. Mine was sewn by a skilled little dressmaker for a fraction of that but was every bit as pretty. And I modestly admit I had a lot of success in it.

While Shirley stayed with her mother at the Dorchester, I stayed at the livelier and hard-to-get-into Cavendish Hotel. The Cavendish was owned by Rosa Lewis. She catered only to people she knew or liked. No stranger could just walk in. She had been a favorite of the royals. In fact, King Edward VII had often dropped in for dinner. Rosa had grown up poor, one of ten children, and was raised to become a maid or a cook. Well, a cook it was to be, and she took to it with a vengeance. She apprenticed herself to a chef and really learned the business. She took all the steps to master the art. She started out scrubbing pots and cleaning sinks, moved up to learning a repertoire of sauces, and then advanced to sculpting pastries. Her reputation as a superb chef gave her entrée to most of the titled and moneyed families in England, who clamored to partake of her skills. Staked by the deep pockets of her friends, she took over the Cavendish Hotel. And it's where she died, full of years and success, in 1952. I can still see her patrolling in her wheelchair, rolling down one hall and up another. If Rosa liked you and knew you didn't have much money, she'd tack part of your bill onto another customer who had some to spare. Prince Moritz of Hesse, a great pal of Shirley's and mine, waltzed in to the Cavendish, recommended by Lady Oakes. He came clean with Mrs. Lewis telling her right up front that he was broke. I was also given Lady Oakes' stamp of approval so I was admitted at the same time, and La Lewis didn't bat an eye. She put us up for practically nothing, which was very nice and extremely appreciated. I was more than a little intrigued by Moritz, or "Maurizio" as his intimates called him.

One fine night, Shirley, Maurizio, and I went to the notorious Boodles club. Of course, none of us were members, but I had a vague feeling that the French ambassador was so I took charge and took a chance. We strode up to the front desk, where I boldly declared we were friends of Ambassador Massigli. The head porter beamed and said, "Ah, what luck, Mademoiselle . . . Monsieur l'Ambassadeur is also here tonight!" Forsaking even a shred of dignity, we ran out before we got thrown out. Or worse, I would have had to face the ambassador or his wife, Odette, whom I'd only met once, and briefly at that. Anyway, Maurizio and I always had a wonderful time together. Those were the days when the world was our oyster. We kicked up our heels dancing till dawn, going from club to club, listening to jazz all night, and, when waking the next morning, instead of nursing a hangover, we'd start making plans for another night of wassailing. I remember that after every one of these glorious nights, Maurizio would make me promise that I would never ever forget this romantic interlude. And I haven't ever forgotten painting the old town red with a young royal.

Yet another great friend I made in Paris was Sue Cardozo, an American. Sue was simply stunning. Super intelligent and attractive and had been Frank Sinatra's guiding light for many years. She eventually married Paul de Brantes and abandoned her fascinating life to become the Marquise de Brantes and settle into a more mundane life. That was a quite a loss, in my book, but I guess Sue brought a bit of luster to the Château du Fresne in Touraine. Her Chatêlaine's life came to a doleful finish when she was evicted from her house by her own children in her eighties when her husband died after fifty years of living there. A much later "foreign" friend from Paris was a painter named Moriharu Shizume, a marvelous Japanese artist whom my mother brought into our lives about forty years ago. Mummy had met him at a Calder opening in Paris and asked him—a perfect stranger—to come and spend Christmas with us in Battenville. The poor fellow had no idea how far away Battenville was. He flew to New York, grabbed a cab at Kennedy

Airport and, four hours later, arrived at our doorstep with a bewildered Indian driver, and a $325 bill. On top of that, the winter's worst snowstorm hit us so there was no way the cabbie could go back, and he ended up staying for the whole weekend. As so often happened when my mother created bizarre situations, everything turned out in a friendly and interesting way. The Indian was a wonderful cook, which came in very handy.

At any rate, Mori became an intimate of the family, and I ended up representing his work in the United States. I gave him a few exhibits at my gallery, and they were really successful.

To this day, he still paints and is a major success particularly in Japan, where he is the protégé of Mr. Toyoda (of Toyota Motor Cars and Toyota City).

But I digress. As school progressed I had to put in extra work late into the night just to keep up. I started losing weight, even coughing up blood, until I finally (and tardily) realized I must be seriously sick. And I was. Somehow, I had contracted tuberculosis. Somewhere in the metro or in classes or on the street, somebody must have coughed in my face, and that's all it took with this highly contagious disease. It was Henri Deschamps, whom I was dating, who arranged that I get X-rayed. My mother thought it was quite unnecessary. Well, there it was, big as life, a huge cavity in my right lung.

Even before I could finish my thesis, I was shipped off to a TB sanitarium in Switzerland. I languished in that hospital for an endless year. It was in Leysin and was called "Le Belvédère." The miracle cure for tuberculosis in those days was lots of fresh air. No moderate exercise, not *any* exercise. They simply bundled you up in a chaise longue and abandoned you to a terrace, all the live-long day to "rest." We would dress for dinner—ladies in long dresses, gentlemen in black tie. Every night! A musical ensemble played for us all through dinner. Patients included Russians, Germans, a sprinkling of French, Swiss, English, and many Indians and Pakistanis. And some of these patients had been there for *years*. A few had their own entourage, friends servants, musicians, hairdressers, etc. It was all pretty grand. One prized patient was Sir Stafford Cripps, Great Britain's Chancellor of the Exchequer.

A highlight of each day was when the huge black chukka birds came flying around to battle each other for breakfast crumbs. To me, they looked like circling vultures casing the joint to see who was going to expire next. And indeed people died. We would notice an empty seat in the dining room, the grim signal that another companion was gone and there would be a tightening of the ranks. But my luck held as it has so often. While I was there, they discovered the first wonder drug to fight tuberculosis, PAS. I was one of the first patients to be given large doses of it. The effects were unbelievably fast.

I picked up strength, and added some weight. Best of all, it meant the end of all the talk about a pneumothorax, the deflating of the lungs, a dire threat that hung over my head all during that dreadful time. To help pass the time away, I found a wonderful guitar teacher who had had a severe bout with TB himself. As a consequence, he had both legs amputated. He would come up from the village on a sled pulled by two dogs. The moment he started strumming his guitar, you quickly forgot about his missing legs. He taught me to play, but though I got pretty good at it, I quickly went back to my piano, which was my first love and a steadfast companion all my life. I even tried my hand at composing, which I had already started doing at Friends Academy, writing, among other things, the class song for my graduation.

In 1960, Jackie Kennedy invited me to the Democratic Convention in Los Angeles. Then she became pregnant with John, Jr. and had to cancel. But she told me to attend anyway. I invited Shirley Oakes to come along. She knew Jackie when they both went to Vassar, but she hadn't been invited so she was very happy to go. (Jackie didn't like Shirley all that much even though she had chosen her to be one of her bridesmaids.)

Shirley picked me up in Edmonton, played a few rounds of golf with Jean, met my son Marc, who was her godson, (I had asked Shirley to be Marc's godmother, probably a little hangover guilt on my part for stealing Jean from her so long ago in Nassau.), and then she and I took off for California. In L.A., we stayed with Ted Jameson, former undersecretary of the navy. Ted was famous, or infamous, for having wrecked a DC 8 while swerving to avoid a flock of birds while landing. (The Air Force wasn't all that happy about wrecking a plane worth millions.)

Since Jackie wasn't at the convention, we had no arranged invitations to any of the convention parties. No matter, we successfully crashed the best of them, one after another. One, in particular, was rather fun. It was a ladies' luncheon at Tony Curtis and Janet Leigh's house - a hundred "ladies" had been invited but somehow a thousand showed up. Their neighbor, who happened to be a Republican, was roped into having his backyard used for the overflow. Frank Sinatra, who was meant to sing at the event, had to stand on the diving board to croon a tune or two. He had master-minded most of the Inauguration parties very efficiently; but this one had really gotten "out-of-*his*-hand." In all that confusion our "crashing" the party went by pretty unnoticed. And it was a crazy mélée but an interesting phenomenon to absorb. The day of Jack's acceptance speech, for which, once again, we didn't have tickets. Shirley said she didn't think we should go; but I thought differently and dragged her to the open space of the Memorial coliseum.

We waited until the band struck up the *Star-Spangled Banner*, and everyone leapt to their feet. While they all stood at attention, I marched us both into the box behind JFK, where Bobby Kennedy was sitting. He was so nonplussed at seeing us; he simply motioned us to sit down. And so we did and had a bird's eye view of history in the making.

CHAPTER 11

Edmonton, Alberta, Canada

Back in Edmonton, I enrolled in a course at the University of Alberta to learn Russian. I also decided it was high time to resume my piloting career. I had learned to fly in Boise, Idaho, while getting a divorce; and now I wanted to hone my aerial skills in the blue skies of Edmonton.

Jean and Sandy owned a little one-engine Cessna 170 that I could practice in. I still remember its call letters: Echo, Tango, Papa. I loved calling them out, "Echo! Tango! Papa!" to announce my every takeoff and landing. In no time, I was comfortable at the controls. Feeling myself free of gravity, soaring alone in the wild blue yonder was a sense of freedom never matched on the ground. Getting away from everything was almost as satisfactory as banging on a piano!

Gold Bar Farm.

Maman at Gold Bar.

Véronique, Marc, Jackie.

Gold Bar Farm.

Jean also owned an open-cockpit Tiger Moth biplane, a feisty little craft I'd ride along in while he performed daredevil acrobatics that scared me to death. I kept my trembling knees pressed against the sides of the cockpit to keep from falling out. I can still remember how the passenger door didn't close tightly so he improvised a wire coat hangar as a flimsy latch. One time, when my mother was visiting, he took her up, but she was horrified by this makeshift door-handle and disapproved of his happy-go-lucky attitude toward aviation safety. Once I was comfortable flying the 170, I graduated to the Cessna 180 then to the grander and much more powerful two-engine Cessna 310. In fact, we often flew the Cessna 310 all the way to Nassau, just the two of us; and there, at Christmastime, we would fly over the leprosy compound at the Western end of the island and drop presents out of the sky to those poor isolated souls whom nobody would dare go to visit.

For a while, Sandy lived with us downstairs; and most days, both he and Jean came home for lunch although their office was about an hour's drive away. So that meant organizing breakfast, lunch, and dinner every day. It seemed like we hardly finished with one when it was time for the next. Somehow I coped, but much as I liked Sandy, I was glad when he finally moved out and into his own digs. It lightened the household duties a little and gave us some blessed privacy.

After I divorced Jean de La Bruyère, I moved to New York City with my four children, where we lived in an apartment at 1000 Park Avenue. Soon, I started going out with Yusha again. He was as sweet as ever. We went to wonderful parties all over town, but he always preferred having dinner at home. He would arrive from Newport lugging a steak and a bundle of logs to grill it on in my fireplace, and that was fun too.

Meanwhile, Yusha became very interested in the American University of Beirut. I remember that at some point, the University asked Yusha to help raise some money. One of his targets was a sheikh who had graduated from AUB.

Sheikh Shakhbut Bin Sultan Al Nahyan was not just any old sheikh. He was the eldest son of sheikh Sultan II bin Zayed Al Nahyan, ruler of Abu Dhabi from 1922 to 1926. He succeeded his uncle Sheikh Sago I bin Zayed Al Nahyan. Shakbut was the ruler of the emirate of Abu Dhabi until August 6th 1966, when he was deposed in a bloodless coup. His brother Sheikh Zayed Bin Sultan Al Nahyan became the emir of Abu Dhabi and eventually rose to become the undisputed leader of the United Arab Emirates.

A Saint-Jean-de-Luz : le chargement de la Dyna. 5 000 km de campi...

Yusha Auchincloss, Jackie, me.

Jackie Bouvier doing her laundry in an out-door "Laundro-mat"
on the way to Saint-Jean-de-Luz

Yusha Auchincloss and me
at Bailey's Beach, Newport.

Bailey's Beach,

When Yusha met with him at his palace, the sheikh had a hawk perched on his shoulder. Yusha asked if he could take a polaroid photo of the sheikh and his hawk. The sheikh agreed. Then when the flash went off, to Yusha's horror, the hawk shat on the royal shoulder. But the sheikh shrieked with laughter and told Yusha how delighted he was because the falcon hadn't done anything like that in days. They had all been very concerned about the bird's constipation, but now, thanks to Yusha, everything was all right, and please, how much money did he want? Yusha had been hoping for a few thousand dollars. He got a million.

I always enjoyed living in Manhattan. My apartment was close to the Lycée Francais. It wasn't large enough for all of us once my daughter Mary joined us so I rented the apartment next door. By knocking out a wall in the kitchen, we gained two and a half extra rooms. Mary moved in on my side of the apartment, and the little ones slept on the other side with their Swiss nurse, Vreni, who had been with us for a few years and stayed quite a few more.

My children kept me pretty well-anchored, and we had a very busy and happy life. I gave a lot of dinner parties and dined out a lot. At this point, I met Michael Mooney, a senior editor at *The Saturday Evening Post*. He was fun to be with and a great talker. He was divorced and had three slightly unruly children. A serious bout with polio had left him severely lame, I guess this brought out the Florence Nightingale in me. We seemed compatible. We liked the same books and enjoyed the same people so after a short courtship, we decided to get married. This brought our brood of seven children together, which proved to be a disaster. It was like blending oil with water.

I bought a house at 176 East Ninety-third Street. I figured it was plenty big enough to accommodate everybody. (The Mooney boys came to us on weekends.) Michael's three boys were 101 percent American, and my four were still essentially French in outlook. Mike's youngest son, Christopher, was autistic, and my son Marc, who was the same age, was often paired off with him in games or other activities. This didn't work well at all, and I know Marc was really unhappy about the situation.

On the other side of the coin, my daughter Véronique flirted with the boys, especially Laird. I remember catching them kissing one day and telling her it wasn't too good an idea. She told me she had gotten the idea seeing Mary kiss Michael Jr. (some excuse!) Another thing she used to do, which was less wild, was to systematically turn the thermostat way up in defiance of her stepfather, or maybe to attract his attention.

That winter, my mother was staying with us. Michael and I went off to the Book Fair in Frankfurt, and she called us there to report a true disaster: In a few catastrophic nighttime hours, our Ninety-third Street townhouse had burned to the ground. At first when she told me, I thought maybe she had had too much champagne, but the story was all too true. The children were safe (although Véronique had risked her life by rushing back into the burning house to successfully rescue my jewelry). Nobody, not even our dog was hurt, but our house and furnishings and belongings were just about a total loss. Some furniture was saved; but it needed extensive and expensive repairs and anyone who's gone through a fire knows you can never really get rid of the smoke smell. All in all, a very traumatic experience.

Starting with the fire, things began going downhill between Michael and me. I had bought the house with my own money, but when the insurance money came through, Michael claimed half of it. Then and there, I asked for a divorce, and once it went through, I never saw him again. We all felt relief. The children and I went back to our happy life together. I rented an apartment at 1088 Park Avenue, and thank God, we still had our Battenville house.

The cause of the fire was never discovered. The assessors presumed it was an electrical failure. I always thank my lucky stars that my mother was there when it happened. The only thing left of my beautiful grand piano was the metal plate with its Steinway serial number on it. I have that sad memento still. The piano had been given to me by a not-so-secret admirer when I lived in Saanen. Every Friday, punctually at three o'clock, a dozen white roses were delivered there, all the way from Lausanne. One Friday, at the stroke of three, there was the usual knock on the door. There were the roses, but this time, they were on top of a grand piano. I was beside myself with joy and wonder even though I had to take down a couple of doors to get it into the chalet.

My mother had been the first to detect the fire. She was going downstairs at about 7:00 p.m. on her way to the opera, when, on the first floor, she saw the library curtains going up in flames. The children were a floor below, having dinner, and she frantically rounded them up and got them out on the street. Never one to overlook details, she told the nanny, who had a habit of wearing transparent shirts, to put on something less revealing and to hurry up about it. Our neighbors, rising to the occasion, took in all the children that night and cared for them until I got back from Germany the next day.

As soon as I got back from Germany, I packed up the children, my mother, the nanny, and the dog and drove them all straight upstate. I felt the children needed the respite of a familiar and normal home, considering the trauma they'd been through. After the long drive, when our headlights picked out the front of the house, Marc burst into tears. He was convinced that since the Ninety-third Street fire had destroyed his toys in Manhattan; maybe his toys he had left in Battenville had disappeared too. It was touching to see his joyful reunion with his favorite stuffed bear "Nou nours" and "Linus" and "Peanuts."

When Michael's children didn't come to New York on the weekend, we'd often go skating with them at the Beaver Dam Club on Long Island. That was Mooney territory. They had their friends, and they resented our invasion. They all skated like Olympians, and my children didn't, which made it tough all around. Their other club, the Seawanhaka Yacht Club, was on Center Island. Michael's family did a lot of sailing there and loved it; but mine, again, didn't.

CHAPTER 12

Nassau

Though of my mother's generation, Josephine Bryce was another great friend of mine. She was Huntington Hartford's sister. She and her brother were heirs to the A&P fortune. (At one time, this made Jo the second richest woman in the United States. I forget who was first.) Unfortunately, Huntington lost millions upon millions through his lascivious, misguided ways. When the A&P stocks plunged, he bailed out. Jo, because of family loyalty, held onto her stock, losing many millions in the process. Of course, that just meant she was less rich, not in any way poor. Nonetheless, her accountant at some point told her that she really had to cut down her expenses, and evidently, she said "Well, maybe I can cancel my magazine subscriptions," which rather non-plussed the accountant!

Jo's daughter Nuala (who later married Senator Claiborne Pell) and I attended Bennington at the same time. I first met Jo in those college years when Nuala invited me to her mother's house in Vermont, but I didn't get to know her well until much later on. Our growing fondness was cemented in Nassau. At the time, Jackie Kennedy was staying with Jean and me "at Sea Horse," a house we had rented. It was a tiny place. Jackie loved coming there to get away from the Kennedy Palm Beach compound, and she would get off the plane with just a small carry-on bag and swimming fins.

One night, we took Jackie to the Bahamian Club for dinner, dancing, and gambling. I noticed a very good-looking man approaching us. Jackie got up to speak to him then introduced us to this Aztec god. (He was half-Peruvian and really did resemble a bronzed deity.) He was Ivor Bryce, Jo's husband, and invited us to lunch the next day at "Xanadu," their beach house at Lyford Cay. "Xanadu" was the most glamorous beach house I had ever seen. It had mother-of-pearl furniture, Coramandel screens, and damask and velvet ottomans all over the place. Jean and I were frequent guests at Xanadu, and Jo often invited me there after I was divorced. At one point, that first time, Jo suggested to Jackie that she bring JFK along some time.

Jackie whispered to me, "Can you imagine Jack in that den of iniquity?"

You bet I could. With no trouble at all.

I met many interesting types in Nassau. One day, I was sitting at a table by the Lyford Cay Club pool, and I saw Truman Capote at the next table, all by himself feverishly going through some papers. A sudden gust of wind blew away quite a lot of them, and I will never forget how this little figure of a man started darting around the pool trying to retrieve them and screaming "My manuscript, my manuscript. Will somebody get those pages out of the pool?" Well, in I dove, and when I gave him the dozen or so pages I had fished out, he thanked me profusely and asked me to have lunch with him. The "manuscript" happened to be the final galleys for *In Cold Blood,* the book that really made him famous. Our paths would cross again many times. We had quite a few mutual friends. One of them was Gordon Wholey, who had an interesting pad above the restaurant PJ Clarke on Third Avenue. He had a swing, which was hung in such a way that it could with a kick of a foot swing out onto Fifty-fifth Street and, with another kick of a foot, swing out onto Third Avenue. Gordon would love doing that to surprise the passersby below. Truman tried it once and never again. He said he was too famous to risk his life that way. We spent many interesting evenings there, swinging or not swinging.

At another poolside in Nassau, I met Sean Connery. A friend of mine had rented out her pool for the filming of the movie *Thunderball,* the first James Bond film. The script called for Sean to be attacked by sharks in that pool and the poor man had to do take after take to get that scene right. My friend and I were right there, obviously breathless, whenever he came out; and we always had a towel or a little glass of something ready to encourage him. Unfortunately, my friend often had more than just a little glass, and she had to be fished out of the pool quite frequently. Luckily, no harm came to her or to Sean, whom I got to see in a lot of other scenes.

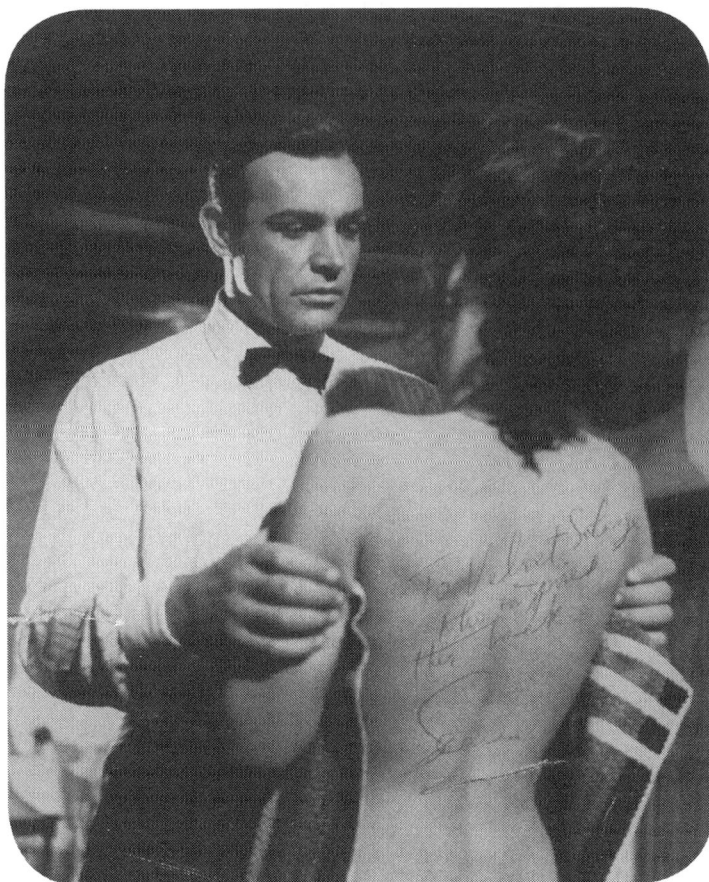

Sean Connery photo dedicated to Velvet Solange

Sean had a hard time pronouncing my name and asked if he could call me Velvet. He had seen a stripteaser on Forty-second Street in New York who went by the name "Velvet Solange," and thought she was "a little bit of all right," that was fine with me. I didn't care what he called me; but it did raise a few eyebrows.

At Christmastime that year, Jo invited us to Black Hole Farm in Vermont, and I returned there many times when I became single again. And, serendipity of serendipity, Fred and I now live in that magnificent place.

Jo was determined to find a good husband for me and kept producing different possibilities, sort of like a cat dropping captured canaries at my feet. She would extol my, oh, so many virtues, always carrying on about what a good mother I was. (I remember one of these swains saying that

that was not particularly what's he had in mind!) Foremost on her list was her ex-brother-in-law, J. Gordon Douglas, Jr; but that didn't work out. She assured me that he came from a good old New York family bla bla bla. He kept plying me with that good old New York family jewelry which I sported for a while but gave back to him, saying I thought that it should go to his daughter, Dita. She was a good friend of mine and we remain friends. She is an excellent artist and I recently arranged for her to have an exhibit of some of her wonderful horse paintings at gallery 668.

CHAPTER 13

Battenville Farm

During one long-ago weekend at Black Hole Hollow Farm in 1965, I had my five-year-old son, Marc, in tow, and Jo had some rather grand houseguests. including Princess Margaret, who had been brought along by Dru Heinz (of fifty-seven varieties fame), Ian Fleming, the creator of 007 James Bond and other interesting types. HRH drank nothing but "Famous Grouse" whiskey. She sent a case of it before her arrival, and Jo was very grateful when the case showed up because the whiskey disappeared at a fast rate. Anyway, I thought I should get Marc out of the way for a bit. So I took him for a long drive, and he began to get grumpy. That's when I spotted a sign: "Battenkill Inn 1779." We went in.

It was a beautiful old house. While we were having a cup of tea in the cozy Dutch Oven Room in front of a blazing fire, I heard that this charming spot was going bankrupt. And something clicked. Something magical. Something crazy. I sped back to Black Hole Hollow Farm, raved to Jo about it, and told her I was going to buy it.

She went into high gear. We discovered it was listed with the real estate people as "a stately homestead with eighty acres on the Battenkill River, fifteen rooms, a cow barn, a silo, and a hay barn." She called her lawyer, John Briggs, and made an appointment with him for the next day. I met with him and got the deed for the property a few short months after. January 10, 1966, to be precise.

Never mind that it had been converted into a restaurant and that all the downstairs rooms were dining rooms. Never mind that there was a horrible built-in bar in the Dutch Oven Room, that there were "Men" and "Ladies" plastic signs on the bathroom doors. So what if I had no furniture to fill it, that the whole place was a mess? So what if one four-poster bed, a dining room table, and a sideboard were all that had been left behind. I'll let you in on why owning this house was so important to me. I had long felt that bringing up children in New York City without the relief of weekends away was not a good idea for parent or child. I read somewhere that the recent epidemic of attention deficit disorder probably sprang from city children being denied the physical and psychological benefits of unstructured bodily contact with the natural world. The priceless chances to watch my children climbing trees, wading in a brook, tumbling in the grass, lengthening their steps, literally getting down to earth made the purchase of Battenville even more meaningful to me.

My mother had a beau who was a plumber. Paul Warfield was his name. He had been CEO of the U.S. Lines and, when he retired, he bought a house in North Bennington, sight unseen, and found, when he moved in, that it had a lot of plumbing problems. Appalled at the cost of the repairs, he learned the trade and very quickly was helping his friends and acquaintances with their plumbing. He was a charming fellow and without any trouble at all became the darling of the North Bennington single and even married ladies, who, reluctantly, would have to fall back into the woodwork when my mother came around. I asked him to go over to Battenville to look at the house and tell me what he thought of it. He wrote me a long letter, basically telling me that it would be a horrendous mistake to buy it, mentioning all sorts of structural problems, the noisy and smelly paper mill across the way belching away and spewing chemicals into the Battenkill River, making the fish go belly-up under the bridge, the two county roads the house was on, obviously creating noise also, no view from the house. The plumbing, of course, then came eaves troughs, downspouts, and gutters that needed repair, the heating costs which would be astronomical for a house that big, the repainting of the house which would have to be done every four or five years to the tune of $400 to $500, the railroad tracks going through the middle of the property which, though it had only one freight train going on them once a day, might develop more businesses in the future, the hilly acreage which was likely to be more picturesque than useful, the $600-a-year taxes which were bound to go up the minute I paid $ 35,000 for the property, the insurance coverage—all very negative and discouraging, but I didn't listen to any of it and asked him to fix the plumbing for starters.

I could tell he was very much in love with my mother. The problem was that his brother, Ted, was also in love with my mother. But Ted had an extremely jealous wife, and that complicated things even more because when he wanted to communicate with my mother, he had to go through his brother!

My happiness was unbounded. There was only one drawback to owning the house: Since I now had a place of my own to go to, I had no excuse to stay at Jo's. Even so, buying it was probably the best thing I ever did because although the children and I were happy in our apartment in New York, the place in Battenville was different. This house was something else. Even more than our Manhattan apartment, this was *home*.

I think I remember every drive we took, my children and I and Jackie's dog, Zookie, piled up in my little 1963 Alfa Romeo for the two-hundred-mile trip. The huge restaurant kitchen had been torn out so we had no kitchen at all for the first few months and cooked things in a huge cauldron that hung above the fire. Hotdogs, potatoes, eggs, anything that could be boiled in water. And one in a while, we even baked bread or a pie in the Dutch oven. But that was rare, very rare.

Another Battenville problem was that when I became Paul Warfield's twenty-five-miles-away neighbor, he would often drop in unannounced, his violin tucked under his arm, and ask me to play really difficult duos with him. He had an incredible Antonio Stradivarius, which had been made in 1692, But even that great instrument didn't help his mediocre playing. It was insured, he told me, for half a million dollars. He developed carpal tunnel syndrome and couldn't play anymore; and thank God, that was the end of that, and I could continue to play my piano in peace and tranquility.

We'd eat and talk and laugh then sleep like logs with the sun acting as our alarm clock. We'd hit the ski slopes at Stratton Mountain first in line when they opened the lifts then ski all day till dusk. Back home we'd go, then we'd drive to Bromley on Sunday for another grand mountain to conquer. Sometimes, we skied at our little local mountain called Willard, where *après-ski*, you could relax and warm yourself around a roaring central fireplace. When we left, we'd each tuck a log from the huge woodpile under our arms. I hardly ever had to buy firewood. The owner knew about our petty larceny, but he didn't seem to mind, he even encouraged it!

When my mother first came to stay, she was appalled that I had no help, in or out of the house and quickly acted upon it. She spotted an attractive young man mowing the lawn on the neighboring property (Soldiers' Rest Farm) bounded out of the car and asked him if he had any free time to come over to her daughter's place which was a mess . . . and that's how Johnny Woodard came into our lives. He arrived the next day with his lawn mower and very rapidly became part of our landscape. To this day, he mows the lawn for my daughter and does a million other things like mind the gallery, keep intruders out etc. etc. and besides all that, has been through the years a great friend and is definitely part of our family.

Jean de La Bruyère was baffled when Battenville became mine. He simply couldn't get over my pulling this off! How could I possibly buy this house on my own? I guess it was sort of a miracle. I am glad that my daughter, Véronique, now has it—she and her four children. I think she loves it as much as I ever did: maybe more. Even if she doesn't live there for the rest of her life, at least she has a refuge to call her own. Or, as I have always called Battenville, a haven.

And one time, it really became a "haven." I often lent Battenville to friends, and on one occasion, I lent it to the French Consul in New York. He and his wife had invited me to party after glittering party at the Consulate, and I had no way of reciprocating equally in New York City. So one evening after one of these parties, I told them that if they ever wanted to get away, my house upstate was theirs for the asking. I never dreamed they'd take me up on the offer because Battenville—"Les-Bains"—was definitely not their cup of tea. But to my surprise, the very next day, Madame La Consule was on the phone exclaiming how marvelous it would be to go to Battenville for a few days of peace and tranquility so she could work on the book she was writing. And of course, she'd bring her butler and cook along so she could really rough it.

Well, she showed up all right with the butler and cook but without the husband. And for a very good reason. It turned out that a certain politician in Albany was enjoying her diplomatic privileges, and since Albany was just around the corner, my humble little farmhouse was mighty convenient. So much for "havens." For one brief moment, I considered erecting a plaque on the Southwest side of the house, proclaiming: "So and so slept here"—and how!

One day, a friend, Charles Byron, told me he was starting a gallery and needed some help. I jumped right in as one of his investors. (There were already three big investors, and I became the fourth and much smaller one.)

Battenville Farm.

My mother at Battenville Farm
in famous snow leopard coat.

I loved the work. Byron had a good eye, and so did I. We picked out exciting artists to promote like Agnes Martin, Pedro Friedberg, Yves Corbassière, and Marino Marini; but the gallery didn't make much money so one day, I suggested to Charles that we should invest in some pre-Columbian art and see if that would sell. He agreed, and off I went to Central and South America and came back with a great trove of primitive figures. We never sold many, which, in a way, was lucky because I ended up with a really nice collection, which I still take delight in today.

Importing art was more or less legitimate in those days, and the rules were far less strict. Even so, I was always careful to pile a lot of personal gear on top of those objects to avoid trouble with the customs agents. But they never really bothered me, certainly not the way they would today. I was also working with the Coe Kerr Gallery, finding them pictures and sometimes putting them together with buyers. That was both fun and lucrative. We not only represented Andrew Wyeth and Jamie Wyeth but also had major Impressionist paintings.

CHAPTER 14

The Saratoga Gallery

I was a pretty free agent. It wasn't a nine-to-five work, and it was very interesting. But what I found to be much more exciting and rewarding was discovering and encouraging artists, which is really what inspired me to start my own gallery. It's amazing how all of a sudden I was meeting all these interesting and talented people who wanted me to show their work. I must admit there were a few who were bummers too; but I managed to ward them off and only took on the artists I thought were really good. Compromising was not the name of the game. I will never forget one time, in Gimbel's basement, at a dreadful art show a friend of mine had dragged me to, noticing a wonderful (in my not so humble opinion) watercolor. I said to my friend, "Now *that's* the only decent painting in the show. It's so charming and delicate, it must have been painted by some little old lady with baby blue hair." Well, from behind me, I heard this booming, masculine voice say, "Well, lady, I did it" I turned around and found not a little old lady with baby blue hair but a strapping, very good-looking hockey player. He told me his name was Reeve Schley III, and would he be interested in having a show in my gallery this summer? Why, yes! And so it was that Reeve and his family came to stay with me in Battenville. He hanged his paintings and sold everything in sight. This was in 1972. He has become ever so successful, with exhibits in major galleries; and some thirty years later, he is having a retrospective show in my daughter's "Gallery 668," the successor of the Saratoga Gallery. I'm glad that I had the eye to discover some really good painters like Reeve Schley way back then.

The Saratoga Gallery I started on Union Avenue was the first art gallery Saratoga had ever had. I came about finding a location for it in a strange way. At a party one night, I overheard some people speaking of improving the image of their college. My ears perked up, and I introduced myself and asked them to tell me about their college. Well, it turned out that when Skidmore College moved to their new campus, they sold the houses they owned on Union Avenue to some Italians who wanted to found a school where Italian Renaissance history would be taught. They named it Verrazzano College and were very proud to have it be the first college in the United States to be named after an Italian (I guess they didn't know about Columbia University, which was named after Christopher Columbus). But they hadn't been able to attract many students. I asked them what they did with their buildings in the summer, and they told me they just shut them down. And that's when I suggested having a gallery in one of the buildings and, under their auspices, having interesting art exhibits which would give their new school a little kudos. Well, they thought it was a splendid idea, and I found myself with a three-story mansion free of rent. This house was at 125 Union Avenue where Diamond Jim Brady had lived. He had built a tunnel to the house next door, where his girlfriend, Lillian Russell stayed for the racing season. She and Diamond Jim apparently worried about shocking the populace with their antics and, this way, were able to disguise their trysting. The next year, I was given another house of theirs at 48 Union Avenue, kitty-corner from The Reading Room. This house was called the Van Deusen House. It had once belonged to Sam Riddle, owner of the legendary bay, Man o' War. Sam Riddle used the place to throw a humongous mint julep party every year on the anniversary of Man o' War's death, and he would play a record of the great horse's funeral. I picked up on that idea and gave my own Man o' War parties. They brought in a lot of people. I suddenly realized I loved being an entrepreneur. Especially a successful one. Even if I had to mix batches of mint juleps in the bathtub, which I did. (They were very good and helped the sales of paintings no end.)

The trick, I knew, was to get the horsey set to come to my parties. The owners and breeders and trainers and interconnected celebrities. Marylou and Sonny Whitney, Paul Mellon, Kay and Walter Jeffords, the Mathers, the Ogden Phippses, CZ Guest, Cortright and Tootie Wetherill, and Penny Tweedy, owner of the super-horse, Secretariat. (He, like Man o' War, was nicknamed Big Red.) They all came, and, God bless 'em, they bought pictures.

I got New York galleries like Knoedler and Wildenstein and Coe Kerr to lend me important paintings on consignment. (Munnings, Herring,

Stubbs, Alken, etc.) And if even just one of those paintings sold, the costs of my whole operation were more than covered.

Another "horse" person I got to come there was E.P. Taylor, the illustrious Canadian breeder. This not-so-sweet tycoon had a strong crush on me and would lend me wonderful paintings from his collection. These, of course, were not for sale but added a lot of glamour and excitement to my shows. One of his pictures, a particularly spectacular Munnings, was featured in a local newspaper article and reported to be valued at $70,000. (That's nearly a million in today's market.) In this case, the publicity was double-edged because I had to double the security I had for the gallery. (Actually, what this came down to was that my secretary, who was already my security guard, had to invite her boyfriend to sleep over at the gallery with a gun under their bed on the first floor.) They seemed to like the idea so that was good!

Around this time, Paul Mellon asked me to have a show for an English artist he liked, John Skeaping. So I arranged a big show for Skeaping, and his paintings went flying out the window. Not only because they were good (they were), but because buyers knew he was Paul Mellon's protégé. I remember throwing a black-tie dinner for Skeaping in one of my barns in Battenville. More than a hundred people came, and it was a smashing success.

One time, I gave C.Z. Guest a party to introduce her new book, "My First Garden." C.Z. called to tell me Andy Warhol was staying with her and asked if it'd be all right to bring him along. Not only would it be all *right* . . . I quickly ran an ad in the local paper announcing that Andy Warhol would be at C.Z.'s opening. People came in *droves*. Oh, a lot of them were hippies and beatniks, hardly the types to buy art, but they added a lot of color; and the publicity was great.

The next year, I joined forces with John von Stade who had a wonderful gallery called the Essex Gallery in New Jersey, and knew everybody in the racing world—our partnership was a great success. We never argued over anything once, which is rare in gallery circles.

That same year, 1971, I was asked to chair a benefit to raise money for the United Nations School. I agreed and called the show "Young Artists" and found fifty-five unknown (and young) artists from all over the world to contribute their works. The exhibit was at the Union Carbide Building on Park Avenue in New York, and I got Alexander Calder to create the poster for it. To get it, my mother and I went to Calder's house in Saché, a few hours' drive from Paris. Sandy was kindness itself and showed us all sorts of gouaches to choose from. We finally chose one from this embarrassment

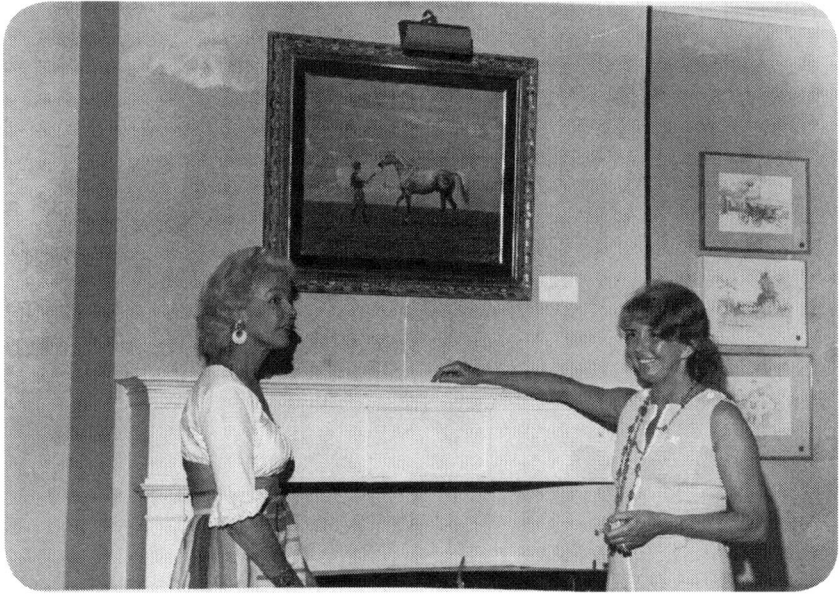

Tauni de Lesseps and me in front of E.P. Taylor's
Munnings, 1973.

Article by
WILLIAM JAEGER
Special to the Times Union

COUNTRY GALLERY HAS BARN, BATS AND LOTS OF ART

BATTENVILLE - Dream up the perfect art gallery. Go ahead.

A place in the country, maybe? Near a stream, big trees and gardens all around, not too far from Saratoga Springs and the Northway, but not too close.

Add a timeless 18th-century hay barn, perfectly renovated. And professional lighting that angles down onto rustic, horizontal pine boards where the work will be hung. And lawn to spare around the barn where people can mingle, and nearby a sparkling pool for ambiance.

Too good to be true? Not at all. Solange Herter has made it happen, creating a little utopia for the arts in Battenville, in the center of Washington County, an hour from Albany, and even closer to Saratoga Springs, Williamstown, Mass., and Bennington, Vt.

The farm entered her life fortuitously. "I overheard the place was going to be sold," says Solange Herter, *"and on an intuition I bought it. It's the best thing I've ever done."*

"It's a cultural addition to the neighborhood," she says, standing in the barn under the rough-hewn stairway that cuts through the airy space above. "Art opens up all doors; there are no social barriers."

Solange Herter, born in Paris and with children on both sides of the Atlantic, was formerly the Countess Solange de la Bruyere, and was always surrounded by art. Now married to retired physician Fred Herter, she makes clear the gallery fulfills a personal need, to surround herself with art and artists. She says, "I prefer artists to bankers."

In her gallery, called Gallery 668, art in a range of attractive styles, made by regional artists of all stripes, rotates through eight weekly shows all summer. Now in its second season, the gallery, which closes after Labor Day, is becoming something of a social must for those in the know, and each opening has more than 100 visitors. It coincides perfectly, of course, with horse-racing season, and is part of the fiber of the summer blossoming of the area.

Sandy Calder and my mother
at Saché.

Me and Sandy Calder
signing posters at Saché.

Article from the *Times Union*

————————

'Young Artists, '73'
works now on display

By SHELLEY RILEY

The weather was beautiful for the official opening of the July exhibit at the Saratoga Gallery, 125 Union Ave., Saratoga Springs, and a pleasing crowd attended the preview reception for the "Young Artists, '73" exhibition which will be on display in the gallery throughout the month.

Hostess for the reception was the gallery's director and chairman of the "Young Artists '73" art advisory committee, Countess Solange de La Bruyère. With her, greeting guests, were Mrs. D.G.W. del Rio, exhibition administrator, and Gustavus Ober, public relations director.

Space for the Gallery, located in the former Van Deusen house, is being donated by Verrazanno College and proceeds of the July exhibition, which just closed after a month at the Union Carbide Building in New York City, will benefit the International Play Group, a non-profit school in New York City for international families temporarily residing in the city. An average of 600 children attend the school yearly, ranging from six months of age (in the Creche programme of the school) to five years.

On hand for the opening reception in Saratoga Springs were two of the artists whose works were being shown — Akiko Shirai of Japan, whose medium is etching and intaglio, and Alberto Ycaza-Vargas of Nicaragua, whose oil paintings, done in earthy tones of brown and black, attracted much attention.

Of the nearly 500 works in the exhibit in New York City, approximately 95 were brought to Saratoga Springs, most of which are being shown at the Saratoga Gallery, with the remainder on display in the Patron's Room, Hall of Springs, Saratoga Performing Arts Center. The gallery opening was set to coincide with the opening of the New York City Ballet at SPAC.

Members of the preview committee attending the reception included Newman E. Wait Jr., past president of SPAC, and Mrs. Wait; Dr. Joseph C. Palamountain, Jr. president of Skidmore College, and Mrs. Palamountain; Lewis A. Swyer, president of SPAC; and George A Dudley, administrator of the New York State Council on Architecture.

Other area residents attending included Mr. and Mrs. John Petrella, Miss Remigia Foye, and Jane Marshall, all of Saratoga Springs; Hortense Calisher and Curtis Harnak of Yaddo; Dr. Emma S. Albach of Hadley.

The Saratoga Gallery

REVIEWING THE EXHIBITS — Countess Solange de La Bruyére, left, director of the Saratoga Gallery, and Mrs. John Petrella review the Alexander Calder poster that was commissioned to honor the 1971 exhibit. The poster to honor the 1973 exhibit has not yet been completed by Spanish artist Juan Miro, but orders are being taken for lithographs.

FROM CHINA — The only artistic endeavor to come from China as a part of the Young Artists '73 exhibit in New York City and currently at the Saratoga Gallery. 125 Union Ave., Saratoga Springs, is this ivory carved scene encased in glass. The exhibit will be on display throughout the month of July.

Miro poster for "Young Artists '73" show.

Fred, my mother, and me at 1984 Whitney party.
Canfield Casino, Saratoga Springs.

On the front lawn of Battenville with
Cornelius Vanderbilt Whitney.

of riches. I took it back to Paris, where the Atelier Mourlot made it into a poster. Having Calder's poster helped us raise over a million dollars. I had also somehow convinced the Chinese government to send me a piece of art for that 1971 exhibit. It was a dreadful cork sculpture, made in a factory, where Chinese artists had to produce their work on an assembly line; but it was the first piece of art to leave Communist China and that piqued some interest. Barbara Walters got wind of the news, and she asked me to appear with the sculpture on her show.

Barbara had her crew construct a mock-up art gallery, where I appeared and explained the "Young Artists" show to her TV audience. I then took phone calls that came in from all over the world. They were mostly price inquiries about that cork sculpture from China. We sold it for $3500 to the first caller, which was probably a mistake. Had we auctioned it off, we could have gotten much more. I was fearful Barbara Walters might give me a hard time because we shared a beau, Alexis Lichine, the great wine expert. (Sharing a beau does not make for great warmth between two women) And, indeed, when she started to give me a bad time I countered by correcting her pronunciation of my name. Barbara didn't speak French and had no idea how to pronounce either "Solange" or "de La Bruyère." She blushed and stammered and had no choice but to behave herself after that, apologizing for her mispronunciation. Lichine later married Arlene Dahl, which was just as well!

Afterward, I brought the whole *Young Artists* show up to Saratoga and had a really successful exhibition there. A feat I repeated in 1973. This time, the exhibit included twelve Calder tapestries, and I sold them all. They were spectacular, and I wish I had bought a couple myself, but the "song" they were going for was still too high for me. You can't cry over spilt milk, but I should be allowed to weep a little about the opportunities I had to buy art I liked but couldn't afford. I would be very rich today. So be it.

In 1973, I asked Miro to do the poster for another *Young Artists* exhibit. But dealing with Miro was a world away from dealing with Calder. I didn't know the great man and enlisted the help of a friend, Daniel Lelong, whose gallery, the Gallerie Maeght on Avenue de Messine, represented Miro in Paris. He agreed to take me to Miro's modest little house in Palma, Spain. His wife was toiling away in the kitchen, where I suspect she spent most of her life. Miro had a very red face, and Daniel asked him about his scarlet complexion. He explained that since his politics were at violent odds with the Spanish government, when he went to the bullfights, he had to sit in the unpopular side of the arena, in the glaring sunlight. Franco had his own imperious ways of putting dissidents in their place. A side note: The Calder gouache from which I had made his poster and which I simply adored was stolen when Fred and I moved out of the Dakota in 1980. My heart was broken. Then almost thirty years later, in 2008, the Calder Foundation called to tell me my missing gouache had shown up for auction at Christie's. I called a lawyer who specializes in recovering stolen art, and he froze the sale. And we're still hoping to get it back. The present "owner" paid $4000 to *somebody* for it twenty years ago. Today, it's worth *sixty thousand dollars!*

We had bought the Dakota apartment from the famous opera singer, Cesare Sieppe and it looked rather like a setting for La Traviata—lots of red velvet and damask on the walls, huge crystal chandeliers from the ceilings, in the master Bedroom, right over the bed etc. We sold it to another musician of quite a different caliber-Billy Joel-or we thought we had sold it and went off to Europe, where on the dusty beach in Saint Tropez we read in the Herald Tribune that Billy Joel had been rejected by the board. We had already bought another apartment and we had to wait approximately six months before we could get rid of the Dakota, and that was quite a bummer. It is strange that Billy Joel was not acceptable there as people like John and Yoko Lennon, Roberta Flack and Lauren Bacall were already firmly ensconced on the premises.

Another time I asked for Sandy's help was in 1975. At my suggestion, he had made some posters for George McGovern's presidential campaign, and I went to Saché to get them signed. These posters were to be sold at a fund-raising party Pat Lawford was throwing at Joe Allen's Parisian hamburger place. The poster was supposed to read "McGovern for McGovernment." But the type was too big to fit on one line so it read:

MCGOVERN FOR MCGOVERN
MENT.

Unfortunately, in French, "*ment*" means "lies." Everybody at the party laughed about it except for Pat Lawford, who didn't think it was funny. Years later, I met McGovern at a dinner at the Sultan of Oman's palace, and he was nice enough to tell me he thought that that had been all right. Artists could make mistakes! I doubt if the poster had anything to do with his lopsided loss, but if it did, he certainly didn't hold a grudge.

Even with my gallery's growing success, I was growing weary of my grueling routine: Early each morning, I'd get up to have breakfast at the Saratoga track and "shill" (luring potential customers back to the gallery), have lunch in town, usually at the Reading Room, head off to the races each afternoon, again gathering a following to bring back to the gallery, drive back to Battenville to change for still another dinner in Saratoga, and then back again late at night to Battenville to catch a little sleep before starting the same grind again the next morning. I grew totally exhausted on this merry-go-round, so I started a gallery in one of the eighteenth-century barns on my Battenville farm.

A local architect, Timothy D. Smith, had just finished building the Bennington College Art Center. I hired him to update the second barn, which was Scottish. The first barn, the German one, had already been renovated by George A. Dudley, another renowned architect. He was the one who chose the site for the UN building in New York. The interior spaces were, and are, magical, with every eighteenth-century architectural detail left in place yet somehow emphasized. These remarkable architects saved the barns from deterioration . . . and even eventual destruction. That makes me very happy and proud.

CHAPTER 15

My Mother's Death

My mother died peacefully in her pretty four-poster bed at my Battenville house on the thirty-first of March 1989. As I was about to leave the house to drive to New York the day before, something eerie happened. At the last minute, I couldn't find my car keys. Her nurse and I looked everywhere but to no avail. It gave me a sort of a premonition that I shouldn't leave, but suddenly, we found the keys on my mother's bed. I must have left them behind when I went to say good-bye, maybe unconsciously, not really wanting to leave.

I had a doctor's appointment in the city which I had to keep. I intended to drive straight back to Battenville that night, but in the afternoon I got the phone call that Mummy had died. I've regretted, to this day, that I wasn't there to hold her hand. But a friend told me, and I half believe it, that my mother probably planned it that way or, rather, would have liked it that way to save me from the final anguish. All my life, she protected me. For me, going through life always meant going through life with *her*. For as long as I can remember, it had always been the two of us, protecting each other. Then, in a second, my world changed, and I was stunned by the sudden emptiness. I was alone with a sadness that no one else, neither husband nor child, could assuage. For nowhere else would I find the unconditional love that she so endlessly dispensed.

I had inevitably included my mother in every aspect of my life. To me, her presence was as normal as breathing, and she always—*always*—rose to the occasion. I fondly recall one time when Marylou and Sonny Whitney gave their August party at the Canfield Casino in Saratoga Springs. The invitation asked all the ladies to wear white. But Mummy didn't have a white evening dress with her so she wore a grey one, saying that at her age she could wear anything she wanted; and she was the star of the party. Even MaryLou, who hated to be outshone, bowed to that! Another time, when she was well on in years, Mummy went to Japan as the guest of her great friend, Marguerite Dortu, who was the curator of the Musée d'Albi, the Toulouse Lautrec museum in France. Madame Dortu was bringing all the Toulouse-Lautrec paintings from the museum for a show in the Tokyo museum. My mother was, as always, a great hit. I have a funny photograph of the brother of Emperor Hirohito staring at her shoes, or was it at her legs?

It was a great success, but it all came to a screeching halt when a very important painting called "Marcelle" was stolen. The curator of the museum committed hara-kiri, and the whole French contingent had to attend his funeral and eat the cookies that contained his ashes. That's right: his *ashes!*

Mummy came back reveling in all these tales like a young girl after her first salvo in the world.

In 1961, when Jackie conquered Paris during Jack's presidential tour, she invited me to the official reception dinner that President de Gaulle had for them. The only catch was that Jean de la Bruyère, my then husband, who was supposed to be my escort, was back home in Edmonton. So I simply brought my *former* husband, Henri Deschamps, along instead. In the receiving

The emperor's brother, glancing at
Maman's knees.

line, Jackie's eyes opened wide when she saw me with the wrong husband. But since I had already confided that I was having problems with Jean, she wasn't all that surprised. The only problem was that Jean's, not Henri's, name was on the place card; but it didn't seem to bother Henri at all.

I remember that when I first told Jackie about my marital troubles, she casually tossed out a mind-boggling idea. To solve my problems, Jackie suggested that Jack maybe could have Jean *extradited!* I was never certain whether she was kidding or not. Anyway, it didn't go any further.

To get my divorce from Jean, I got myself a good lawyer. He was the afore-mentioned celebrated Sol Rosenblatt. His clients were a combination of the very rich and the very famous. He was Shirley Oakes' lawyer, and she recommended him to me. Some of his other clients were less stable and perhaps more intriguing figures like Ann Woodward, who everybody thought had shotgunned her husband to death. He got her off. And the always sun-glassed Carmine de Sapio, Tammany Hall's behind-the-scenes dictator. And Sam Giancano, the gang lord who ran Chicago while his moll, Judith Exner, romped around Jack Kennedy's White House. Ironically, even while acting as a mouthpiece for menacing Mafia types, Sol was Chief Counsel to the Vatican's far-flung and super secret organization, Opus Dei. Maybe because his wife, the very, very Catholic Estelle, was a friend of the Pope's. When their two sons served in World War II, they changed their last name to Russell. They figured, if the Germans captured them, they'd have a better chance if named Russell instead of Rosenblatt. Rosenblatt was a firm believer that any client, whatever their guilt or innocence, deserved the talents of the greatest lawyer on earth. And that lawyer, of course, was Sol Rosenblatt. When he told me that by exposing Jean's loose and amoral behavior, he could get me a huge alimony settlement, I was shocked.

"But think about the bad publicity!"

Sol answered, and I remember his answer so well, "Honey, what makes headlines today lines the garbage cans tomorrow."

He was right, and I was probably wrong, but nevertheless, I never did allow him to reveal what I called Jean's "dark" side. The result of that was I didn't get a great settlement for myself, but I made certain the children's education would be well taken care of right down to and including archery and fencing lessons. This was an almost absurd condition, but Sol agreed to putting it into the separation agreement. To this day, I can conjure up the image of my adorable little ones, Jackie and Marc, fencing mightily against each other. I can see them kissing their swords, lunging at each other, and shouting with glee when one or the other would "touché" the other and shout the word out. I don't know what good it did them in their lives. Maybe they do. Anyway, they have continued sparring.

I did, once, give in to Sol's advice and agreed to have Jean followed so that we could sue for divorce on the grounds of adultery. It was arranged that on a given evening at the Bahamian Club, I would tap Jean on the shoulder and give the detective who had been put on the case positive identification. Unfortunately, on my way to the tap, I gave a big hug to a friend of mine. The detective mistook the hug for the tap and proceeded to follow my friend for forty-eight hours, and the mistake cost me a pretty penny. But I must say that when Sol and I saw the report, we were quite impressed by my friend's activities; and later, when I told my friend what had happened, instead of being angry, as I thought he might be, he was thrilled that his prowesses had been well-recorded. Ah! Men!

CHAPTER 16

Jacqueline Kennedy

Jackie Kennedy was a peerless friend. Back in 1976, I had my first problems with cancer. After an operation for a melanoma, I was recovering at Columbia-Presbyterian Hospital. I was there for a long time and she'd faithfully drop in to see me. We'd talk about much deeper subjects than the schoolgirl discussions we'd had in the past. She realized I was facing a life-threatening disease and that I was more than a little scared. Scared enough to want to talk about it but only to very few people, and Jackie was a really good listener. Fred and I went to stay with Jackie at Martha's Vineyard the summer before she died. She seemed so well—swimming in the icy ocean, walking briskly up and down her private beach, taking us to Gay Head to watch the sunset, giving wonderful dinner parties with interesting people like William Styron and George Plimpton (and his ninety-two-year-old mother). One couldn't possibly have thought there was anything the matter with her health or that there would be, very soon. When I found out that she had non-Hodgkin lymphoma, an almost-always non-forgiving disease, I wrote her a little note saying something about how many advances had been made in the field, etc., and that cures were happening, and she immediately wrote me back a beautiful letter on that baby blue stationary of hers, downplaying her illness and saying that it was nothing at all and lauding me for having shown such "great courage and dignity" in facing mine twenty-five years before though she, of course, knew she was dying.

"Twenty five years before". I had fallen in love with my superb and very handsome surgeon, Fred Herter, even though his scalpel had wrecked my upper leg. I'll never forget Jackie's response when I revealed my new love. "Oh, the son of the secretary of State!" She said it as though that was the most prestigious title in the world. Much more exalted than Jack's "Mr. President." I saw her do the same thing to an awed twelve-year-old Cathy Sulzberger. I was staying with Cathy's parents, Punch and Carol Sulzberger, as I usually did before I had my own Manhattan apartment. Jackie had invited me to Camp David, and I brought little Cathy along to meet her at the presidential suite on the top floor of the Carlyle Hotel. The plan was we'd leave from there and head off to Camp David. Cathy and I bumped into the King of Morocco, who stepped out of the elevator just as we stepped into it. The king had just presented Jackie with belts and bracelets encrusted with glittering rubies and sapphires and emeralds. These priceless treasures were strewn haphazardly all across the coffee table, and little Cathy was hypnotized by the dazzling sight. So was I. But the point of the story is that when I introduced Cathy, Jackie said to her in her breathless murmur, "Oh, when I think that your father is both the president and the publisher of *The New York Times*, and Jack is only president."

She had a unique way of making everybody feel important even while effacing herself. At any rate, the Secret Service gathered us up (including the king's jewels) and got us into Marine One, the presidential helicopter that whisked us to Camp David. This rustic retreat is anything but rustic. It's a glorious spot, half-a-mile high and one hundred fifty acres in the Cacoctin Mountains in Maryland. It was created by FDR, and every president since has used it as a secluded getaway. There are a dozen or so comfortable cabins. And however relaxed it may look, the camp is guarded more tightly than Fort Knox.

During our visit to Camp David, there was obviously something important going on. I overheard some muttered references to Cuba but didn't pay any attention. What was much more important was that Jackie was teaching me how to back-comb my hair, which her hairdresser, the great Kenneth, had just taught her how to do. I had never teased my hair before, and what a revelation! All that *volume*. It gave one a whole new look. I was amazed to see Jackie Kennedy's full panoply of cosmetics. Flasks and vials and tubes and jars all lain out before her arrival and ready for her to use. No wonder I was more impressed with all of that than with any undecipherable mentions of the Cuban problem.

The Bay of Pigs invasion took place shortly after I was back home in Edmonton. Jackie called me the day American troops suffered the humiliating defeat at Castro's hands. She wanted to talk to someone about the disaster, and she was so happy she'd gotten through to me. (She had called her mother first, but Mrs. Auchincloss was busy playing bridge and couldn't possibly be interrupted by something as trivial as an impeachable blunder by her son-in-law.)

When Carol and Punch Sulzberger married, I was the only friend they had in common. Punch and I became friends in Paris while he was married to his first wife, and I had known Carol in Hollywood in the '40s (when we both were hyperventilating over Victor Mature's beautiful body, which he always oiled thoroughly before diving into the pool at her parents' place, which made the water rather slimy). Punch, with all the responsibilities he had, took time out to fulfill his creative side. Whenever I stayed with them at 1010 Fifth Avenue, he would make, either a ceramic doorknob with my name on it for the guest room, or a beautiful wooden plaque that said "Welcome Solange", or he would pin a poem to the flowers in my room . . . all very endearing . . . He had a great sense of humor. Once, when I told him how much the Kennedys admired him and his newspaper, he quipped back, "Never mind the admiration, tell them to buy a copy!"

Carol was very protective of me, always worrying that I was spending too much money on my children and would end up not having enough money to even go to the movies! To compensate, she introduced me to lots of interesting people from *The New York Times* (who could take me to the movies).

One of them was Sidney Gruson, whom Carol was determined I should marry. Sidney was a brilliant journalist, had won a Pulitzer for his reporting in Poland, and was way up there in the *New York Times* hierarchy. But I didn't really take a shine to him. And he failed the acid test I'd come up with to determine a beau's character. My challenge was to take them to spend a weekend in Battenville and see how they reacted to the primitive life in the boondocks. Well, Sydney failed miserably. After only twenty-four hours, he announced that he had had a phone call from his office and had to get back to New York. What he didn't know was that the phones in the house were out of order (cell phones didn't exist.) That was the end of that!

Another person who often came to see me while I was at Columbia-Presbyterian Hospital was the Rt. Reverend Paul Moore, the Episcopal Bishop of New York, a great friend of Fred Herter. Fred had brought him to me when I had asked for a sympathetic clergyman I could talk to. A Roman Catholic priest had paid a call on me (which was his want as I was registered as a Catholic in the hospital rosters). It had been a terribly depressing visit as this kee-kee little priest started speaking to me about my mortality, confessing my sins, and getting absolution—all that jazz. Not very cheery. But when I saw those two tall Greek gods—Fred and Paul—walk into my room the next day, things

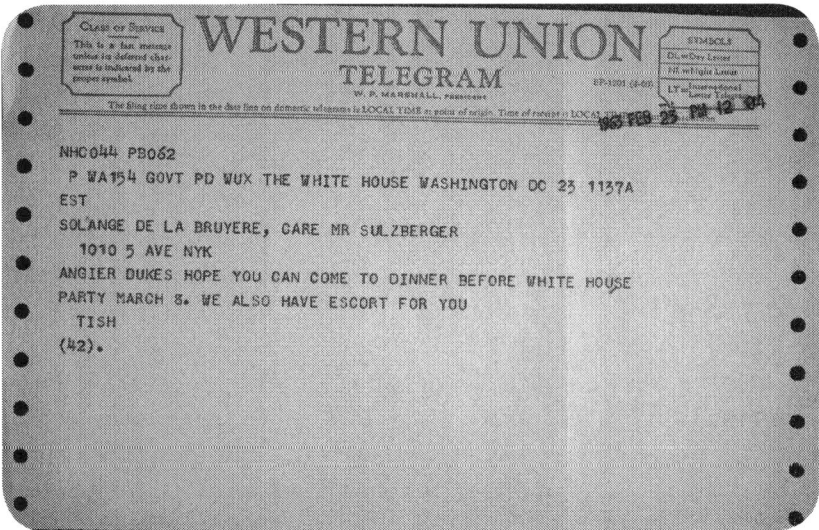

White House invitation from Tish Baldridge
(Jackie's secretary). (I wonder if the White House provides
escorts today).

President Kennedy and Jackie.

brightened up no end. In fact, when Paul Moore put his hand on my head to give me a blessing, I had—for the first time in my life—a deep religious uplifting moment. He came almost every day. A year later, he married us at the Cathedral of Saint John the Divine, kindly and bravely overlooking the fact that Fred and I had a few divorces between us. It was a lovely wedding; about two hundred friends and relatives came to wish us luck and cheer us on our way. There was a wonderful reception afterwards at the Dakota given by our friend, George Davison Ackley; and then we flew to England and spent our honeymoon at Moyn's Park, Jo Bryce's castle in Sussex—in separate rooms, on separate floors as was the English custom, which meant we had a lot of climbing to do, up and down the stairs. We had spent our first night at Claridge's in London, where, somehow, I lost my nightgown. I wrote a letter to the manager about it, and he answered me in a very funny tongue-in-cheek way that many lady guests had done that in the past in his hotel but that, in his experience at least, no ladies had ever left their nightgowns behind on their honeymoon and that my beautiful nightgown was nowhere to be found.

CHAPTER 17

The Cathedral of St. John the Divine

New York Times article by Charlotte Curtis
A First for the Cathedral

St. John the Divine hopes to emulate the fund-raising successes of the public library and the zoo.

THE sign posted just inside the Episcopal Cathedral of St. John the Divine is inescapable. "We are a community as well as a cathedral: Caring for the hungry, homeless and jobless; Educating the young, supporting the elderly." And that's not all.

The cathedral has an elementary school, a textile works, its celebrated stone cutters (recruited and trained from among the city's disadvantaged youth), outreach programs, concerts, chapels devoted to each of the city's ethnic groups, a soup kitchen with food grown in its own gardens, a theater, shelter for the homeless, a theological institute, platforms for political debate, interfaith services and an ecumenical board of trustees that proudly includes Jews. Perhaps no religious institution is more inclusive.

And, like all big public institutions, the cathedral needs money. Its board has launched an $80-million endowment drive. And next May, at the height of the spring social season, it expects to stage its first benefit dinner dance.

"Probably not black-tie," Solange de La Bruyère Herter, the French Roman Catholic who volunteered to do the party, had said. "With 600 or 700 for dinner. A thousand the top price for each couple. A celebration of the 100th anniversary of the plan for the cathedral. We haven't worked out the details. But I think it's possible."

Mrs. Herter is the wife of Dr. Frederic P. Herter, professor of surgery at Columbia University, and daughter-in-law of the late Christian Herter, a Secretary of State. She knows what she is about. Two years ago, working full-time for six months, she raised more than $1 million for Columbia medical scholarships. She thinks she can do it again.

"All she wants is a full-time assistant," said the Very Rev. James Parks Morton, Dean of the cathedral. "She's really quite amazing."

The Dean, freshly returned from his summer holiday, was in his handsomely Gothic office in the bishop's residence donated by J. P. Morgan. The hot September sun streamed through the arched windows. He and Jocelyn Kress Turner, a new trustee, had just come from a tour of his 13-acre domain. He wore a short-sleeved shirt with his clerical collar and khakis.

"Solange is calling it a church supper," Mrs. Turner said. "But it will be an extravagant church supper."

"The extravagance will be the beast itself," Dean Morton added. *(He often refers to the cathedral as "the beast," hails associates "How art thou?" and categorizes friends as beasts, birds or sacred animals)* "And the extravagance will be the singers. The food will be picnic fare."

The two reminisced about less spectacular church suppers they had known. "Everybody brings fried chicken and there's no dessert," Mrs. Turner said. *The Dean smiled. Clearly, this is to be no such gathering. Whether they use tents or dine in the synod house, the evening is to begin with drinks and end in the cathedral with a major concert.*

"We can't talk about the singers," Dean Morton said. "We're still negotiating. But they'll sing inside and then again on the front steps for the entire neighborhood."

Columbia is across the street, and the neighborhood is a mix of shops and faculty housing. Unlike parish churches, the cathedral has a wide variety of regulars but no true congregation.

A century ago the Morgans, Bloomingdales, Astors, Fishes, Belmonts, Millers and Vanderbilts were among those who raised the money to build the cathedral and assure its financial stability. Up until World War II, the old families quietly made up the annual deficits. Now, many old families have left the city, or the church or they simply don't have the money. Construction was allowed to languish. There was no fund-raising until Dean Morton arrived in 1972.

"We're two or three years behind Brooke Astor and Annette Reed, who actually got people to go to the New York Public Library," Mrs. Turner said. *She is a handsome woman with old-fashioned credentials, a Kress of the dime store fortune.* "They put the library *on the map. We want to do for the cathedral what ladies like Enid Haupt did for the Botanical Garden and the zoo."*

And they may well do it. Nine years ago, on Easter Sunday during the city's fiscal crisis, Bishop Paul Moore Jr. of the Episcopal Diocese of New York, delivered a sermon comparing big companie's leaving town to rats leaving a sinking ship. The next day, Felix G. Rohatyn, a leader in the fight to save the city, phoned his thanks.

The cathedral began its corporate fund-raisers that year, honoring Mr. Rohatyn. Shortly thereafter, he became the cathedral's first Jewish trustee. Now there is a Dean's Council of activists and Philippe Petit, the resident high-wire artist, is in the rafters, practicing. He has vowed to help celebrate by dancing his way up a wire strung from the cathedral's front-door to the highest window above the altar. "On Ascension Day," the Dean said. As if explanations were necessary.

Mayor John Lindsay and me.
St. John the Divine Benefit.

When my mother died, I needed help for handling my grievous loss, and I went to see Paul Moore. I met with him for numerous teas that were more like counseling sessions. His bottomless compassion and, more importantly, his sensible guidance helped me get out of the depths. Even today, decades after her death, I still miss my mother physically, actively every day. It's the unshakable sense of loss that has been with me since I got the awful news that all of us fear getting about a loved one.

A few years later, Paul asked me to chair the benefit to celebrate the one hundredth anniversary of St. John the Divine. I was already on the board of the cathedral, and I leapt at the chance. I quickly formed a noteworthy committee, boosted with Jacqueline Onassis's name at the top. We decided to hold a black-tie picnic supper, and I suggested we add some games to the program . . . maybe Bingo. Some uptight, fellow board member drew herself up to her full height and declared:

> "Only the Catholics play Bingo." Really attractive. Paul Moore struck her down, and we played Bingo, like good Episcopalians, at the centennial. Then I suggested that Philippe Petit, our artist in residence, perform his high-wire act inside the cathedral. The wicked witch of the West piped up again:

> "What if he crashes to the floor and splatters his blood all over the nave?"

Philippe Petit and me.

With the Dean of the Cathedral, James Morton.

Letter in St. John the Divine centennial program.

When Bishop Moore asked me, a Roman Catholic and a foreign one at that, to orchestrate a benefit for the Centennial of St. John the Divine, I thought he was speaking to the person on my left (see photo above).

Though it was Paul Moore who introduced me to the Cathedral–and I shall always be grateful to him for that–many others, particularly Dean Morton, have helped me understand what this extraordinary institution is all about.

The training of young artisans in stone carving and in classic methods of construction for the completion of the original Cram towers are appealing facts of the Cathedral's activities, and this is just one of the myriad and imaginative ways in which the Cathedral has reached out to so many in this city.

The words "community," "ecumenical," "service," "care," "courage," and "joy" as they are embodied in the works of the Cathedral family have new meaning for me. Truly, this is what a great church should be about and I am proud to be in some small way a part of it.

I feel so very lucky that it was me Bishop Moore addressed a year ago and I want to thank him from the bottom of my heart for giving me this privileged opportunity.

I must thank all those who have worked so hard to bring this evening about and everyone who has purchased tickets to tonight's event, and to the impressive roster of advertisers who have supported our Commemorative Magazine.

We all salute St. John the Divine—on this first Centennial.

New York
June 1986

Sincerely,

Solange Herter

Mrs. Frederic P. Herter
CHAIRMAN

Philippe performed a sky-high number actually on Ascension Day while a thousand people watched, transfixed; and once again, my event raised over a million dollars, which went toward building the missing front tower. And Philippe Petit didn't crash to the floor.

Jackie often gave small, intimate parties at the White House. Those parties were sometimes hatched late in the day after Jackie got a glimpse of JFK's frame of mind. So depending on how the president was feeling, the invitations were often sent out as late as 6:00 p.m. They were considered command performances even if accepting them required frantic rearrangements of schedules. (In order to accept one of these very late invitations, Hervé Alfandéry, the French ambassador, told me he once cancelled a dinner for fifty at the French Embassy. When she heard about *that*, Jackie was appalled, particularly since her dinner was for eight people.)

But of all the Kennedy White House parties I attended, one is indelibly etched in my mind. And here's why: It was a black-tie private little dinner dance for about a hundred people in my honor. Jackie often "used" beards as an excuse for a party, and I was the beard that night.

As the guest of honor, I was seated on Jack's right at dinner and on my right, I had Jack's Harvard buddy, Lemoyne Billings. After dessert, I asked him if he knew where the nearest loo was. "Absolutely," he said. "Follow me." He led me down to the basement and pointed to a door. I sailed right through and found myself in a *men's* room with huge Victorian urinals lining the walls. There was no one else there, thank goodness, and I thought, *What the hell? I can pee anywhere? which* I did. Then I went to wash my hands; and while I was scrubbing away fast to make my getaway . . . plunk! One of my earrings fell into the sink and down the drain. I was wearing important diamond earrings that I treasured and had taken out of the safe just for this occasion. I ran out of there, yelled at Billings that his joke wasn't very funny, and demanded he call for a plumber. Immediately! He went searching for one while I stood guard outside the door. Two dark-suited plumbers arrived. After a lot of men came and went, my plumbers emerged, and I jumped on them.

"Did you manage to get it out?" I asked.

But these two men weren't plumbers at all. They were Lord Ormsby-Gore, the British ambassador and his aide-de-camp. Though taken aback, they smiled and moved on. (The real plumbers soon fished out my earring, thank God.)

A week later, in Newport, Jackie ask me to join her in a game of tennis—mixed doubles. And our partners were, who else? Ormsby-Gore and his aide! The ambassador looked me up and down and smiled:

"Aren't you the young lady who was standing outside the men's room last week, asking each gent if he could get it out?"

I said "Of course, I was." And despite that, I was soon put on the guest list of the British embassy. It was always terrific fun to go there. I also went to the French embassy often.

The French ambassador, Hervé Alfandéry, and his decorative wife, Nicole, gave great parties. He had a way of mimicking people, which was inimitable. His best imitation was of Lyndon Johnson. It was not flattering, and Jack would ask him to do it again and again. One of my favorite embassies was the Moroccan embassy, where everybody always seemed to walk around looking extra happy and smiling. It was only later that I learned the reason: the Moroccans habitually added hashish to their popular brownies.

At another White House party, this time in the upstairs family apartment, Jackie told me we would only be seven or eight for dinner. As I was ushered in, I thought I was the first guest; but then, I saw a little man happily rocking away in Jack's famous rocking chair in front of the fireplace He was the recently widowed Spanish ambassador, Señor Guarrigues, a gregarious man about town. I introduced myself and quickly told him that he was in the president's chair. As he jumped out of it, Jack entered the room. He glanced at his chair, rocking away by itself, looked at the ambassador and then at me but didn't say a word. The Spanish diplomat later wrote me a letter to thank me for not telling on him. During that dinner, I was reminded once again at how much the Kennedy men were entranced by movie stars. (Like father, like sons, I guess.) When Jack and Bobby heard me mention that Elizabeth Taylor and I were neighbors in Switzerland and that our children went to school together, their ears perked up, particularly when I added that each morning, on my way to taking my girls to school, we could hear Liz through her open windows, cursing like a trooper. (She was married to Richard Burton at the time, and the two fought constantly even at that early hour, turning the air blue with their swearing.) But Jack and Bobby didn't care about Liz's cussing. All they wanted to know was what she was wearing and if she looked sexy that early in the morning.

I had moved to Gstaad, right after my divorce from Jean de la Bruyère and rented a châlet in a little village on the outskirts called Saanen. My pockets weren't exactly overflowing at the time, and Saanen was a very inexpensive place to live. (My daughter Mary had been in a Gstaad boarding school for a year for her asthma problems, and when I moved there, I was able to enroll her as a day student instead of as a boarder.) The king of Belgium's children went there. Of course, this didn't guarantee high academic standards, but security was assured.

Châlet Aellen was Heidi-like. I had a good cook, and I found a nice Swiss nanny called Vreni, who had just graduated at the top of her class from the best nursing school in Switzerland. She had long blonde hair and rosy, apple cheeks and was just wonderful. In the summer, just below our châlet, Yehudi Menuhin practiced his violin in the little church there. Can you imagine the bliss of listening through our open windows as the great maestro played his Stradivarius, his resonant sounds flying up our way?

Jean's mother was in nearby Berne, where her husband, Phillippe Baudet, was the French ambassador. We often spent weekends at the embassy, which was not only extremely pleasant but gave the children a sense of family continuity. Jean dropped by our chalet once in a blue moon, my mother somewhat more often, and friends visited from all over. In the winter, there was superb skiing, and the summers were glorious. We lived quite unnoticed in our modest chalet until the U.S. ambassador began delivering packages from the White House for Jacqueline. With all she had on her mind, Jackie never forgot her godchild's birthday. The three Christmases she was first lady, she sent marvelous old prints of the White House, signing them in her distinctive looping penmanship, "To Jacqueline from Jacqueline, with love."

That inscription reminded me of when I'd asked Jackie if she'd be my daughter's godmother. "Of course!" she agreed, but with one proviso. "She must always be called and call herself 'Jacqueline' and never 'Jackie.' All my life, I've regretted that people never called me by my real name."

She was endlessly generous and always sent *me* presents too. Often for no ostensible reason except sheer friendship. When Fred and I were married, she gave me the most beautiful kidney-shaped silver evening purse by Elsa Perretti. I treasure it to this day and think of my beloved friend whenever I carry it. The children and I took many long hikes in the mountains, picking wild flowers, and yodeling our vocal chords to shreds. We were a one-hour hop from London or Paris so we had the best of two worlds—the cosmopolitan and the remotely rustic.

But back to the Marie-José school, Liz Taylor's sons, the two Michael Wilder boys, were there at the same time as Mary and Veronique and were holy terrors. I remember how they'd pack stones inside snowballs then throw them at the girls. Liz's daughter, little Liza Todd, Michael Todd's daughter, was in Véronique's class. The two of them got into a terrible fight once over whose mother was the more glamorous. Liza claimed that she had come out of the most beautiful tummy in the world. Véronique countered that *she* had emerged from the most beautiful tummy in the world. Their fight escalated until they were tearing each other's hair out. All this took place at the ripe old age of *six*. It was funny for me to recall what friends Liz and I had been back at Hollywood High, talking about everything in the world except which one of us had "the most beautiful tummy in the world."

After Jackie left Washington for good and decided to live in New York, she moved to 1040 Fifth Avenue. Just four blocks from where I lived, at 1000 Park. At first, hers was a strictly secluded life. But then, encouraged by Bobby Kennedy, she started having little dinner parties, and often invited me. The cast of characters was fascinating and eclectic, to say the least. Gore Vidal, Fellini and his wife, Giulietta Masina, David Selznick, Peter and Pat Lawford, Arthur Schlesinger, Ronny and Marietta Tree, Dick Goodman, Ken Galbraith . . . Margaret Truman, Clifton Daniel, and always somebody from that week's headlines. Faithfully in attendance was Bobby. (For some reason, Ethel Kennedy didn't often attend.)

After one of those dinner parties, Jackie asked Bobby to walk me the few blocks to my house. And something happened that's always stuck in my mind. I wore very high heels in those days, which only accentuated how much taller I was than he. When we got to the first street crossing, I stepped down into the street while he was still standing on the sidewalk. He asked me, rather sheepishly, if we couldn't keep walking like this. That way, he wouldn't feel badly about being so short. It sounds silly now, but we continued our two-level stroll after many other dinner parties. It even became a standing—or walking—joke between us. He seemed to be quite insecure and was also very self-conscious about his unruly hair, forever running his hands through it.

Despite her endless wardrobe, Jackie always wore the same dress at those dinners. And it was an unremarkable dress—a yellow shantung, sleeveless, shift with lots of gold buttons. I finally asked her why she didn't wear something different. She shrugged, "Oh, it doesn't matter. I always change the guest list . . . except for you and Bobby . . . so not many people have seen it twice; and I'll wear it until it unravels."

After Jackie married Aristotle Onassis, her guest list then included a lot of Greeks and café society types. And later with Maurice Templeman, her great friend of her last years, a lot of little African kings who spoke about diamond mines and things came for dinner.

At three o'clock sharp every Friday afternoon in New York, Véronique and I were picked up by Jackie and Caroline Kennedy and whisked up to Lincoln Center, where Jackie had organized a ballet class for the little girls. I doubt if our daughters appreciated it, but Jackie had asked the great Russian dancer André Eglevsky to take charge of the neophytes. The world-renowned Russian dancer brought in stars like Maria Tallchief to teach and encourage our budding ballerinas. (Tallchief was then prima dancer at New York City Ballet and was married to Balanchine. She later founded the Chicago Ballet.)

At one of our dance sessions, the usual pianist couldn't show up. And I was called on to substitute for him. So there I was, center stage, banging out Chopin Waltzes when all the lights went out. I thought somebody didn't like my performance. To my great relief, I found out it wasn't my fault and that every light in New York city had gone out, paralyzing all of Gotham. It was the big blackout of 1965. Jackie's ever-present retinue of Secret Service men pounced on Jackie, the children, and the rest of us and hustled us into her car.

We sped away, careening through the streets of Manhattan. This was extra scary because there were no traffic lights working at any street crossing. Jackie, Caroline, and Patricia and Peter Lawford's child, Sidney, were dropped off, and then Véronique and I were taken to my apartment. (Ordinarily, we would have been unloaded first, as ours was the first geographical stop, but as always, Kennedy family members were rushed to safety at the first sign of danger.)

That night, I had invited some friends for drinks at my apartment; but because of the blackout, I was certain that nobody would brave the darkened streets and show up. Taxis were scarce, elevators didn't work, most flashlights had long since given up the ghost. But people at the bidden time arrived, puffing a bit from their eight-floor climb and into the soft welcoming light of many candles.

We had a lovely time sharing our blackout adventures until one last guest arrived. It was Rudolph Nureyev, none the worse for the climb but slightly the worse for the drinks he had already consumed. (He was known to claim that vodka relieved the constant pain in his dance-damaged feet.) Nureyev immediately began working the room, accepting the homage of my awestruck guests. He also began plucking the most expensive broaches from ladies' jackets and pinning them onto his own, proclaiming, "Now I am decorated like a wild West sheriff!"

The flattered and star-struck women were delighted at the little game until Rudy made a bound toward my front door, quite unencumbered by all that loot. I stopped him and had a hard time convincing him to return his ill-gotten gains. My friends had gotten more and more nervous about their Cartier, or Tiffany, or Van Cleef and Arpels baubles. Can you imagine explaining to your insurance broker that Nureyev had danced away with your jewelry during the New York blackout? (I have had the thought that more often than not, the proud victims of Rudolph's larcenous fingers just let him keep the gems. How else could one account for the enormous fortune he left behind, even taking into account his $10,000 fee for each appearance?)

Nevertheless, I went to see Nureyev dance every chance I had, and I bless him for every move he made. There's been nobody like him (not even Baryshnikov) who set our pulses racing and emotions flying. Clear as day, I still remember one of his magical performances in Swan Lake. That stellar night, Jackie had invited Fred and me to dinner with Maurice Templesman. We lost track of the time and even thought the restaurant was close to Lincoln Center. We missed the opening curtain.

As we entered the hall, an usher told us we couldn't be seated until the end of Act I. This brought the manager, who had been awaiting Jackie's arrival, rushing up and inviting us to follow him. At this, an irate patron, who'd also been barred from entering, started yelling, "I'll be *she* gets in!" It was an ugly scene. The woman followed us, screaming all the way to the manager's office. While we watched Act I on the in-house television, the woman stood outside, making sure we hadn't been sneaked into the theater itself. She made me think of the "Tricotteuses," the women who, knitting all the while, stayed outside the Versailles Palace gates, clamoring for Marie Antoinette's head. The thought helped me understand how often Jackie's life was encumbered by that sort of thing.

We went to see Nureyev backstage. Now listen to this: After all the bowing and scraping and hand-kissing, those calculating Tartar eyes zeroed in on me. And he said to me, "Tell me, as a reward for my performance, could I have Tchaikowsky's original score of Swan Lake I saw on your piano when I last was in your apartment?" I guess he hadn't been all that drunk playing the part of the sheriff at my cocktail party.

I mumbled a few "maybes," but after we left, Jackie told me not to give such a precious thing away because he'd only sell it and squander the money. So I didn't.

I remember another similar, awful scene involving Jackie. It was in the Caribbean. We had both just gotten off the Cristina for a walk on the island of Montserrat. A sort of creepy beatnik followed us, demanding an autograph from Jackie. She pretended not to hear, but he kept hounding away. Luckily, the security men from the yacht overheard the fuss and came running up to get rid of him.

The incident made clear to me that one of her reasons for marrying Onassis must have been in seeking the very protection from the kind of scene I'd just seen. The Secret Service stopped guarding her and the children two years after the assassination.

Another time I remember all too well was when my children and I were again pounced on for security reasons. It was in Mexico. We were staying at a house in Acapulco, not far from one that Jean de la Bruyère had rented. One day, my friend, Georgette Minelli called. She asked if I could possibly join her and her sister at the president of Mexico's beach compound for lunch. Her sister was married to Miguelito Aleman, the son of the president.

Georgette tactfully explained that Mexico's first family was a bit stuffy, and maybe it would be best if Jean didn't come along. (Jean's colorful reputation obviously had preceded him.) At any rate, I packed up the children, and off we drove for a day at the beach.

Well, I have to tell you, a "day at the beach" it certainly wasn't. First of all, the compound itself was protected in a way Fort Knox could only *dream* of. The place was oozing with Uzis and bazookas. The Aleman men, sporting the skimpiest of bathing trunks and slathered with enough suntan oil to pollute the Gulf, befouled the air with their huge panatelas, hunkered in front of an enormous TV set watching an ear-busting soccer match.

The women lolled poolside, watching the children. Endless attendants set up a buffet that could feed a township, constantly replenishing the guacamole, the tacos, the refried beans, and tortillas.

Then BANG!.Out of the blue, there was a single gunshot. Quick as a flash, scores of armed and uniformed men sprang out of nowhere and dive-bombed all of us flat on the beach and around the pool. They brandished their weapons and gesticulated madly. And the cause of all this riotous reaction? Apparently some hapless guard's gun had misfired. Woe betide him.

At length, the mélée subsided, heartbeats slowed, breathing resumed, and we all got back to the guacamole.

President Aleman, like all feared dictators, demanded an army of visible and hidden protectors. For himself and for his family but the whole episode added a *frisson* of excitement to a casual outing.

At the end of the day, as we were leaving, I noticed a huge yacht pulling up to the Aleman's private dock. And to my amazement, onto the gangplank stepped a dreadful little man named Bernie Cornfeld. He was warmly embraced by Miguelito. Walking in single file, right behind tiny Bernie was a bevy of bikini-clad bimbos. They made up a tawdry retinue, one bearing Bernie's drink, another his boom-box, another his backgammon set, another his snorkel. Oh, Bernie was really a class act right down to his painted toes.

Bernie Cornfeld, or *Cornie Bumfeld*, as I dubbed him, always wore a jester's cap just in case people didn't realize he was such a jerk. I bet he even brought it along with him when he was incarcerated. He was sent up the river a bit later for an embezzlement scheme involving his company, the infamous IOS. And to think they were worried about Jean's reputation!

CHAPTER 18

The Cristina

Once, out of the blue, Jackie called me from Greece and asked, "Could you please drop everything and come to help me?" Ari's beloved son, Alexander, his only son, had just died. Instead of letting the professional test pilot try out the new plane his father had just given him, Alexander insisted on taking the controls himself; but due to some mechanical failure, the plane crashed, and he was killed. The pilot was unharmed. Ari was out of him mind with grief, and Jackie was convinced that the only thing that might help him was to get him on his yacht with a handful of close friends and just sail away from everything. Of course, I immediately agreed to go. Flying from New York to Paris, I boarded Olympic Airlines for the flight to Dakar. Jackie had also asked JFK's press secretary, Pierre Salinger, and his wife, Nicole, plus a friend of Bobby, Felix Mirando. From Dakar, the Cristina sailed across the Atlantic to Martinique, a long haul. It was a bad time of year, the seas were rough, and the Cristina was not a sea-worthy ship. She was top-heavy and always rolled alarmingly in heavy swells. Ari was drinking himself into a stupor every night, bemoaning his fate and cursing the gods like a figure from a Greek tragedy. The only thing that seemed to assuage his grief was playing poker. So every day, after lunch, he, Pierre, Felix, and I would play. We were an off foursome: Onassis couldn't concentrate, Pierre and Felix were poor players, and I had a solid grasp of the odds. The pots were huge, and I, taking full advantage of the situation, won lots of money, which I kept stashed away in the safety of the Cristina's safe. Which was fun to make forays. When we got to Guadeloupe, I told Jackie I had to go back to France to pick up my son for his school holiday. I had never missed doing that. But Jackie begged me to stay. She asked if we couldn't somehow arrange for Marc to join us. Very quickly, plans were put into gear, and my mother had Marc picked up at his boarding school in Normandy and whisked off to Brussels by bus (the Paris airport was on strike), where he boarded an Olympic Airways flight to New York. There, Jackie, who had left to attend one of John-John's basketball games, picked him up in turn and flew with him back to the "Cristina." Simple as that and a lot easier than dealing with a travel agent.

Marc arrived on board with his Astérix comic books. These juvenile books impressed Onassis no end. They were adventure stories based on Roman history, written for children but at an adult level. Ari lost himself in these stories. He was never an avid reader, but he *devoured* this simplistic approach to these historic tales. They became a great diversion for him and helped take his mind off his troubles. I remember him telling Jackie how he wished John-John could read these gripping books. He was convinced Astérix comic books could revolutionize the way young people learned Roman and Gallic history, and he was right. Today, an Astérix movie is being made as we speak.

During this cruise, the "Cristina" stopped at many islands. On Martinique, we had a wonderful lunch at the jeweler Pierre Schlumberger's house, which was a lively spot. I remember watching dozens of black ladies carrying bundles of Porthault linens on their Porthault turbaned heads, scurrying back and forth. Another stop was Montserrat. After Jackie went water skiing, she and Ari decided to take a stroll on the beach. When they got on shore, a car mysteriously appeared and offered them a ride around the island. They accepted, which is unbelievable when you think about it, and eventually reached a very pretty villa. The driver explained that it was the nicest one on the island, belonging to a rich American lady, and that it was for sale. Her staff was under orders never to disturb her before noon. So Ari and Jackie explored the whole house (except for its mistress's bedroom). Then they left. Eventually, the lady of the house woke up and was probably livid with her help for obeying her instructions and kicked herself for snoozing away while the world's most famous couple was roaming from room to room.

Our captain hadn't gotten permission from local authorities, which he was meant to do for us to go ashore. This led to a big problem. When the Onassises were back on board, a couple of police launches suddenly roared up. About two *dozen* policemen boarded the Cristina. They had spotted the party from the Onassis yacht landing on the beach without permission and were just doing their follow-up duty (with the utmost glee, I might add, as they ogled everything in sight). They demanded to see our passports, and I'll never forget how Jackie handed hers over like a little girl who had done something wrong. Can you imagine the tongue—lashing the Cristina's captain got from Onassis that night? Poor man, he was a sweet little Egyptian who spent most of his time trembling in his boots. And for good reason. Ari was always yelling at him about real or imagined mistakes: an imperfectly coiled hawser, a broken deck chair, whatever. Ari was very tough with anyone who worked for him. Down to hounding his chef about the weight and price of a bushel of potatoes. In fact, the chef was great at his job. But during that trip, I was the only passenger who enjoyed his bouillabaisses or his robust onion soups. That's because everyone else was seasick. Anyway, after the episode in Montserrat, Ari renamed the island "Mon Caca." ("He was rather coarse!")

In 1978, Cristina Onassis gave the ship to the Greek nation, and it was used by the president of the Republic and by the prime minister to receive honored guests but only for a short time as the maintenance changes (four hundred seventy thousand Euros per year) were too heavy for the country to sustain. The ship was left to die in the port of Piraeus and put up for sale in 1995. It took three years before an intrepid businessman, John Paul Papanicolau, bought her for 3.4 million Euros. He spent thirty-nine million Euros to restore her. In 2001, she became a floating hotel for nostalgic tourists who can spend three hundred fifteen thousand Euros a week on the renamed Cristina O.

The cabins were made much smaller, and there is now room for thirty-six passengers who can exercise on the lower deck in a newly installed fitness center, Jacuzzi and al, which would really have upset Onassis, as he, (like Churchhill, his frequent guest on board) detested sports of any kind.

The only thing Cristina Onassis took off the ship were the El Greco painting, which had hung in her father's study (and whose authenticity was and is questionable) and the baby seals' penis stools which were in the bar and the jade and ruby Buddha who shook his head and stuck his tongue out at you as you passed him (which amused Ari a lot). A sad ending.

I was never able to discuss my health problems with my mother. She somehow could not come to grips with malady. In fact, I think she was actually ashamed of it. Many Europeans, share that habit of denial as opposed to the Americans who speak about it openly (often too openly). I know that when I had my first cancer operation and her friends pressed her for news about me, she'd just say I had a bad cold or something. Her response was even more lackadaisical when, a year later, I had another bout with cancer—a mastectomy this time. When Fred tried to gently break the bad news to my mother, she merely shrugged and said, "Well, Solange will just have to change her way of life, that's all." Who knows how to interpret her insouciant manner? Maybe it's a helpful attitude to have.

As the sole passenger
on an Olympic Airways flight
from New York to Dakar.

Marc and me by the Cristina's
swimming pool.

Cristina swimming Pool.

At the stern of the Cristina.

At the stern of the Cristina.
Ari Onassis, Jackie, me, Pierre Salinger,
Nicole Salinger, Felix Mirando.

Ari Onassis, me, Felix Mirando,
and Pierre Salinger, playing poker.

Jackie and me in her little boat
at Martha's Vineyard
the summer before
she died.

In front of Jackie's house
in Martha's Vineyard.

By this time, I was romantically involved with Fred, which meant that ethically, there was no way he could perform my surgery. He arranged for a friend of his to operate on me. Philip Wiedell was considered superbly qualified for this type of operation. He was often called the "Ice Doctor" because of his chilly, highbrow attitude. I didn't like him one bit. Actually, his aloofness was a shock, but I tried not to dwell on it. Instead, I considered myself lucky to have an admirer or two who were still in the periphery. I knew that a lot of women who underwent my procedure found their men were soon running for the hills.

One faithful admirer was Bill Matheson, a man I had been going out with fairly steadily before I met Fred Herter. Bill was a brilliant lawyer and great fun, and, although he fought it, an incorrigible alcoholic. Once in a while, he'd make an effort to go on the wagon, and he would drink gallons of Diet Coke, hurling the empty cans into faraway wastebaskets, which made a terrible racket . . . really attractive. But they didn't make enough noise, I guess, because I married him anyway. It happened in Paris ever so privately and ever so briefly. The only guests at our wedding were my daughter, Véronique, who brought a huge bouquet of daisies, and my mother. Véronique liked Bill, and my mother thought he was wonderful. My previous husband, Jean de La Bruyère, was also approving on the sidelines because he'd heard that Bill Matheson had made a ton of money acting as Florence Gould's lawyer. I guess he liked the idea that Bill, and not he, would be responsible for me in the future. But the marriage lasted only a few months for all too obvious reasons.

Even before he was exalted by the mystique of the presidency, Jack Kennedy was always a little aloof. At the same time, he was also scintillating, interested, interesting, and a delightfully human mélange of quirks and idiosyncrasies. For example, he *loved* to play Monopoly. But the only steady opponent he could count on was his Harvard roommate Lemoyne Billings. That's because Jack played all games like a man possessed. Since the game was called Monopoly, Jack wanted a *monopoly*. That meant not only Broadway and Park Place but even the lesser real estate like Vermont Avenue, and he wanted hotels on all of them so the rent he could charge would wipe out all other players as we inevitably landed on his lots. His game was so competitive he scared the rest of us away. (He played just as hard at scrabble, croquet, poker, checkers, or chess, and he hated to lose. A trait he inherited from his old man, I suppose.)

JFK's antennae were always exquisitely attuned to gossip. Here's a typical example: While I was staying with the Kennedys in Palm Beach in

1958, I announced that I was on my way to Paris, Missouri, to meet up with a favorite uncle of mine. Jack raised a cynical eyebrow then asked me if I didn't have a DDS (deep dark secret) to share. With a maidenly blush, I laughed it off.

The truth was that I *did* have a DDS. There was no uncle to meet, not even in Missouri. Instead, I was flying off to Mexico to meet Jean de la Bruyère. When she heard about this, Jackie took me off to Elizabeth Arden and bought me a beautiful plastic and straw belt (plastic was very new in the fashion world) for good luck; and it worked because Jean and I were married a year later.

Jean and I had met when I was visiting Shirley Oakes, at "Jacaranda," her mother's house in Nassau. Actually, Jean was sort of a beau of Shirley's at the time. But Shirley had lots of other beaus so it didn't really matter all that much when he dropped her for me. One of her favorites was member of the Bahamian Parliament, Bobby Symonette. There was also a very pale Italian named Mitia Guerrini staying at Jacaranda, who was interested in Shirley. She'd often ask me to keep Mitia occupied while she was off cavorting with Symonette on the other side of the island. Not much fun for me, and maybe not for Mitia either, come to think of it. He got a very bad sunburn as I dragged him all around the beaches.

Anyway, I fell in love with Jean. He was staying with his partner's father, Sir John Mactaggart, and drove all around Nassau in a noisy little red MG. He was always roaring up in his rented hot rod as if it were a Ferrari, and coming to a screeching halt in front of Jacaranda to pick me up. I don't know if he was trying to irritate Lady Oakes, but he certainly succeeded. She constantly complained about that "nasty little Frenchman" whose nasty little car made so much noise in her driveway.

Jean de la Bruyère and I were married twice.

The first time, on the longest night of the year.

The second time, for a nice balance, on the shortest night of the year.

I got my US divorce in Boise, Idaho. Back in those days, if you established residence in Nevada or Idaho, you could get a divorce in six weeks. I planned to spend those six weeks with Mary in Sun Valley, the ski resort Averell Harriman had just opened. I also had the idea that mountain air would be salubrious for Mary's asthma. But just as we arrived, the place closed for the season. So we traveled on to Boise, where a nice man called Judge Givens took my case. Mary and I stayed in a dreary little motel where I washed her diapers nightly, draping them on the radiator in our tiny room to dry. The most exciting time of our week was the Friday night dinner with Judge

Givens and his wife. Mrs. Givens was ever so delighted to have some exotic French company. I can still recall how she would rush down the stairs in her best black dress, aglitter with rhinestone jewelry to greet us. They were a sweet and compassionate couple, though Judge Givens worried a lot about my being able to cover his fees! My French divorce, called an *exequatur*, took longer to obtain so we had to keep our marriage a secret. The only person who found us out was my mother. She had seen a letter to me from Jean, with the salutation, "My darling wife." Mummy and I and little Mary were in a hotel in Switzerland. The letter was just lying around and so she read it. It gave her quite a shock. I swore her to secrecy, and to her credit, she didn't break the silence that surrounded my marriage. (Probably scared that I'd end up in prison as a bigamist.)

Our first wedding took place in New York's City hall with just a couple of janitors for witnesses and a kindly judge who gave us an apple to speed us on our way. As a matter of face, he threw it at us as we were leaving. It was Christmastime, December 21; and judge, janitors, and everyone else couldn't wait to get home. We stayed at the Sherry Netherlands Hotel. Some friends of mine, the Warrens, took us to the St. Regis Roof for dinner, and that was it. Just the four of us, and we danced and danced and danced. I remember rushing out of the Sherry Netherlands Hotel the next morning in the dress I had worn the night before. It was a very pretty champagne-lace evening dress—thank goodness it was short—but quite *décolletée*. So people did look strangely at me as I hurried across Fifth Avenue to Van Cleef and Arpels to buy a pair of cufflinks as a wedding present for Jean. At 10:00 a.m.! It was all very romantic. Luckily, Louis Arpels himself, whom I knew, happened to be there that day, and he helped me get past the bug-eyed sales people who had never seen an evening dress waltz into the shop first thing in the morning. (Among the staff was a little Bourbon Prince I happened to know. I had seen him in Hyannisport a few years before, laden down with a dozen Van Cleef and Arpels engagement rings for Jackie to choose from. But since he was polite enough not to recognize me, I returned the courtesy.)

For our second ceremony, at the French Consulate in New York, there was a larger cast of characters. Jean's mother, Christiane Baudet and her sister Gilberte Fenwick, my mother, of course, and my voice coach, Maurice Jacquet, and his wife. (He had been Grace Moore's coach and was quite adamant that I should forsake marriage and have a singing career.) Jacquet once arranged for me to sing a solo in a concert at Carnegie Hall. I gave my rendition of *L'Automne* by Fauré. "L'Automne aux 'ciels brulants, aux horizons perdus." A very difficult piece. Afterward, he came back stage to tell me: "You will be a second Grace Moore!" Of course, he had already said that when I was about to be married to my first husband. He told him my career was more important than his, but it didn't work out that time either. And yet . . . and yet . . . maybe I should have followed his advice. But I knew that it took a full five years to develop a voice to its maturity, and I didn't see how I could devote that much time to singing.

My mother knew the importance of good coaches and always found great ones for me. Starting with my uncle, Charles Panzera. While I was studying for my law degree in Paris, he took me under his wing, helped me in focusing my voice, improving my performance, and polishing my diction. Uncle Charlie was a very tough teacher and was blessed with very little patience. He thought I had a very good voice potential for light opera or lieder. Not grand opera. He coached me to sing many of the works he sang himself—Beethoven, Duparc, Debussy, Schumann, Schubert, Fauré. I even made a recording, and he laconically pronounced it "pretty good." Which, coming from him, was high praise indeed. (Unfortunately, all my vocal aspirations had to be put on the back burner when I developed TB and my lungs had to be given a long, long rest.)

As I progressed with my piano studies in New York, my mother signed on the great Berthe Bert, who had studied under the virtuoso, Alfred Cortot. He was the definitive interpreter of Chopin and had devised a unique approach to teaching the works of Chopin, which he incorporated into a marvelous book, *The Methode Cortot,* with technical insights that the advanced student can still profit from. Berthe Bert not only passed on to her student's his exquisite mechanical skills like fingering and subtle use of the pedals, but she also helped one plumb the *emotional* depths of Chopin. Her teaching techniques were unorthodox, to say the least. For example, to seriously tackle loudness and softness and to assure a light touch, she made me play while cupping a small orange in the palm of my hand. It was even harder to do than it sounds, but it developed a delicate, almost feathery touch. Under her tutelage, I certainly progressed and conquered almost all of Chopin's works. At one point, Berthe Bert actually asked me to give up tennis because she said, "I think your right arm is growing stronger than the left, which is giving your right hand a harder touch." Of course, I never considered *that* for a minute.

As a wedding gift, Jean's partner, Sandy Mactaggart gave us a red convertible Thunderbird. It had a removable hard top and two port holes. That was one jazzy set of wheels. Jean and I drove it all the way from New York City to Edmonton with a Maltese Terrier and a Fornasetti wastepaper basket between us. It was a long haul over really fascinating country from

East to West. I remember one stop in the Badlands of South Dakota, where we square-danced the night away in a hay barn. It was here that I got my first inkling of Jean's wayward eye when I saw him flirting quite openly with one of the waitresses. It was a warning precursor of future times.

Sandy Mactaggart and his father played an important role in Jean's life . . . and indirectly in mine. Sir John's father had backed Sandy and Jean when they went into business together. He was a Robber Baron of sorts. He had built tenements in Glascow; and when people couldn't afford the rent, which was part of his scheme, he would foreclose on them—not a very nice thing to do but fruitful, I guess. We always stayed at Sir John's house in Nassau even when he wasn't there. For some reason, the four of us went to Cuba together. This was before Castro took over. We were an unlikely quartet: Jean, Sandy, Sir John, and me. Jean and I were live wires, but Sandy and his father personified the uptight Scotsmen. So I always thought it odd that we would end up each night at all-night nightclubs. Especially the one that featured a native performer known as "Superman." Superman was almost supernaturally endowed, and he left no holes (and I don't mean "holds") barred in performance after performance. The show was beyond disgusting and totally tasteless, but this was the uplifting cultural event that the Batista regime encouraged to build tourism. Maybe. But I know that when we got back to our comparatively humdrum lives, I certainly never described those acts to my friends and neighbors and I can't imagine anyone else doing so. So how could that build tourism?

Me and Thunderbird in the Badlands,
South Dakota.

CHAPTER 19

The South of France

Another great pal I made in Paris was the irrepressible Patricia Cavendish. Our friendship was sealed when I was shipped off for "rest" in Vence in the South of France. It was to take care of more TB complications. I stayed in the house of a very nice woman who was a friend of the Langrognes. The poor woman did her best to entertain me. She had wonderful dinners served *al fresco* in her lovely garden (I remember delicate grilled sardines), but her guests were much older than I, and it wasn't much fun. Pat realized that I was in the doldrums so she would make the one-hour drive from Cap d'Antibes to whisk me off in her quinze chevaux Citroën, pedal to the metal, driving madly but beautifully along the coast. We'd have a splendid lunch at La Fiorentina, on the very point of Cap St. Hospice, the greatest villa on the Cote d' Azur and then she would drive me back.

Pat's half brother, Rory Cameron, had transformed it from a Victorian mediocrity to a Palladian masterpiece. Her mother, Lady Kenmare, was the most extraordinary and exquisite creature. Extremely beautiful, she had married often and well. Her long line of husbands, Roderick Cameron, Lord Waterpark, Lord Furness, Viscount Castleross, the Earl of Kenmare, had all died shortly after she married them. (This led the wicked Somerset Maughaun to rename Lady Kenmare "Lady Killmore.") Witty but not really funny, though she would openly talk about it and laugh about it. To me, she was utterly enchanting, and I was fascinated by her. Even with a score of servants around, when it came time for the salad course, Lady Kenmare would get up from the table and make the dressing herself at the sideboard. It was a weird concoction of Coleman's dry mustard and sweet Nestlé's condensed milk which was anathema to the French; but was actually delicious. She had a generally vague approach to life and didn't look always precisely focused. I remember she turned to Henri, sitting next to her at dinner one night, and said sweetly, "You must come and stay with us sometime." We had been there for a week.

Lady Kenmare was so stunning that when she ambled through the Monte Carlo casino, the high-stakes players would stop their games just to stare. She never seemed aware of the flutter she caused. Everything about her was majestic, particularly her walk. And she had a way of staring off into the distance . . . at something only she could see . . . far beyond the horizon. I found out later that this pensive and inattentive mysteriousness look was simply because she was incredibly myopic.

When she herself gambled, it was always for huge amounts; and as far as I could see, she always—*always*—won. One night as she arrived at the main table, she was, as usual, positively dazzling. She was wearing a clinging white dress that looked like she'd been sewn into it. Around her neck was the famous Furness three-tiered diamond necklace, a wedding present from Furness, along with the Furness tiara of large pink diamonds in her hair. The Aga Khan, one of the richest men on the planet, looked up from his game and complained, "My dear Enid! Could you not make a more discreet entrance? Next time perhaps you could just wear a basic little black dress and not throw us off our game?"

I always thought Enid had a lot of courage to marry Lord Furness, who had been accused and tried for murdering his first wife. She disappeared at sea, last seen on his yacht. Had he been found guilty, he would have been hanged by the neck, but fortunately, with a silken rope. That's one of the perks of being a peer of the realm.

W. Somerset Maugham lived with his boyfriend in his retreat, "Villa Mauresque," right down the hill from "La Fiorentina." Almost every day, Willie (as Maugham was known to his friends) would trudge up to play bridge and exchange exotic gossip. Often, Pamela Churchill would come zooming over from Beaulieu in a Riva speed boat with people like Gianni Agnelli or Prince Rainier or Rainier's father. The latter wanted to marry Lady Kenmare, but to no avail. Other drop-ins were the glitterati of the twentieth century: Woolworth heiress Barbara Hutton, the Duke and Duchess of Windsor, Princess Grace and the Hollywood crowd, including Cary Grant.

Being on the fringes of all of that certainly helped me shake my blues away and come back to life. Later, when I was all better, I stayed at "La Fiorentina" a lot, and I still can conjure up those magical and indulgent times. When Pat's mother died, her house was bought by Mary Lasker (who knew how to care for it) and then by the Harding Lawrences (who didn't).

In Kenya, Pat kept a lioness cub in the house. Once when I was visiting her, I watched, horrified, as that enormous beast suddenly whirled, leapt on Enid, and began mauling her. Frantic servants pulled the lion off her, and she, bloody but unbowed, patted the big cat's head, calmly had her arms bandaged up, and carried on. A Masai warrior was hired to look after the cub, but he wasn't always on top of things. One day, Tana, the fast-growing lioness, jumped out of the bush and pounced on a couple who was staying with Enid. They were in the midst of some torrid love-making. The terrified woman went into shock, causing her pelvic muscles to contract so tightly that the amorous gentleman was unable to withdraw. A little problem, which they needed help to be extricated from, which was even more awkward, as they were not married!

Pat wrote a beautiful book called "A Lion in the Bedroom," which has had great success and is being made into a film as we speak. She also adopted a full-grown baboon and a chimpanzee. They slept in her bedroom, and, when I asked her if she wasn't scared, she serenely said, "Oh, no. Why should I be? They always wear diapers."

Back at the time of my visit, Pat was in love with a handsome white hunter, Stan Lawrence Power. I always thought it strange that she was enthralled by this man, whose everyday business was slaughtering the magnificent animals that she so adored. Actually, she stopped him shooting animals. While I was there, he took us on a week-long safari photographing zebras, Thomson gazelles, warthogs, delicate dik-dyks. Pat eventually built a tourist lodge on the Rogewino River banks in the Tana River Basin. It was the first African district game reserve after Independence. When she ran out of money, she asked for my help. I sent her all the cash I could. In gratitude, she sent me two magnificent snow leopard pelts, which I had turned into a marvelous coat that I still have and treasure. Her lioness Tana roamed free on the reserve.

Pat Cavendish
and her baboon, Kalu.

Shifta bandits (Somalis who were killing everyone) invaded the area and utterly destroyed the just-finished lodge, and Pat and her boyfriend were lucky to escape with their lives. After that, the white hunter went back to his wife, and Pat and her mother gathered their horses and moved on to South Africa, lock, stock and barrel, leaving Kenyatta in charge.

Her Thoroughbred farm, "Broadlands Stud," in Cape Town, South Africa, was, and is, a veritable sanctuary, with:

    65 dogs
    26 cats
    28 velvet monkeys
    12 goats
    8 pigs

2 bullocks
26 mice
umpteen macaws,
and a much-loved baboon, Kalu

They all roam around her place, as do the glorious horses grazing in rolling pasture or safe in their commodious paddocks. At any rate, Broadlands is a truly idyllic spot, and Pat is still living there. She recently created a foundation to provide for her flocks of pet macaws after she dies.

Years later, I took a tour of the grand gardens of the South of France. It was an English tour so there I was, with a bunch of prim old English biddies; and thank God one wonderful American girl, Betsy Wills, who became a great friend. Well lo and behold, one of the gardens on our list was "Le Clos," which belonged to the couturier Givenchy and was once on the grounds of "La Fiorentina." We strolled through the faultlessly manicured alleys of trees, all their trunks artfully white-washed (a procedure introduced by Rory Cameron to discourage bugs). During our walk, I noticed an elderly gardener staring intently in my direction. As I looked back at him, something jogged my memory, and I realized he had been the head gardener of "La Fiorentina" back in Lady Kenmare's day. We fell into each other's arms, causing no end of eye-rolling and tsk-tsking among the English lady gardeners.

Jean de la Bruyère and his partner, Sandy Mactaggart, were adventurous entrepreneurs. That's why they bought God Bar Farm shortly after they moved to Edmonton. It was a former cattle ranch, built in 1905, with much land that bordered the city limits. It was a solid, snug house built of brick. I always thought of it as the Third Little Pig's house, which is funny, in a way, since Jean's and my third child now owns it. It was surrounded by a vast acreage, where long-horned Angus cattle roamed. Part of it bordered the Saskatchewan River, and you could still see prospectors along the shore, panning for gold with their sluices and sieves.

Jean and Sandy were gambling that, as the province of Alberta grew, their acreage would be incorporated into the city limits and explode in value. Which is precisely what it did.

Their happy-go-lucky appearance belied the shrewd businessmen underneath. Both, truly, had the Midas touch, especially Jean; and almost every one of their ventures turned to gold. Of course, it didn't hurt that Alberta was at that time the land of milk and honey. They moved there straight out of Harvard Business School, and I joined them two years later when Jean and I married.

SOLANGE BATSELL HERTER

Jean had a very cold-blooded, cold-hearted attitude when it came to money. I'll give you an example that still angers me. He had cajoled my mother and my friend Josephine Huntington Hartford Bryce to invest a large chunk of money in some development in Edmonton. Nothing more was heard about it for a couple of years until Jo asked Jean how the project was doing.

Jean simply shrugged and said it hadn't worked out. Jo pressed him, "How could that be when land values had soared?" Only after Jo's lawyers got involved and put their foot down did Jean return the money, Jo's first and eventually my mother's. But he gave back only the original investment, with no interest and no share in what must have been significant profits. Not exactly cricket. Jo complained about it a lot. My mother, typically, never mentioned it. As far as she was concerned, nothing more could be done about it, and that was *that*. Although insouciant about large expenditures like this, she could keep an eagle eye on small financial doings. Here's a typical example:

In 1986, the Morgan Bank wrote her, telling her that if her checking account balance fell below $10,000, she would be charged a fee of $250 each quarter! My mother thought it absurd to keep more than a few thousand in her account and wasn't about to start paying fees. She wrote right back, tartly informing the bank that Ann Morgan, (J.P. Morgan's sister) had opened an account for her in 1935 and promised she would be a valued customer and never have to worry about trivialities like a "minimum balance" or other unfair charges. And this had been true for all these years, and she was outraged that the bank would make such demands on an old customer like herself.

Well, by God, the bank wrote right back, apologizing profusely and assuring her that she'd remain a client in good standing for the rest of her life and that she should ignore their letter. Maybe they took into consideration that she was already eighty-two years old. (And didn't figure she'd live to be ninety-one.) But never mind. She took great pleasure in her success at setting the bank straight. My mother kept up her friendship with Ann Morgan. She would often take me along to have tea at Miss Morgan's splendid house at Fifty-seventh Street and Sutton Place, where the Dutch Embassy residence now is. It was just down the street from our apartment at 33 Sutton Place. I remember spending hours in the downstairs bathroom, counting the glittering gold mosaics that lined the walls.

But I digress. Let me reveal another time Jean displayed his warped sense of fair play: One night, in Edmonton, we had dinner with Edith and

Curtis Munson, whom I'd met through Mrs. Auchincloss in Washington DC, where they lived part-time. (Mrs. Munson had a wonderful vegetable garden where she would encourage friends to come and pick vegetables that she then would make them pay for.) After dinner, Curtis took me into the garden and pointed out a large piece of land across the Saskatchewan River that was up for sale. They dreaded some developer getting his hands on it and throwing up some ugly apartments, which would destroy their view. I went to see it the next day, and it was a truly lovely parcel bordering the river. Well! I had just inherited some money from my grandfather and decided then and there to invest in that property. I talked it over with Jean, and he insisted on buying half of it with me. I agreed. We ended up refurbishing a little shack on the place where we would have riverside picnics. I had such a good time decorating it and even installed a marvelous eighteenth-century black-and-white mural depicting the Palais Royal in Paris.

When we divorced, I told Jean I would like to sell my half of the property. He said okay. It seemed that Sandy wanted to buy up the land to build a house on it for himself. I left everything in Jean's hands. When I got the check from the sale, it was for precisely my original investment. Not a penny more than the money I had first put into it. This was a full five years after the original purchase. I had it appraised and found the property had gone up in value *ten times*. When I confronted Jean with this fact, he coolly pointed out that this was the partnership agreement that he and Sandy had. Whatever one bought or sold to the other, it would be at the original price. (Never mind that I owned half of the property and that I was not a 'partner.' *The Edmonton Journal* in a recent article states that the property today is worth 23 million dollars—if that doesn't say a lot about agrandisement, I don't know what does.) There was no recourse. It wasn't fair at all and I certainly could have used the money to supplement my meager alimony.

Jean had earned his *new* fortune on his own starting from scratch, and it was almost an obligation for him (and certainly a joy) to show it off. In what you could only call a *nouveau riche* way, though he was not from a *nouveau riche* background. For example, when he chartered a yacht, it had to be the biggest one available. This obsession went all the way. If we approached a harbor and he spotted boats with taller masts than ours anchored there, on we would sail to a different harbor, where we would be the big fish. Is that slightly Freudian?

Jean's posturing was funny, I guess, but repeated too often. It got on my nerves. Yet at times, Jean could be generous. I'll never forget one marvelous surprise. Jean asked me what I wanted for Christmas. I told him I really needed a typewriter. Sure enough, right under the tree Christmas morning was a huge cardboard box with Remington stamped on the outside. But inside, no sign of a typewriter. Instead, I found a sumptuous mink coat!

And when I was diagnosed with cancer and had absolutely no medical insurance whatsoever, Jean took care of all the bills at Columbia-Presbyterian hospital. I was very grateful.

Reversing the coin, when Jean needed a serious cancer operation, he came to Fred; and it was Fred who performed the surgery that saved his life, which went on for another five years. The only drawback was that gave him time to remarry, which certainly changed the terms of his will.

Fred and I went to Edmonton to see Jean before he died. Before dinner one night, with his usual flair, he went down to the cellar and brought up an extraordinary bottle of wine he had been saving for a "special celebration." It was a big physical effort for him to do this; but then he had great courage, even, and maybe particularly, in the face of death.

Somehow, the "men" in my life always got along. In turn, Henri Deschamps saved Fred's life when he rushed him to the American Hospital in Paris for a thrombosis problem.

In Paris, I had met the artist Jean Pierre Allaux at the opening of one of his shows. I thought Allaux was a very good painter, and he and I became good friends. Jean wasn't too impressed until he learned of all the portraits Allaux had done of prominent people. That's when he commissioned him to do mine. I was three months pregnant (with Jacqueline) at the time and didn't take too kindly to the idea of traipsing up to Allaux's Monmartre studio every morning to pose for hours.

But I went through it, morning sickness and all. Allaux and I talked a lot, and I think he got the gist of a certain unhappiness in my life. He painted me against a backdrop of a large stone wall bordered with sunflowers. (Sunflowers are called *tournesols* or *soucis* in French, which means "worries." And I think he was aware I had my share of them.)

Anyway, when Jean saw the finished work, he raised Cain and sputtered that he couldn't believe that *he* wasn't included in the portrait. He thought that was part of the deal. (Even though he had never even posed!) He flatly refused to pay for it until he was included in the picture too. Allaux was flummoxed but then solved the quandary perfectly while getting a little of his own back. He painted Jean as a satyr, lurking evilly in the bushes behind the sunflowers. It was not a bad likeness either.

Jean never paid for the painting, but Allaux very kindly gave it to me. It still hangs in Battenville. And it still says it all!

Jean kept a Rolls Royce in Paris and would let me use it when I came to town if he wasn't in town himself, and that was a nice arrangement. One day, after a jazzy luncheon with friends at "Chez Allard" on the Left Bank, I suddenly realized that I was late and had to dash to the airport to catch a plane back to New York. I blithely asked if anybody would like to take my car. Paloma Picasso, one of the guests, put her hand up; and I tossed her the keys, gave her the address of the garage, and ran out the door. Well, a month later, Jean called me in New York from that garage, asking where the bloody hell his car was. I tracked Paloma down in Spain where she was, with the car, happy as a clam. She had named it "Guermantes," she told me, and just loved it and wanted to know what she should do about putting it in her name. I was flabbergasted and explained to her that it wasn't my car to give and asked her to bring it back as soon as possible. That would be very difficult, she said, because she planned to stay in Spain for another month or two with "Guermantes." And she was serious. My mother knew her mother, Françoise Gilot, and I had to ask her to interfere directly to persuade Paloma to return the car. She wasn't about to do it herself; she claimed she had just broken her leg so we had to send somebody with some sort of official documents to pick it up and return it to a very mad ex-husband.

The next incident with the Rolls Royce, about a year later, was even more unfortunate. I had once more borrowed the car, in Jean's absence, to go to Claude Monet's house and gardens in Giverny with my mother and Fred. Fred insisted on driving and, at some point, sailed right across a gate-stopper in a driveway and wrecked the whole muffler system. It took time to repair it locally, and, when Jean came back to Paris, the car was still in the Giverny mechanic's garage. It was badly repaired and had to be sent to England at great expense, and, then and there, Jean stopped my alimony payments, which he had never bothered to cancel even after I had remarried. That was really a bummer. I think the fact that he found out that it was Fred driving the car is what really made him go berserk.

At school, Jean and Sandy's mentor had been the formidable French General Doriot, and his advice to them was as brief as it was accurate: "Gentlemen, if you want to make money . . . *real* money . . . there are only two places to choose from: Venezuela or Western Canada."

For Jean, it was a no-brainer: there was a lot of appeal in Doriot's idea of Venezuela probably because he was certain the girls in sultry Caracas would be sexier than the girls in frigid Edmonton. He also spoke fluent Spanish. But his Scottish partner vetoed that approach so they ended up in Canada and started their company and called it MACLAB. They soon bought Gold Bar Farm, aforementioned, from a Mr. Gallagher.

Gallagher lived on the farm alone, with only his spinster daughter, Margaret, for company. I'll never forget her excitement at moving into a house in town because at last she could have "her own boudoir" there. I remember thinking, with the kindness of youth, *Poor thing. What could she possibly use a "boudoir" for at her age?* It was so pathetic. (She was probably all of forty years old.)

The cattle, which were picturesque and valuable, smelled to high heaven and attracted swarms of voracious flies. They were soon sold off, and part of the land was parceled out for development. Jean and Sandy built hundreds of low-income houses—matchbox houses—as I called them. A tall white fence to ensure our privacy was built to surround the property. Not surprisingly, the people in the matchbox houses were jealous of the huge abode. They didn't take kindly to our guests or us gallivanting about on the tennis courts and the swimming pool and the horse barns. Some of those little houses weren't so well-built either. I remember Jean roaring with laughter when he heard that paintings hung on the walls of one of these houses swayed back and forth because the walls weren't built straight. Also (more laughter) as he recounted how water was coming out of some of the electric outlets of another house. Those poor benighted people! It's a wonder they didn't burn our house down.

Much too often, the local teens would scale the fence, romping through the forbidden territory, the more adventurous ones sitting on a lovely old wagon I had placed on the front lawn. We endlessly had to shoo them away.

Jean gave me *carte blanche* to fix up the old house, and I went at it with verve and vigor. First, I pulled out all the beautiful old mahogany trim and sliding doors. I knocked down walls and moved windows. Then I painted everything—and I mean *everything*—a dazzling white. I was determined to really "modernize" the place. To make matters worse, when my drastic improvements were finally finished, I invited poor, prim Miss Gallagher to tea. I'll never forget the look on her face when she walked into her old house. I can still see her, blinking her eyes and dropping her by-now-astonished jaw. Gasping, she obviously couldn't comprehend how—and even worse, *why*—it had been transformed from its gloomy Victorian splendor into an over-bright space with curtains made of mattress ticking and TVs swinging out of the walls. She mumbled something about "how really unnecessary it had been for her to have dusted the whole place before she moved out."

She then beat a hasty retreat, and I never invited her back. (I never made such redecorating mistakes either.)

To keep the household running smoothly, I advertised for help in the Paris edition of *The Herald Tribune*. After dozens of interviews, I finally settled on a Danish couple. The husband, Igun, had worked at the Danish court and was a tad overtrained as a butler for Edmonton. Can you imagine the reaction of our informal friends, ringing the doorbell and having it opened a split second later by a solemn Igun, wearing spotless white gloves and a disdainful expression? Igun's wife, Bertha, was at best a mediocre cook, but we weren't all that fussy. I had to make both of them disappear whenever Jean and Sandy invited business types for dinner. After all, in Edmonton, not even bankers had butlers and maids running around their houses. So we certainly didn't want to show ours off, especially while Jean and Sandy were trying to negotiate loans from their banks. (For the same reason, I pretended that I'd prepared all the cooking, atrocious as it was, and Jean acted as bartender.)

Only slightly smaller than Texas, Alberta itself is home to fewer than four million people. Edmonton in the sixties had a population of less than three hundred thousand, which, interestingly enough, happens to have been the population of the capital of France in the eighteenth century.

In those days, Alberta was a dry state so of course, everybody drank every chance they got. The law was strictly upheld, if not observed. Woe betide the citizen who got stopped with an open bottle of rye (the whisky of choice in Western Canada) in his car. He'd be hauled right off to jail and nailed with a stiff fine. Anyway, people kept showing up at our house and drinking a great deal, which probably helped them ignore the bad food. It also helped them lose their shirts at poker, which we played a lot of!

Our house was somehow a Mecca for interesting people. I remember a Frenchman who was the head of French Petroleum. I had sat next to him on a flight to Edmonton. We chatted, and I invited him for the weekend. He instantly accepted, sight unseen. He knew it would beat staying at the old MacDonald Hotel (part of an uninspired chain built by the Canadian Pacific Railroad, with sub-par food and poorer service, but it was just about the only hotel in town, except for some miserable greasy spoon establishments.)

After his first breakfast with us, he took a dim view of Bertha's kitchen talent. And, in self-defense, taught me how to make *perfect* scrambled eggs. To this day, it's the only kitchen skill I have complete confidence in. (You have to take the pan off the fire and add a raw egg at the end.)

One summer, a couple of years after Jean and I had separated, I traveled back to Gold Bar Farm so I could be with my children. Our divorce agreement gave Jean custody of the children for two long months during the summer *if* they were accompanied by a nanny of my choice. It wasn't exactly a lark for me to go back to Edmonton, but I missed my children and longed to be with them. Also, I wanted to make sure that they were happy there and that the nanny could cope. I relegated myself to noisy mealtimes in the kitchen with the children while Jean and his for-the-most-part unattractive friends had an even noisier time in the dining room. Of course, the children couldn't wait to escape poor dull Momma to sneak in and eavesdrop on Jean and his fascinating (to them) coterie.

But I was saved by Sigismund von Braun, brother of Werner von Braun, the Nazi rocket physicist who defected to America when the war ended. I had met Sigismund in Paris a few months before at a party in the German Embassy. (He was the German Ambassador to France), and in passing, I had told him I was going to Edmonton and mentioned there was good polar-bear hunting in the Northern territories and gave him my address. Well, one fine day, without warning, he showed up on our doorstep loaded for bear, you might say. And, much to Jean's annoyance, Von Braun and I took off for the tall timber.

Von Braun planned no casual trek. He had organized the expedition with Teutonic efficiency. Backpacks and guns and complete camping equipment. It was all so exciting and such a refreshing change for me. My enthusiasm wasn't even dampened when our overloaded little seaplane crashed into a lake way up north. (We were so far north in fact, the compass needle had lost true North and just spun and spun.) We were stranded and out of touch with civilization for forty-eight hours. By searching around, we discovered a cache of food the government places around the Northwest Territories for just such emergencies. The food was high up on stilts so the wild animals couldn't get at it. Lots of beans and chickpeas and hard tack.

Unbeknownst to us, Jean had sent out an all-point alert reckoning our location. Before we knew it . . . maybe a bit too soon . . . a rescuing seaplane came swooping out of the blue and picked us up. And just like that, we were back in civilization. Bear-less, wolf-less, but thank God, not lifeless.

I know both from letters and hearsay that Jean never got over the fact that I left him or, should I say, had the good sense to leave him. I surely would have become a vegetable had I stayed put under his thumb and not had the courage to get up and go, four small children in tow. In a funny way, I think he admired me, even respected me, for doing so. As much as

Jean pursued women and carried on "chercheing la femme," I don't think he really liked women. For example, his take on girls' education was that they didn't need any and that as long as they knew how to arrange flowers properly and keep their nails well-manicured, that was fine. Véronique managed to override—even defy—this silliness and went on to post-graduate work after college. Jackie didn't, though that angel—in disguise, given half a chance, could have run IBM or GE single-handedly. But she's applied her intelligence to many other things and is a star at running her family And probably running both IBM and GE on the side!

My first child, Mary, was born in Paris on July 23, 1953. I have always thought of her since the word "go" as the most *debrouillarde* (coping with everything) person in the world. Mary's birth had been a difficult experience. Doctors feared lingering and contagious TB Koch germs and would not even allow her to be in my room. It was heartbreaking, and the danger was real. (The year before, I required an abortion because the fetus might have been affected by my tuberculosis.) Then infant Mary developed an infection, which necessitated an operation on her back. She was kept in a neonatal ward, in and out of danger, for weeks on end. So balancing the joy of having a beautiful baby girl was the helplessness I felt at not being able to be near her. Our only contact was visual, and I would look at her beautiful eyes through the glass window into the nursery hour after hour. My second child, Véronique, I had in New York by mistake. A special delivery, you might say. She was born at the wrong place, a month ahead of time. February 28, 1957. Pregnant with Véronique and with Mary, nanny in tow, we were flying back from Nassau to board the *Queen Mary*. Certain the baby would be a boy, we preferred to have him born in France. That way, he'd have no military obligation in the United States. We were all staying in New York overnight. I was only eight months along and had even gone waterskiing just the day before on Lake Cunningham in Nassau so everything seemed fine.

Suddenly, in the middle of the night, I had to be whisked off to the Polyclinic Hospital, the only hospital where we knew anyone from the staff—a certain Dr. Mendelsson, whom we had met in Nassau. Jean, with his usual bravado, declared that if he delivered a boy, he would pay him twice his fee. If it was a girl, he'd receive not a penny. I don't know what ever came of this proposition; I was too embarrassed to ask.

For my part, again, I wasn't allowed to hold my baby girl or do the normal newborn things because she had to be in an incubator for her first weeks in this world. She had enormous blue eyes and extraordinarily beautiful feet. My little *trésor bouclé* who always reminded me of the limerick. "There was a little girl who had a little curl right in the middle of her forehead. When she was good, she was very, very good. When she was bad, she was horrid." Except she was never horrid, just wonderfully naughty once in a while. Once she was strong enough to travel, off we flew to Paris, where we rented Rory Cameron's wonderful flat Rue de 'l Université. There was a towering stuffed giraffe in the living room, with its head poking through the ceiling and into the bathroom above. A charming touch unless you're not used to sharing the bathroom with a giraffe. The Shah of Iran's youngest sister lived on the top floor. "The Red Princess," she was called, and she was dyed-in-the-redwool communist. She wore red alligator shoes, and all day long, she received scary-looking types, traipsing up and down the stairs. Very intriguing.

Both my last two babies were born in Edmonton. Jacqueline arrived on April 24, 1959, Marc on April 25, 1960. "Irish Twins, as siblings born a year apart are called. Both were baptized by the snowflakes landing on their noses on their way home. Even Jean, who was fairly subdued after the birth of his daughters, lightened up considerably when he finally had a male heir. Daughter or son, it made no difference to me except maybe I felt happy to have this new man in my life who wouldn't be as temporary as a husband might be . . . Someone, possibly, who might fill the emptiness my father's death had left in my heart.

Speaking of babies, I should tell you about my promise to Jean's father, Jacques de la Bruyère. He had asked me for lunch after Jean told him we were going to be married. He was very kind to me even though he didn't relish the thought of his son marrying a Catholic—and a divorced one at that. He explained that the La Bruyères came from old Huguenot stock, which traced itself back to the Musketeers. The Huguenot La Bruyères had the title of "Marquis" but were demoted to the title of "Count" after the war against the Protestants (in Henry IV's time). I used the "Countess" title sparingly—mostly for hair appointments or restaurant reservations or raising money for charity. It seemed to help. One place that really impressed people was in upstate New York, where they had indirectly heard about it, at Willard Mountain, our little local skiing place. The children would ask my children if they were descendants from kings and if they really had blue blood running through their veins. My future father-in-law went on to say that until now, no La Bruyères had *ever* married outside their religion. He also told me that his son could be very difficult and erratic and hoped that I would try to stay married to him, at least until we could produce a male heir to carry on the family name. I promised him I would. And even though I'd had more than enough of Jean after the birth of the two girls, I stuck to my word and finally produced the *dauphin*. When I think back, that was really quite honorable of me. After all, Jacques de la Bruyère had died by then, and there was nobody to hold me to my pledge. But to me, a promise is a promise. However, even that beautiful baby boy couldn't hold the dissolving marriage together. Particularly since Jean had spent the first three months of my last pregnancy in Tahiti, living openly with a "Vahinée" and had no compunction about talking about it. Upon his return, laden with dreadful Tahitian oils and silly straw hats, he even brandished a cigarette burn the woman deliberately made on his hand so he wouldn't be able to forget her. How utterly charming.

But let's go back to life in Edmonton. My hands were full with children and running a complex household. Luckily, I had the Hungarian Revolution to jazz things up. This Slavic upheaval brought a steady stream of fun-loving Hungarian refugees to Canada. I met lots of them; and with song and goulash and humor, they helped one get through those long Canadian winters. During some of these unbelievable windchill seasons, the thermometer often plunged to *forty below zero!* Those winter temperatures are what prompted us to start spending our winters in Nassau. We would spend a couple of months there because Mary and Véronique weren't in school yet. But back in Edmonton, I did organize a little school in the guestroom at Gold Bar. There, I taught my children and their friends French and English songs and nursery rhymes. I also read to them stories and fairy tales, mostly in French. They really loved it, sitting up at their little desks, attentively, in front of my upright piano which I had shipped all the way up north from Sutton Place.

I remember one starstruck night in 1957 when, instead of seeing the usual Northern lights out of our windows or the lights from the CIL Factory, our immediate neighbor, we saw out of Mary's third-floor bedroom window Sputnik, which the Soviets had just launched. The joke was that when the Russians first saw it, instead of going "Beep-Beep-Beep" as Americans did when they saw it, they went "Ha-ha-ha," since they had beaten us in that race. To think that it was only four years later, on April 12, 1961, to be exact, that the Soviets again made history by sending Yuri Gargarin into space, the first man to accomplish this feat. And again, I was with Mary. We had gone to Long Island to see about buying a horse for her and on the way back stopped at a motel, got a room, and watched the whole magical spectacle. I spent a lot of time alone and thinking things over, on that third floor. That's because life on the first and second floors had slightly disintegrated.

CHAPTER 20

England

Jean always had a roving eye, but when he started bringing his girlfriends home, I decided I'd had enough. So I moved out, heading off to London with the children, in a swift trial separation. Jean would leave Edmonton every month or so to join us in England. He'd perfunctorily play with the children, maybe comment on how many bouquets of red roses were around, ask who they were from, and then head back to Canada, disgruntled about the red roses. We were living at 65 Eaton Square on two floors of a charming townhouse. It came with a perfect butler, who did *every*thing. I enrolled Véronique in a little kindergarten, where she learned to sing a lot of English songs. I remember her singing "In and Out the Windows" with her adorable French accent. An English nanny took care of the children, and I was finally a free agent. And loving it.

I had many English friends and was invited to a ton of parties that were certainly more fun than parties in Edmonton. There were concerts and theaters and night clubs too. My favorite haunt was Annabel's, above which was Aspinall's place called the Claremont club. After dinner, my friends and I would go up there and gamble. I got to know John Aspinall quite well. He had just gone through a divorce and reveled in telling me the hows and whys of it. Then one Friday night, he invited me to spend the rest of the weekend at his house in Kent. I accepted. I was more than a little surprised when he pulled up to get me at Claridge's, and the doorman, opening the door of Asper's Rolls Royce, had to move two huge cord balls to one side to make room for me. The cord balls were for his gorillas, which he kept in Kent and which his ex-mother-in-law cared for. But that didn't shock me.

What *did* give me a turn was watching John Aspinall play with the big apes and kiss them full on the lips. That threw me off a tad.

One night at the gaming tables, I won so much money the house couldn't pay me. I was playing chemin de fer with some world-class gamblers. I mean real heavy-hitters like Baroda, Major Sterling, Ali Khan, casually wagering a thousand pounds a pop. As the stakes rose, John Aspinall, who was watching me from across the room, signaled me to get out of the game. (I thought he meant while the getting out was good.) Of course, it was definitely not the thing to do and hardly good form to leave the tables when you're so far ahead. But get out I did, smilingly offering some lame excuse about having a headache. This didn't go over well with my fellow gamblers; but after all, high-stakes chemin de fer is *not* a popularity contest. It didn't take long for me to discover the real reason "Aspers" wanted me out of the game. I had broken the bank! And it would be disastrous for him if I continued winning.

Early the next morning, there was a rap on my door at Claridge's. There stood John Aspinall, carrying a big brown paper bag. It was full, not with money but with pomegranates . . . the fruit of love, thank you very much. He also handed me four checks for ten thousand pounds each, all postdated. It took a long six months for those checks to clear. There were obvious ups and downs in the gambling business . . . but when the ups were up, Aspinall was forever bestowing precious baubles on me. He came to New York once with a huge diamond ring tucked into his pocket. That's when he proposed marriage. But I thought it was too much of a risky proposition. Ah well, with my forty thousand pounds ($160,000) tucked safely in my pocket, I felt pretty secure; and I vowed never to gamble such high stakes again. And I've stuck to it.

In 1972, Winthrop, my favorite of the five Rockefeller Brothers, invited me out to "WinRock," his nearly boundless ranch on Petit Jean Mountain in Arkansas. He was hosting the 15th Annual Santa Gertrudes Cattle Auction. The Santa Gertrudes are hardy cattle from Australia, and Winthrop was introducing them to America as a breed that could withstand drought conditions. But the auction wasn't going too well, bidders were just sitting on their hands, and Win asked if I couldn't liven things up a little. Well, they brought out an enormous bull, snorting and pawing the ground. He was Lot Number 8. Eight is my lucky number so when the bidding slowed down, I raised my hand then sat back, waiting for someone to outbid me. Instead, nobody budged except the auctioneer who slammed down his gavel. And I suddenly owned a cute pet that was no bigger than a two-car garage.

In Jean's arms at BHHF, 1963
(vaguely separated).

At Black Hole
Hollow Farm.

Josephine Bryce,
Douglas Fairbank, Jr.,
and me in Acapulco.

His breeding name was WRFeller, and, weighing a ton, he cost about fifteen bucks a pound, on the hoof. At $30,000 he was way outside my range. But a bid is a bid, and nobody was letting me off the hook. I had the crazy idea of shipping this stud back to Battenville to graze my lawn and save my mowing costs. But the shipping would have put me even further in the hole. So I asked Winthrop what he thought of the idea of keeping my bull on his ranch for breeding purposes or something. With a leer, Winthrop told me that he'd rather keep me than keep my bull. Very subtle, that cowpoke humor. Well, we made a little arrangement, and the bull stayed while I moseyed on my way. That "little arrangement" involved Lucius Beebe's private railroad car which Win thought would look good on my railroad siding in Battenville, spittoons, fringed lampshades, and all. It was a great idea, but it meant a lot of commitments, which I wasn't prepared to deal with so it stayed on Petit Jean Mountain, where it is still in the museum. I still regret the spittoons!

But Winrock was a splendid spot, both inside and out. Every guest bathroom, and there must have been a dozen, was stocked with the complete line of Elizabeth Arden cosmetics. And there were massive display cases in the central hall, showing off the jewelry collection owned by the second Mrs. Rockefeller. It was as if Harry Winston had moved to Arkansas. Of course, the cases were kept locked and, sadly enough, Mrs. R. was usually often too far in her cups to open the doors and get at her gems.

Another note: Years later, Fred and I moved to 1 East End Avenue, into the apartment that had been the Winthrop Rockefellers'. There was an unseemly out-of-place door in the drawing room giving onto the kitchen. Win had wanted quick access to the pantry to get to the ice for his drinks at all times. We quickly got rid of it.

CHAPTER 21

Henri Deschamps

I remember like it was yesterday the first time I laid eyes on Henri Deschamps. It was 1951, and we met on the boat/train platform at the gare St. Lazare. My grandmother knew Henri's aunt, Colette Langrogne, because they both were involved with "Chez Pérette," a women's exchange in Paris. Henri and I got to know each other on the *De Grasse,* sailing over from France to America. He was devilishly handsome, looking like a young Louis Jourdan, the most glamorous French movie star of that time. He was an intern at the Faculté de Medicine in Paris and was on his way to New York to study at Columbia-Presbyterian Hospital on a medical scholarship. I guess you could call ours a shipboard romance. He shared a Manhattan apartment with several other gay blades. (One of them was Paul Le Perq, who soon became a powerful financier and subsequently President of the Brooklyn Academy of Music and the head of the New York Public Library.) But back in those days, their main diet was home-cooked rice, because they couldn't afford anything else.

During that voyage, Henri and I once met in the ship's doctor's office, where I was getting a smallpox inoculation, which I'd failed to get before sailing. I remember him watching attentively while I was injected on my upper thigh. I guess my thigh was okay because he soon became a regular caller at the Sutton Place apartment. And he was next in line to sit beside me on the three-seater blue couch. We swiftly moved from talking about our past, apart, to planning for our future together. A future, I was soon to find, that included his family.

The Deschamps family had a very different approach to the values of life than my mother had. They talked a lot, and I mean a *lot,* about their lands and their silver and jewelry and furniture and other possessions. These were all material things that my mother couldn't have cared less about.

It is a French tradition that, at the dinner on the day before the wedding, a basket is presented to the bride filled with family jewelry. Henri's mother had died and left him a lot of jewelry, and this beribboned basket held some very nice pieces. I was pleasantly surprised and very impressed. Only later did I find out that my mother owned just as many treasures and a lot *more* on her walls. She just never talked about them. Bourgeoise, she wasn't.

My mother's lawyers convinced her that I should get married outside of French jurisdiction . . . for tax reasons mainly . . . and so it was decided that everyone would travel to Belgium for the civil wedding. We had a Dawint cousin, Tante Marcelle, whose husband Marcel Durlet was a banker. We stayed with them in Woluwe Saint Pierre, and our wedding ceremony was conducted at the Hotel de Ville in Brussels in front of the colorful flower market. It was very picturesque, and the whole French contingent came by train to attend and be fêted with three days of endless lunches and teas and dinners. The Durlets were very charming, and I liked their sons, Fernand and Claude. I allowed myself a fleeting flirtation with Fernand; and a little later, my cousin Odile married his brother Claude so it all sort of stayed in the family.

We decided to have the church portion of our wedding during the summer of '51 in Talloires, Savoie. By a marvelous coincidence, the mayor of Paris, Missouri, a chicken farmer, was in Paris, France, meeting with forty-seven other mayors from forty-seven American towns also named . . . *Paris!*

Officiating the gathering was the Mayor of Paris, France, Pierre de Gaulle, who was President Charles de Gaulle's brother. He had invited all these other mayors of all these other Parises to come to the "Ville Lumière."

I invited the Missouri mayor and his wife to the wedding. They came and made quite a hit. Next to the stolid French, they were quite an exotic couple.

Mine was a storybook wedding. There was a cortege of six bridesmaids and six ushers led by Henri's two little half-brothers then all the parents, all the grandparents, and a host of relatives slowly walking all the way from the church to "La Pirraz," the Deschamps house. And there we had a very pretty reception set up in the garden. My poor mother, who was footing the bill, was horrified to discover that Henri's stepmother named Rose of all things, had ordered flowers from the south of France because she claimed she could get them more cheaply there. (Instead, those flowers were terribly expensive and ugly, to boot.)

For Henri and me, our honeymoon was certainly not a bowl of cherries. First of all, I needed injections twice daily for my T B problem. We motored in our new little car, a Quatre Chevaux Renault, to Austria. Henri unilaterally assigned me the job of navigator. He handed me a bundle of formidable-looking maps. When I unfolded them, they took over all the space in the front seat. They were bafflingly complex, and I couldn't make head or tail of them. So, to hide my ignorance, I boldly called out directions for Henri to follow. But as the miles piled up, our location became more uncertain. After one more baffled look from Henri, I burst into tears and confessed. Just because I'd made a *very few* minor miscalculations way, way back, it seems we were a little bit farther away from Austria than when we'd started. (The silver lining to all this? I never had to act as navigator again.) But Austria itself was another problem:

To me, Austria meant Salzburg and *music*.
To Henri, Austria meant *fishing*.

We spent the entire first week of our marriage on some godforsaken river plagued by clouds of hungry black flies far outnumbering the fish. After seven days of fishing—bliss for Henri, hell for me—I realized this was no way to go, and I put my foot down. So although we had no tickets, I dragged Henri to Salzburg's Festival Hall every night. True, we were ticketless, but I had an ace-in-the-hole. He was Herr Doffer, the owner of the little inn we were staying at. In my broken—or even fractured—German, I described my plight.
"Nicht problem!" Herr Doffer said, He worked at the concert hall, and we met him there each night and, as the conductor lifted his baton, Herr Doffer would spot empty places and usher us to wonderful orchestra seats. He worked this miracle by night. I plied him with chocolates by day until even I was Mozarted out, and we headed back to France, our heads saturated with music.
Though Henri and I struck this concert/fishing balance, it struck me as a worrisome beginning to marriage joy. Doesn't it seem strange that we hadn't discussed the particulars of *our* honeymoon?
On our return to Paris, we moved into an apartment at 180 Rue de la Pompe in the sixteenth arrondissement on a huge airy floor in a very nice building just off the Avenue Foch. We had some good furniture that Henri inherited from his mother and a lot of excellent silver (same inheritance) plus

some nice paintings (my contribution). There was only one snag. Fully half of our half-apartment was set aside to be Henri's office, with all his medical equipment like the EKG, X-ray, and other machines. We always had to rush through lunch because our dining room doubled as his waiting room. The table had to be cleared so his patients could come into the Waiting Room and "wait."

One day, I decided to throw a very grown-up lunch for my mother and invited Rose Kennedy, Lady Oakes, Lady Kenmare—all the big cannons of Mummy's generation I knew who happened to be in Paris at the same time. (Mrs. Kennedy told me she had gone to Christian Dior the week before to order a pink suit and matching hat especially to wear at my luncheon. She looked like a little pink rhapsody. She came to Paris twice a year, religiously of course to visit the couturiers.) Well, about dessert time, I tried to rush them through the chocolate mousse so I could whisk them into the living room for their coffee. But as I was sliding the doors closed, the hyrax that was sleeping in a scarf around Lady Kenmare's neck woke up. The rodent jumped to the floor and ran into the waiting room. Bedlam broke loose as my distinguished guests had to mix with Henri's more mundane patients.

We often had to go to the Langrognes' château in the Loire Valley. It was called "Les Grotteaux" and was really charming. It was built for one of François Ier's counsellors in 1515. They shared the château with Tante Colette's brother, Bernaud Renaud. He was a true eccentric. His favorite trick was to don the caretaker's hat and pretend to be the guide for visitors, who were allowed in once a week, taking them around the grounds and inventing licentious stories about its history. At tour's end, he'd doff his hat and take tips. He visited a lady girlfriend in Blois every Tuesday and Friday. She ran an umbrella store, and he always came back with a few "bumper shooters." He hid them as best he could; but it wasn't easy; and often, when you opened a closet door, dozens of them would fall on your head.

Poor fellow, one couldn't begrudge him his idiosyncracies. His wife, Annette, was a stupefyingly dull peasant woman from Lorraine whose only joy and interest was growing the vegetables she sold in the local market. I guess she needed the extra money because of Miss Umbrella. During one tour, a rich Texan asked Uncle Bernard if he could provide him with the blueprints for the château so he could duplicate it back in Austin. Uncle Bernard was thrilled. He never thought of asking for a fee. He merely watched patiently as the American architects, draftsmen, and engineers invaded the house and grounds for months on end. Probably doffing his hat all the while. As a thank you, the Texan sent a silver teaset from Tiffany!

Henri Deschamps in Paris, the year we met.

Henri Deschamps
on the Lac d'Annecy.

Me, Henri Deschamps
Talloires.

The newlyweds and their parents.
(My mother and Dr. Jean-Louis
Deschamps)

Me and bridesmaids.
Madeleine Deloulme
Yacinthe de Montera
Audrey Bosworth
Shirley Oakes
Olivia Hammerschlag

Henri Deschamps
Casting In the Bois de Boulogne.

We made many a drawn-out trip there, picking apples and living *en famille*. There was precious little social activity except that once a year, the "gentry" were invited for tea. This was a big to-do. Extra help was hired, and *petits fours* were sent from Paris. Why, shoes were even shined.

During one long, tedious lunch, Uncle Ernest proclaimed his belief that doctors, like taxi drivers, should be required to learn all the streets of Paris so they could make house calls. That really was the straw that broke the Camel's back for me. I burst into tears and fled the room. I think that was the beginning of the end of my already shaky first marriage.

My American grandmother had left me a thousand dollars in her will, and, with it, I bought myself a Hillman-Minx convertible. The car was owned by a friend of mine, Donald Coons, whom I'd met at Yale. After his legs were paralyzed by polio, he had his car fitted out with hand controls so he could still drive. This made it an impractical car to sell, which is why I got it so cheaply when he decided to get rid of it. The car was my pride and joy. I used to dash over to my grandmother's and take her for long drives all over Paris. It whirled her away from her humdrum life and gave me added pleasure to make her so happy. Poor, generous, Donald, he rented a house in Biarritz and invited all his friends to visit. Jackie and Yusha and I stayed there on our way to Corsica. One day, we all piled into the car and went to the Chambre d'Amour, a private swimming club, with Donald's college friend, Gordon Wholey, who stayed with him all that summer. He helped and provided companionship (in exchange for the trip abroad). While Gordon was lifting Donald from his wheelchair and carrying him to the pool, a dreadful French woman walked up and objected that a cripple like Donald would immerse himself in the pool and defile it. We left but not before I ripped that woman up one side and down the other, including some sulfurous language impugning her forebears. My friends were quite impressed by my vociferousness.

CHAPTER 22

Fred Herter

My mother was not exactly turning cartwheels when she heard of my plans to marry Fred Herter, yet another doctor. She asked one of her Boston pals, Betty Houghton, just who these "Herters" were. Betty assured her they were the *crème de la crème* of Boston society. This vague description didn't impress my mother, and it didn't assuage her maternal worries. Her take on life was certainly at extreme poles from my future mother-in-law's.

I was put off by my first meeting with my future mother-in-law. She had invited me to lunch in Washington DC shortly after Fred told her we were getting married. I was fifty years old and felt like Wallis Simpson meeting the Queen Mother. I was barely seated when she lunged into the conversation:

Mrs. Herter:"You know, dearie, Fred has no money."
Me: "Oh, that's no problem, Mrs. Herter. You see, I have plenty."

I loved saying it and savored her bewildered expression. But I must say that the exchange didn't particularly warm me to her. I later learned that she had grilled every friend of hers who knew me, which included some of the *grande dames* of Washington, like Janet Auchincloss and Edith Munson.

Jackie Kennedy told me about the grillings. Imagine! At my age! But as it turned out, I got high marks. To be charitable, maybe Mrs. Herter's worry about money was brought on after she heard about Jean's and my lifestyle, which certainly included spending scads of money. Actually, she was a Standard Oil heiress and was quite rich herself. Her father, Charles Pratt, had left her and her sister not only a lot of money but also a beautiful plantation in South Carolina. He had bought it on the eve of the 1929 crash for a dollar an acre. The twelve thousand acres were bordered by the Cheeha and the Combahee rivers, and the place was called the Cheeha-Combahee plantation.

The first time Fred took me there, we presented a problem. Apparently, she and her friends had discussed lengthily whether her son and I should share the same bedroom. (I mean, good heavens! We weren't even married yet!) Anyway, we finally got to share a room but not without paying a penalty. After dinner, that first night when we played charades, Fred and I were given the word "insinuate." In-sin-you-ate. Hmmm. To act out. That word must have been carefully chosen before we got there too.

Fred Herter was a professor of surgery at Columbia-Presbyterian Hospital in Manhattan. He held the Auchincloss Chair of Surgery and had been chairman of the department. Fred's and my worlds were light years apart, and I don't think we would ever, ever have run into each other, except by accident, on the subway or across a crowded room; but when we did, lightening struck.

As luck would have it, I learned I needed an operation for a melanoma and didn't have a doctor of my own. I had plenty of pediatricians for the children. In fact, it was while I was taking Véronique to her dermatologist that fate intervened. I was wearing a short golf skirt, and the doctor noticed a suspicious mole on my lower thigh and suggested I have it looked at. That warning began my search for a surgeon, and I consulted seven of them before I finally encountered Fred P. Herter. And talk about second opinions!

I was told I had to wait three weeks before he could operate on me. When I mentioned this to my friend Jo Bryce, she was furious, called him up, and told him that he should operate on me immediately and that her aunt, Pauline Huntington Harford, had donated the chapel to the hospital. She didn't quite threaten to take the chapel back, but almost. Well, somehow, or by sheer luck, I was scheduled to go under the knife the very next week. Fred was very amused by Jo's intervention, luckily not outraged. And that was that. Or at least it was, eight months later, when after many peregrinations, we got married. So in our case, it wasn't a cloud but the rainbow itself that had a silver lining.

At the time Fred and I were married, we had to sign certain documents, and my lawyer suggested I use a middle initial. I laughed at him. "How could there be *another* Solange Herter in the world?" Well, he was right, and sure enough, another Solange Herter did turn up in Paris, France, of all places, a couple of years later. Evidently, she was née Herter; but I don't know what the family connection is. Fred and I had a very nice tea with her and her husband, a Parisian lawyer, at their apartment on the Right Bank. For good or for bad, our paths never crossed again. She wrote a book "Trop Tendre' l'Áutomne," and I am often asked if I am the author, though it's not at all my "voice".

When Fred retired from the Department of Surgery in 1985, he started writing a book, explaining surgery to the layman. But he never finished it, returned the $100,000 advance to the Arbor House Publishing Company (which nobody had ever done before), and accepted the post of President of the American University of Beirut. He held that dangerous post for six years. (Two prior presidents had been victimized by the war. In 1982, David Dodge was abducted by the Hezbollah and held captive for three hundred sixty-five days, often in solitary confinement. He kept his sanity by using the one sheet of paper they gave him to write a letter on, cutting it up instead into fifty-two pieces and making himself a deck of cards to play solitaire. Two years later, then President Malcolm Kerr was assassinated just outside his office in College Hall.) Americans were disallowed from Lebanon in 1985. And during Fred's presidency, the university was run from the AUB office in New York, and a deputy president who was Jordanian represented him on campus in Beirut.

During those tumultuous years, we nonetheless traveled thousands of miles thought the Middle East, raising money and goodwill for the school. From Jordan to Saudi Arabia to Kuwait to Qatar to Abu Dhabi to Bahrain to Oman to Egypt and Turkey and many times to Cyprus, where Fred met with the faculty deans. They were fruitful but exhausting journeys. We were finally allowed to go to Beirut in 1992, but security still prevented us from living there. Those were exciting days. I remember one night, going to yet another official dinner, surrounded by body guards and the usual retinue, I was seated next to the nephew of one of the trustees, Rafik Hariri, (who, later, in quick succession, became prime minister and was assassinated). Between courses, he told me his uncle was very keen to know Fred better. He had met Fred briefly at a few board meetings, but I told him I didn't think it was possible as we were flying to Paris the next morning.

"That's all right!" he said, "One of my uncle's jets can take you to see him and then get you to Paris earlier than the commercial flight could."

Fred was eager to talk more to this uncle, who, starting as a laborer in Saudi Arabia, had amassed an immense fortune from new techniques in construction and contributed a lot to AUB. He had found that he could build things faster and better and *cheaper* than his competitors. His secret was to ship concrete blocks from France to the Middle East. When the Saudi king heard of this, he had him build *everything:* palaces, mosques, office buildings, apartment houses with billions in budgets, billions in profits.

At the crack of dawn next morning, the nephew picked us up at our hotel in a block-long limousine, zoomed us to a private parking at the airport, bustled us onto a private jet, where we waved good-bye to him with still no idea where we were heading. We asked the stewardess; she wouldn't tell us. We asked the pilot; he shrugged his epaulettes. Well, remembering the old State Department slogan, "When rape is inevitable, relax and enjoy it." we settled into our seats and awaited developments. Soon enough, a large island appeared on the horizon, and the plane began a gentle descent. Though my geographic skills are nil, I saw what looked like the shape of Sardinia below, and that's precisely where we landed.

We were carrying a dozen huge bags of pita bread for Harīrī from Beirut. He claimed there was only one bakery in the whole Middle East that could bake pita bread properly. When we left the plane, we saw five other jets identical to ours, Harīrī apparently used to ferry those people he wanted to see from anywhere in the world. We were sped to Harīrī's yacht.

Harírí was on deck to greet us. He was wearing short little white shorts and had very muscled legs, which I think he liked to show off. Once on board, he asked what we'd like to drink, and I asked for iced tea. It took a full half hour to get it. On came a stately procession of minions, each toting a silver tray, the first bearing a huge bucket of ice, the next a copper kettle, and then about a bushel of lemons, another tray with limes, followed by one with a pile of straws and spoons. Finally, a silver salver laden down with one lonely glass. While I sipped my million-dollar beverage, Fred and Harírí talked, for a half hour at most, but apparently satisfactorily, Then we were back on the plane and landed in Paris an easy two hours before the commercial flight would have gotten us there. Two more limos zipped us home, one for us, one for the luggage, giving us plenty of time to change for dinner.

Fred Herter at his desk
at Columbia-Presbyterian Hospital
the year we met.

Mrs. Herter and me
in Millis.

CHAPTER 23

The Middle East

F.P. Herter shaking the hand of the
President of Lebanon.
Me and Hamilton Southworth
in Beirut.

Yet another sheikh-shake.

Fred Herter, Queen Noor,
King Hussein, me singing the AUB alma
mater in Amman, Jordan.

In Egypt.

Jackie, my mother,
Me, and Fred in
Cheeha-Combahee.

Fred & me in Barbados.

And in St. Lucia.

Our year 2010 Christmas card.

As a twist on "When in Rome, do as the Romans do," I decided to study Arabic so I could hold my own and signed up for a four month "total immersion" course at the UN. I was by far the oldest in the class. A pleasant young Russian student sat next to me and let me copy his notes. (He was so much quicker than I and knew that he had to do well or be sent to Siberia.) Anyway, he helped me a lot; and in gratitude, I'd take him to lunch in his threadbare red suit to thank him. We have kept in touch. He didn't go to Siberia and he is now Minister of the Interior!

For me, learning basic Arabic was a simple matter of self-defense. Most of the women I met during our travels were perfectly fluent in English. Yet after saying "hello," they would quickly and deliberately switch to Arabic, excluding me from their conversations. But I could usually catch their drift, and, in Arabic, could say, "I didn't catch all of what you just said to each other." This really threw them for a loop, made them switch to English, and put me in the driver's seat (just as long as they didn't continue in fast Arabic). But I think they appreciated the fact that I had made the effort to learn their language, which not many Americans do.

The last time I went back to Missouri was in 1992, I was there because I had received a copy of this letter a friend had sent to Donald Rothenberg, President of Missouri's Columbia College, my father's alma mater.

> Dear Doctor Rothenberg:
>
> I am in fact looking forward to receiving an honorary degree from you on May 17th, 1992. You will be interested to know that one of your distinguished Columbia College graduates, Walter Russell Batsell, was the father, now deceased, of Solange Herter, wife of Dr. Frederic Herter, President of the American University of Beirut. She lives in New York. She and Dr. Herter were recently in Bahrain where they stayed with me.
>
> She has kindly decided to donate to your college some interesting and valuable manuscripts from Russia and elsewhere, gathered by her father. You may wish to contact her regarding these, and I can mention this gift in my speech.
>
> (Signed) Charles W. Hostler
> Ambassador of the United States to Bahrain

Fred and I had met so many interesting people in the Middle East, and Charles Hostler was one of them. He was Ambassador of the United States to Bahrain during the Gulf War. We stayed with him for a few days at the embassy; and at all the dinners he gave, he always had me sit on his right, which, in itself, was very flattering. But on the fourth night, I think it was, I found myself running out of topics of conversation and in desperation, asked him where he had gone to school (something I'm not in a habit of doing). When he answered "Hollywood High," I almost fell out of my hot seat. "So did I! So did I!" And two minutes later, we were fast friends and even went into confidential subjects like his having pined after Elizabeth Taylor at Hollywood High School. Well, a few months later, we met up at the Mark Twain Motel in Columbia. I had been hesitating about whom I should give some of my father's papers to (Harvard, the University of Missouri, or the New York Public Library, all of which wanted them), but Hostler had spoken to me so highly of the University of Missouri that I decided to donate these important documents to them. The other two institutions being much better endowed anyway. The University was very grateful.

At the presentation ceremony, it was nice to have Harold Batsell's sons and their mother, in attendance. (A few years later Hostler gave $12 million to AUB. He later told me it was thanks to his friendship with Fred and me. We went to the inauguration of the Hostler center, a glorious new building on the campus; and it was a nice feeling that we had had something to do with it.)

I guess the reason I'm not nervous about writing my memoir is that I've done it before.

At the ripe age of seven. And in *two* volumes.

Penned in my own precocious hand, my profound recollections are reproduced digitally to both astonish and amuse the reader. I refuse to have them translated into English because I think that most civilized people can read French and my descendants, should they not be yet civilized, should make every effort to learn French. Winston Churchill once said that a capable, intelligent person should speak at least three languages. So there you are . . . He also said that if a person spoke three languages, he was trilingual, two, he was bilingual, one, he was American. (So true)

I leave it you, Gentle Reader, to decide whether these early memoirs are more accomplished than my newest one. Maybe I should have rested on my laurels and spared both you and me this recent effort. You will find them at the end of this book.

I have forgotten to mention that I have fifteen grandchildren, four of them brought into my life by two of Fred's children (whom I love as dearly as my own.) Very few men in my life have mattered really except, obviously, the ones I had children with and the one, sadly enough, I couldn't have children with because it was too late, namely Fred Herter. I am grateful for the thirty-three years we have had together. I don't think I could have endured all those years of marriage with anybody else). And we are lucky, at the end of our lives, to be surrounded by loving children and grandchildren and numerous friends. One couldn't ask for anything, more (realistically), and I count my blessings every day and pray (very realistically) that life will go on like this for a while longer.

There, I've shot the bolt!

My four children
and eight out of my
eleven grand children.

CHAPTER 24

The Memoirs of Miss Secret

Livre premier

Mémoires de miss secret

(Solange Bataille)

Cours de Madame Parizot
11, rue Anatole de la Forge
Paris - 17e

1

Chapitre I

Un départ mouvementé...

Il y avait sept ans mon père étant mort un an auparavant, ma mère devait partir en Amérique pour continuer les affaires...

Il y avait des parents dont il faut vous parler chers lecteurs car ils jouent un rôle assez important dans ma vie ;
A Marseille ma tante la sœur de maman appelée Yvonne mon oncle et ma petite cousine Odile à Bellevue (dans les environs de ....) mon oncle Charlie (le frère de maman) ma tante Madeleine et ses deux filles Christiane l'aînée et Ginguette la cadette. Il y avait aussi une amie madame Franklin et non deux Gérard...............
Ma mère habitait avec ma grand-mère donc cela était très naturel qu'en

partant en Amerique elle me confia
à ma grand'mère: ce qu'elle fit...
Mais après deux mois elle envoya un télégramme
disant que je devais aller en Amérique mais
elle ajoutait à la fin ce mot qui effraya
ma grand'mère: "SEULE" et de préférence
sur le Normandie...

Deux semaines plus tard accompagnée de grand'mère
et de ma tante, nous prîmes le train pour
le Havre, je n'avais jamais vu un tel silence
personne ne prononçait mot, car tout le monde
était triste, mais une séparation ne se fait jamais
sans pleurs. Enfin nous arrivâmes au Havre
une ville grise, mais c'était sans doute à cause
de la pluie qui tombait en faisant semblant de
ne s'échapper de ne vouloir nous abattre sous son légère pluviosité

Chapitre II

Voyage sur la Normandie

3

Après avoir traversé en hâte des rues des bou-
-levards etc. nous arrivâmes dans un port... ...
Ce que je vis là me stupéfia. Dès là on
voyait une énorme maison flottante à ... mai... le
... on voyait une chose qui ressemblait à
un bateau, mais n'ayant jamais vu de bateaux
si grand, je me dit que cela devait être
un espèce de phénomène qui n'était pas or-
-dinaire. Enfin lecteurs ne restons point sur
cela et passons à autre chose... ...
Arrivés à ce ... espèce de phénomène, nous entrâmes
par un petit pont et ne ... ... après avoir
demandé à un monsieur la cabine du commandant
nous voici cheminant par des escaliers et des couloirs nous
arrivâmes enfin devant une porte. Le monsieur tapa ...
une voix répondit de l'intérieur "entrez" alors
nous entrâmes je vis en face de moi un grand
monsieur avec des galons sur les épaules. Ce grand
-nieur alla devant lui et lui donnant ...
lettre de mon oncle (car le commandant était
grand ami avec mon oncle ils se connaissaient
depuis très longtemps) Il lut la lettre suivi ...
me tapotta les joues et ayant parlé à grand...

4.

dans son oreille nous partîmes. Quand nous
arrivâmes à la porte il dit que je serais la
reine de Normandie pendant la traversée......
Nous continuâmes ma grand'mère ma tante et moi
à circuler dans ces longs corridors; et brusque-
-ment à un tournant nous vîmes une
marine salle avec des garnitures sur les murs;
remplie de gens qui mangeaient (les passagers)
où des hommes qui adroitement tenaient les
plats d'une main en mettant l'autre derrière
le dos. Alors là dut se faire une cruelle sépara-
-ration; ma tante m'embrassa bien fort et je
m'arrachais de ses bras pour tomber dans ceux
de grand'maman. Oh grand maman; que je
regrettais de lui avoir désobéi tant de fois tandis
que pendant dans un coin elle tâchait de me
dire d'être raisonnable avec des paroles tendres.
Maintenant c'était le dîner moment nous
nous embrassâmes longuement et alors tout d'un
coup comme dressée par un passant grand maman
tourna la tête pour cacher ses larmes et après m'a-
-voir lancé un long regard de tendresse je
la vis disparaître dans ces interminables corridors.

₮ *sanmialier*

Que j'aurai voulu pouvoir courir après elle et
me retrouver encore quelques minutes dans ses bras
maternels. Allais déjà un steward s'avança
vers moi et me dit : " Suivez-moi " ; donc je
fis ce qu'il me disait et le suivit en silence
car j'avais le cœur trop gros pour avoir avec
ce steward qui quoique faisant bien son
habit ne me plaisait guère avec son air souriant
et moqueur ; et des yeux qui avaient l'air de
me dire : " tu te vois malheureuse grand être
au milieu de tout ce monde !! " Quelle humiliation
j'étais prête à me jeter sur lui et lui dire
tu vas te taire oui ou non ; mais j'étais trop
fière pour me battre avec un domestique devant
tout le monde donc malgré que bouillonnant
de fureur je le suivis en rageant. Arrivés au
milieu de la salle je m'installais devant une
petite table où bientôt deux garçons me re-
centrent des chaises vraiment semblables mais
toutes ces choses ne s'arrêtaient pas à mon
esprit je pensais seulement à : home maman !
Ah j'aurais voulu que étant dans ses bras elle
me dire des paroles douces qui consolent toujours

6   mais hélas je n'étais que dans une grande
salle avec ses immenses tableaux et des
personnes qui n'étaient faisaient des courbures et
tout... j'aurais beaucoup mieux aimé être
dans les bras de ma... maman et entendre
sa douce voix me murmurer des chansons
que je savais par cœur mais que je croyais que
ce n'était qu'à grand'maman qu'elles
appartenaient... Aussi quand arriva la
fin du repas ce fut avec un grand soin
que je vis une... me dire d'un ton
très... "je viens de la part du commandant"
elle disait au même... qu'elle aurait dit
"je viens de la part du roi..."...

Le soir arriva vite et quand je me couchais je
cachais ma tête enfouie dans l'oreiller je
pleurais... mais quand j'entendis la...
venir... redoublai mes pleurs et tournais
la tête de son côté mais malheureusement
j'avais les joues ruisselantes de larmes
alors elle... approcha de moi et je
m'endormis...

7

Le lendemain matin en me réveillant je
fus tout à surpris de me trouver dans une
cabine avec des petits hublots (à la place de fenêtres) et de voir à travers ces
hublots de la magnifique mer moitié
verte moitié bleue, et qui avait l'air de
changer toujours à une autre mer plus
belle encore que la précédente, mais,
c'était toujours la même . . . .
Il était neuf heures du matin je sau-
tai hors de mon lit et m'habillai
en hâte; j'avais à peine fini de me
coiffer que la nurse entra dans ma chambre
— J'espère que vous avez bien dormi?
— Oui très bien merci lui répondis — je —
. . . . Un certain un jeune parent de maman vo-
yageait sur le même bateau que moi . . .
et aussi l'après — midi du premier jour
il alla demander au commandant s'il
pouvait m'avoir pour goûter et ainsi
chaque jour je goûtais avec lui et
vraiment c'était épatant car ce qu'il
commandait pour moi était délicieux

Un jour même il télégraphia du bateau à grand'maman 1º pour lui dire que j'allais très bien et deuxième ment à maman pour lui annoncer ma prochaine arrivée. Le cinquième jour de mon arrivée à bord j'étais sur le pont, puisque là le bateau avait été entouré de toutes part par la mer et en tournant la tête je vis un bout de terre alors aussitôt je me précipitais dans ma cabine pour me préparer et 10 minutes après j'étais de nouveau toute prête et m'attendais à débarquer quand je vis que nous n'avions presque pas bougé de place alors abordant un matelot qui se trouvait près de moi, je lui demandais quand nous arriverions et il me répondit sans même jeter un coup d'œil sur moi dans 1 heure et demie. J'étais navrée je regardais autour de moi tout le monde se préparait pour arriver. Enfin au bout d'une heure et demie que j'aurais passé à regarder autour de moi je vis un quai et beaucoup de personnes qui quittaient leurs manteaux. De plus il y avait des buildings, hautes maisons qui avaient l'air de nous souhaiter la bienvenue. Je me regardais sans cesse dans une petite glace que j'avais glissée dans ma poche avant de monter sur le quai, j'étais inquiète. Est-ce que maman me reconnaîtrait ? étais-je bien coiffée ? Toutes sortes de questions se multipliaient dans ma tête quand tout à coup je ressentis une secousse, le bateau avait accosté. Je descendis avec la nurse qui ne me quittait pas et j'eus à peine le temps de dire ouf ! au milieu de cette foule grouillante que j'étais dans les bras de maman.

Je pleurais de joie ; nous marchions toutes les deux l'une serrée contre l'autre et nous fûmes bientôt sur une place où maman héla un taxi. Pendant le

280

10.

trajet je regardais en dehors de la voiture.
Pas un seul arbre ; partout de ces
grands buildings : enfin le taxi s'arrêta
et nous entrâmes par une grande porte
dans un de ces buildings ... nous montâmes [quelques]
marches et nous entrâmes dans un
ascenseur là maman dit quelque chose
au [boy] que je ne compris pas mais plus
tard je sus que cela voulait dire ... "16ème
étage. Nous allions à une vitesse ver-
-tigineuse. Arrivées nous marchions dans
de longs corridors quand maman s'arrêta
et me montrant une porte me dit de
l'ouvrir, je l'ouvris et je vis une jolie
gentille chambre à devais être alors je
sautais au cou de maman et je l'embras-
sais mille et une fois après je déshabillais
car il était 8 heures et que j'avais déjà
dîné sur le bateau je me couchais fis
ma prière et m'endormis d'un bon
sommeil .... Le lendemain matin
en me réveillant je fus surpris de me pas
voir la lucarne de ma petite cabine mais

chasseur

me

quand je vis maman devant moi
toute habillée alors je me suis levée
et tout en l'embrassant lui ait demandé
ce que je ferais ce jour là elle me
répondit tranquillement que j'irais à
l'école à ce dernier mot toute personne
qui aurait été dans cette petite chambre
bien tranquille m'aurait vu bondir
en sautant presque au plafond et
demander à maman !! et mes livres ?
et un cartable ? et des cahiers ? à ces
trois questions maman répondit de plus
plus tranquillement : ?? j'ai été les acheter
hier avant ton arrivée ! alors je dus me
résigner mais je demandais encore une question
Quand est-ce qu'on allait nous prendre notre
petit déjeuner ? — nous devons aller le chercher
dans un magasin où nous déjeunerons : et tu
déjeuneras à l'école car j'ai acheté en
même temps que tes affaires de classe
une petite mallette contenant une
bouteille thermose . . . .
ainsi j'allais chaque jour à l'école

— Hôtel Alex. Weston —
où j'habitais.

je déjeunais à
l'école et je
rentrais à l'Hôtel
Alex Weston
où j' habitais
et là maman
rentrait le soir
et après s'être
... pour
ressortir (car
elle avait beau-
-coup à sortir
car elle devait
voir beaucoup
de gens et ne
pouvait pas
s'occuper de moi)
Donc je restais

seule de 8 heure à minuit dans la petite
chambre que j'aimais tellement et je
dormais tellement bien dans mon bon
petit lit que je m'endormais bien le
soir en regardant à côté de moi le

13

grand lit vide et lendemain matin en
me réveillant je le voyais occupé...
Ainsi chaque jour se passait et comme
j'étais arrivé à Albert-York un mois
avant la fin de l'année scolaire et
quand cette fin arriva et maman
décida que j'irais dans un camp
qui se trouvait dans le Albert guisey
et qui paraît était épatant. Mai cela ne
m'enchantait pas du tout car même
que je ne voyais pas beaucoup maman
j'aimais mieux rester auprès d'elle car
quelque chose me disait que puisque
papa n'était plus là c'était à moi d'être
auprès d'elle. (J'ai oublié de vous dire
que je ne savais pas que papa était mort
et que ne l'ayant pas trouvé auprès de
maman cela m'intriguait énormément
et ayant demandé à maman s'il était
en voyage elle m'avait répondu sur les
larmes aux yeux, mais aussi plus tard
quand maman me dit que mon papa
était mort je me suis rappelé que étant à

New-York avec moi elle avait toujours
parlé du midi et je ne m'en étais jamais
aperçue.

Chapitre III

Description du camp.

En arrivant au camp je vis que
maman ne resterait pas toujours avec
moi et je fus effrayée quand ma
man me montrant une demoiselle
me dit c'est cette demoiselle
qui s'occupera de toi ma
chère pendant que tu resteras au
camp et elle partit. Je comprenais
que nous ne resterions pas toujours
ensembles et qu'il fallait s'habi-
tuer à des séparations nouvelles.
La camp il était une des plus pe-
-tite dans ce camp et je croyais que
personne ne s'occuperait de moi
mais au contraire les grandes

15 m'apprenaient à faire toutes sortes
de choses que je ne connaissaient
pas et qui étaient très amusantes
c'est à dire ou de cueillir des fleurs
que l'an applatit et que l'on sèche
et après en les colle dans un petit livre fait exprès en mettant
leurs noms sous la fleurs indiquée
au alors de tirer de l'arc cet etc
Enfin je passais des jours très heureux
d ce camp qui était vraiment
idéal, mais je sentais qu'il me
manquait 3 êtres qui m'étaient
chers c'est à dire ceux que
dans ma vie qu'ils soient morts
ou pas auraient toujours la pre-
-mière place dans mon cœur.
ces trois êtres je crois que vous
devez les connaître chers lec-
-teurs ce sont mon papa ma
maman et ma grand'mère
aussi quand maman venait me
visiter chaque dimanche au

deux semaines c'était avec une
joie vraiment réelle que j'accourais
vers elle et l'embrassait comme
si je ne l'avais pas revue depuis 6
mois...

Chapitre IV

Une chose assez désagréable
il est inutile de vous dire chers
lecteurs que pour coucher dans ce
camp on couchait 3 dans une
petite cabane en bois il y avait comme
cela des cabanes et des cabanes con-
-tenant chacunes quatre de petites filles.
Donc moi je couchais dans une
de ces cabanes avec deux autres
petites filles dont il y en a une dont
je me rappelle le nom elle s'app-
-elait Barbara c'est avec elle et
moi que se passa cette chose
assez désagréable ce fut plutôt
pour elle que ce fut désagréable car

17

pour moi après avoir été honteuse
comme si j'allais rentrer sous terre
j'éclatais de rire à la consternation
de tout le monde. Voici ce qui é-
tait arrivé...

Dans la chambre de la colonie
je couchais juste à côté du lit
de Barbara et à côté de moi c'é-
à dire de l'autre côté de mon
lit il y avait la fenêtre qui é-
videmment était sans vitres puisque
c'était une colonie et cette fenêtre
je m'en servais souvent au lieu
de la porte surtout la nuit car
c'était trop long de passer par
la porte et d'ailleurs je n'ai pas
honte de le dire je me faisais
souvent attraper à cause de ça.
Le cabinet était un peu plus
loin et il y avait toujours une
lanterne car pendant la nuit celles
qui avaient besoin d'y aller
ne verraient rien du tout pour

18 y aller.

Un soir m'étant endormie d'un bon somme je me réveillais en sursaut pendant la nuit et je sentis tout d'un coup (en même temps que je frottais mes yeux avec acharnement) que j'avais envie d'aller visiter la petite lumière et même que cette visite était très pressée donc je ne fis qu'un bond mais au lieu d'aller du côté de la fenêtre j'allais du côté du lit de Barbara et là la sensation que j'étais déjà là où était la petite lumière s'empara de moi et tout d'un coup m'accroupissant sur le lit de Barbara je fis ce dont j'avais besoin et ce qu'il y avait de très fâcheux pour Barbara c'est que ça que je la fis juste sur sa tête ! ! ! ! ! ! ! Le lendemain matin cela fut vraiment une consternation générale on me punit et vraiment ce n'était pas de ma faute. pourtant je fus puni car je ne pus aller à une excursion organisée dans une montagne proche de dont je m'étais réjouie et je fus désapointée tout en me promettant de faire même en mettant un peu plus attention !!!!

Chapitre V

Départ du camp +

Je me plaisais beaucoup au camp mais comme je vous ai dit dans le dernier chapitre il me manquait ces trois personnes que je chérissais le plus au monde dans un jour que je pensais à eux trois maman vint juste au moment où appuyée sur le rebord de notre cabane je pleurais alors maman arriva et me tenant par la main me dit : "Ma chérie je devine ta pensée : tu

20   voudrais retrouver ta grand'mère
et ton papa mais comme nous
ne pouvons pas retourner en France
tout de suite à cause d'affaires
que j'ai à finir à New-York
je vais t'envoyer à la mer
avec une demoiselle très gentille
que je connais car je ne peux
pas te laisser encore au camp car
il va fermer dans une semaine."
Et elle partit après avoir parlé au direc-
teur de mon prochain départ. J'étais
restée pendre après le départ de maman.
Est-ce que je serais heureuse là-bas?
Et pourquoi maman ne voulait pas que
je reste le reste de l'été avec elle?
Toutes sortes de questions tournaient dans
ma tête enfin je me dis que quoique
je dise où je pense j'irais là-bas...

Une semaine après comme on l'avait
décidé je partais du camp c'est à dire
que le camp était fermé et je me dirigeais

Chapitre VI

Nouvelle destinée

Ce fut au son d'une douce voix
que je me réveillais le lendemain
d'un voyage bien fatiguant la personne à qui appartenait cette voix
c'était Betty, celle qui devait me
garder à "Ocean City" station de mer.
J'étais partie du camp avec ma
mam qui m'avait amenée à
"Ocean City" où Betty et ses
parents habitaient et puis elle
était restée avec moi une
après-midi et le soir m'avait
quittée pour retourner à Philadelphia où ses affaires l'appellaient
quant à moi comme je vous
l'ai dit le lendemain matin
en ouvrant les yeux je vis

22

Betty au chevet de mon lit qui m'appelait tout doucement je lui dis bonjour et me levais :... j'aimais beaucoup Betty au commencement mais à la fin je commençais à l'aimer moins car elle me parlait toujours avec un ton de commandement... je m'amusais beaucoup à la plage avec d'autres petites filles et je passais un temps très agréable car il y avait aussi maman qui venait me voir chaque semaine ou alors chaque deux semaines....

Chapitre VII

Ce qui n'est pas agréable pour les parents

Il y avait un magasin sorte de ...

23   à Ocean City où l'on ache-
-tait toutes sorte de choses ;
un jour en passant j'avais vu
une vitrine de jouets bien ten-
-tante et parmi tous ces jouets
il y avait des révolvers à
réservoir à eau vous pensez bien
que ce n'était pas fait pour se
la jeter à la tête mais seule-
-ment pour le jeter dans une
cuvette ou quelque chose comme
ça mais moi j'avais une autre
idée qui me trottait dans la tête
donc je rentrais en courant à la
maison et je pris mon argent
(car maman chaque semaine me
donnait de l'argent) puis je
revins au magasin et j'achetais
ce révolver après je revins à
la maison en portant triom-
-phalement mon révolver puis
j'allais directement au grenier
là je m'installais sur une chaise

294

24 juste devant la fenêtre puis
j'allais chercher de l'eau que
je mis dans une grande cuvette près
de moi et mon manège commença.
Mon idée c'était d'asperger les
passants. le facteur arrivait
traînant la jambe (car il était
fatigué) moi je me préparais et je
l'aspergeais d'eau de la tête aux
pieds comme les fois précédente
je rentrais vite ma main pour qu'on
ne me voit pas mais il avait été
encore plus vif que moi et avait
relevé la tête alors il a été le
dire aux parents de Betty qu'il
y avait une petite fille de chez
elle qui l'avait aspergé lui et ses
lettres alors moi vois pensez
mes chers lecteurs que je me suis
bien fait attrapée et que je
n'ai plus jamais recommencé après.

FIN

Livre second

Mémoires de miss secret

(Solange Batoul)

Cours de Madame Parisot
11, rue Anatole de la Forge
Paris – 17e

Chapitre I

Départs

Je passais un très agréable été à « Ocean City » mais malheureusement (dans la vie il y a toujours un mais) on m'annonça que j'allais repartir avec les parents de Betty à Philadelphie dans la maison qu'ils habitaient l'hiver. Et que après avoir passé un mois là-bas je rentrerais seule par le train à New-York. Je partis donc avec regret de Ocean City pour aller vers Philadelphie. Nous fîmes tout le voyage en auto. Betty fut assez gentille avec moi pendant le trajet et enfin nous arrivâmes.

Pendant mon séjour à Philadelphie je ne vis rien du tout de cette ville ; tout ce que je vis

297

2 ce fait la charmante et pitto-
-resque petite maison des parents
de Betty. Je ne vous la décrirai
pas car cela serait trop long.
Mon anniversaire est le 8 Septem-
-bre et justement le 8 septembre
je devais le passer à Philadelphie
donc j'étais très contente (car je vous
l'ai dit tout à l'heure c'était à cause des
cadeaux). Enfin le jour du 8
Septembre arriva et j'étais frétillante
d'impatience. La porte s'ouvrit tout
doucement et je vis Betty entrer
chargée de paquets. je courus à elle
et tout en lui disant bonjour je
me précipitais vers les paquets qu'elle
avait posé sur ma table de nuit.
Les cadeaux étaient pour moi tout ce
que je désirais : 1° un petit sac
à main en cuir avec un petit
chien blanc attaché et qui bou-
-geait à chaque petite secousse. Et
puis il y avait aussi une très

jolie paire de pantoufles de la
part de Betty et puis une
grande boîte de bonbons.

Le lendemain matin en me
réveillant je vis fixés sur moi
les yeux de la maman de Betty
qui dès qu'elle me vit réveillée
me dit qu'il fallait que je me
dépêche vite pour m'habiller car
on allait bientôt partir en auto
pour aller à la gare de Phi-
-ladelphie pour que je prenne le
train. Bien je partis, j'avais assez
de peine de quitter toutes ces per-
-sonnes qui avaient été si gen-
-tilles avec moi et d'un autre côté
j'étais très contente de retourner
à New York je fis un très
bon voyage et arrivée à New
York le train s'était à peine
arrêté que j'étais déjà dans
les bras de maman; j'étais

4   bien contente de la revoir car
quoique je l'avais vue une semai-
-ne avant il me semblait que
je ne l'avais pas vue depuis
six mois... je passais encore un
mois à New York c'est à dire
jusqu'à la fin de l'été ....
je vivais une vie normale pendant
ce mois et rien d'extraordinaire
n'arriva ....

Un mois après maman me dit
que bientôt nous retournerions en
France... En effet deux semaines
plus tard un soir que je commençais
à m'endormir j'entendis un grand
bruit dans le couloir c'était les
malles que deux chasseurs apportaient
Maman fit entrer toutes les malles
dans la chambre et ayant dit
merci aux chasseurs elle ferma la porte
je refermais longue mais de temps en
temps quand je les ouvrais je voyais

5

maman debout devant la malle
qui mettait des affaires dedans, enfin
je m'endormis et le lendemain
matin quand je me suis réveillé
toutes mes malles étaient faites mais
pas encore fermées car au dernier
moment on pouvait toujours avoir
besoin de mettre quelque chose. Tout
l'après-midi maman et moi nous
fîmes des courses et vers six heures
du soir maman téléphona à une
de ses amies (qui était Française)
elle s'appelait Odette Abdjoural et
elle était très gentille pour l'aider à faire les malles
Le bateau devait partir à minuit
tapant et à onze heures juste
maman me dit qu'elle avait
oublié d'acheter deux choses je
ne me rappelle plus ce que c'était
mais ce que je me rappelle c'est
qu'ayant appelé Odette je lui de
-mandai si elle voulait bien m'ac
-compagner pour faire ces courses

6 car maman ne voulait pas que je
sorte seule surtout le soir. Alors
Odette me donna une idée épatante
c'était de mettre mes patins pendant
qu'elle se préparait et elle m'entrai-
-nait dans les rues pour faire les courses.
Je trouvais cette idée très bien et
je courus vite mettre mes patins
et je partis avec Odette dès que
nous fûmes en bas Odette ôta
sa ceinture et me la donna en
me disant de surtout ne pas la
lâcher puis elle se met à courir.
Ce fut une course folle que nous
fîmes toutes les deux et en tous
cas maintenant je me rappelle encore
que je me suis beaucoup amusée.
enfin on revint avec toutes les
choses que maman avait demandé,
et nous étions revenues vers onze heu-
-res et demie et maman commen-
-çait à s'inquiéter car on aurait
pu être en retard pour le bateau.

302

7

On arriva juste à temps pour le bateau il était minuit moins dix et on dut se dépêcher maman et moi d'embrasser Colette avant de monter sur la passerelle qu'on allait bientôt lever.

Le bateau s'en va et Colette Yorka devint de plus en plus petit et enfin il disparut de l'horizon.

Nous fîmes un très bon voyage sur le "Bremen". De temps en temps j'allais à la piscine avec maman et vraiment on ne pourra pas dire que je me suis embêtée.

Bing à six jours plus tard on voyait déjà apparaître les côtes de France j'étais folle de joie et juste à penser que bientôt je serais dans les bras de ma mème cela me donnait envie de sauter et de danser en même temps

Chapitre II

Oû je peux dire que je suis heureuse

Je demandais à maman si maman nous attendait au port du Havre ou alors à la gare de Paris mais je reçus une réponse négative pour le Havre et évidemment affirmative pour Paris. J'étais un peu ennuyée que maman ne soit pas venue au Havre mais comme je savais que bientôt je la reverrais !!!!!!!!!!!!!!!!!!!!!!!!!!

Le bateau accosta au Havre et maman me dit que dans une heure nous repartirions par le train pour Paris. Une heure plus tard en effet maman et moi nous étions emportées par le train dans la direction de Paris. Le train s'arrêta et à peine j'eus à jeter un regard sur le

9

qui que je vis maman qui elle
aussi me cherchait alors je courus
à elle et me suis jetée dans
ses bras en pleurant de joie.
Le moment que je passai là dans
les bras de maman et avec
maman à côté qui nous regardait
toutes les deux avec affection
fut un moment où je n'eus
aucune ombre à mon bonheur

Chapitre III

À Paris

La rentrée des classes était le
premier Octobre et j'étais arrivée
à Paris le 20 Octobre et maman
me dit qu'il fallait que je
recommence à aller à l'école.
Avant d'aller en Amérique c'est

312

10

à dire quand j'avais sept ans
j'allais au Lycée Carnot mais
en revenant maman ne voulut
pas m'y remettre car elle trouvait
que je n'y apprenais rien du
tout alors elle me mit au cours
Yvatternier qui est un très bon cours.
En y allant je croyais que l'on me
mettrait en neuvième comme je l'avais
été en amérique mais je vis que
je ne pouvais pas rester dans cette
classe car elle était beaucoup trop
fort pour moi donc on me mit en
dixième où je [...] suivre convenablement
Notre maîtresse était madame KA-
RASICOFF elle était russe.
Nous la faisions assez enrager
mes camarades et moi mais tout
de même nous l'aimions beaucoup.
Je passais mon examen de passage
et je comptais avoir des prix mais
malheureusement juste une semaine ou
deux avant la distribution des prix

Je tombai malade . . . .
J'ai oublié de vous dire mes
chers amis que maman était partie
en Amérique à peu près trois mois
avant la distribution des prix . .

Ma maladie était assez grave c'é-
-tait des rhumatismes articulaires ai.
— que à la fin on dut appeler
maman d'Amérique parce que je
n'allais pas bien du tout alors
elle arriva et une semaine après
qu'elle était là j'étais presque
guérie . . . Enfin le docteur Florent
celui qui me soignait décida qu'il
me fallait l'air des montagnes
pour me retaper, alors maman
trouva que d'abord je pourrais aller
dans les Pyrénées avec ma cousine
et ma tante et que après j'irais
avec . . maman . . . et Odile (ma marraine)
à Luchon .

1112

Chapitre IV

à la campagne

Je partis donc pour Palermé
(là où maman avait décidé que
j'irais passer un mois,) là où
habitait la mère du père à
Odile c'est à dire sa grand' mère.
C'était une très gentille dame.
Je m'amusais énormément avec Odile
et Yesse (mutante, la soeur de maman)
enfin le jour du départ arriva...
Mais avant de vous raconter le
départ je vais vous raconter une
chose assez drôle. La grand mère
à Odile avait un poulailler et dans
ce poulailler il y avait des
poules, des oies, des canards, des
lapins, des cochons, et encore
des tas et des tas de bêtes.
et parmi ces bêtes il y avait
une mère poule et une mère

12/2

lapin qui avaient eu toutes les
deux des petits et ces petits
étaient mignons comme je ne
sais quoi alors Odile et moi
nous décidâmes que ces petits é-
-taient trop mignons et que
l'on ne pourrait pas se séparer
d'eux et qu'il fallait les
emporter mais il ne fallait
pas que ni la grand' mère
à Odile ni Jessie le voie alors
on emporterait un petit canard
et un petit lapin dans une
petite valise que Odile avait
avec de l'avoine pour le canard
et de l'herbe pour le lapin
et alors on les emmèneraient
tous les deux sans que per-
-sonne n'en sache rien et ce
n'est qu'à Suchan qui on mon-
-trerait les petites bêtes
On prépara tout dans la
petite valise et une heure

14

avant le départ nous nous
glissâmes toutes les deux dans
le pyjamillon et nous emportâ-
mes l'une du petit canard
et l'autre du petit lapin
et alors après on courut vite
toutes les deux sans que personnes nous voit dans notre
chambre et nous mîmes les
deux pauvres petites bêtes dans
la valise d'Odile et juste quand
nous aurions fini Jessie arriva
et demanda si tout était prêt
nous répondîmes toutes les douze
ensembles "oui" avec empresse-
ment et nous allâmes sur le
perron de la grille où devait
arriver dans peu de temps le
car qui nous mènerait directement à Buchanville je m'étais
chargée de la petite valise contenant le canard et le lapin
nous parlions quand tout à un

15

coin un coin coin coin coin
retentissant éclata et la petite
valise aussitôt la grand mère à
Odile qui avait une oreille
très fine dit que cela ne
venait pas du poulailler et
que cela venait tout près
d'elle (car j'étais juste
à côté d'elle), elle crut
que c'était un canard qui
s'était échappé du poulailler
et elle courait par ci et elle
courait par là; enfin une fois
qu'elle reparait près de moi
le coin coin coin retentit encore plus vibrant que la
dernière fois alors la grand'mère
à Odile dit que on dirait que
cela venait d'une des valises
et enfin cinq ou dix minutes
après elle découvrit que cela
venait de la valise à Odile
et elle me dit de l'ouvrir

5/2

16

mais moi ayant encore un petit espoir de garder le canard
et le lapin dit que dans cette
petite valise il n'y avait que les
affaires à Odile et Odile aussi
m'approuva fortement en di-
-sant qu'il n'y avait que ses
affaires à elle mais la grand
mère à Odile persuadée que son
canard était dans cette valise
me prit la valise des mains
et l'ouvrit et alors quelle ne
fut pas sa stupéfaction en
voyant non seulement un ca-
-nard mais aussi un petit
lapin âgé de à peine douze jours.
L'indignation lui coupa la parole pour
à peu près une minute et enfin éclatant
« Petites vilaines n'avez-vous pas honte de
prendre ces pauvres petites bêtes (et elle serrait
les deux animaux contre son cœur) et
d'un ton radouci à cause de nos
mines effarées, « Pourquoi donc les avez-vous pris ? »

16/2

17

Nous lui apprîmes toutes les deux (Thérèse
seulement) ce que nous allions plaire.
Gilbert n'eut pas le temps de nous
pardonner ou de nous dire le car
car il lui résonna à dix pas
de nous. Nous n'eûmes que le temps
de mettre les malles dans le car
et de lui donner un hôtel Maison
(qui n'était pas sans beaucoup d'affection)
car toutes les deux nous l'aimions énormément
et je sais que cela nous fit beaucoup de
peine de la quitter... J'ai oublié de
vous dire un inconvénient qu'il y avait
à Palimini; c'était à propos de l'eau.
il n'y avait pas d'eau courante et
toute l'eau que nous avions nous
étions forcés de la pomper de la
pompe, et quand nous voulions avoir
de l'eau chaude il fallait premièrement
aller pomper l'eau ce qui n'était pas
si facile et puis transporter cette eau
jusqu'à la maison et là il fallait
le mettre dans une grosse marmite

18   (devant le feu) et attendre une demi
heure jusqu'à ce que l'eau soit chaude
après il fallait prendre l'eau dans
la salle de bain où nous devions
nous laver dans des bassines (car
il n'y avait pas de bain) alors
vous pensez comme c'était commode !!!
Mais malgré cela nous aimions Pala-
-vini et marraine de tout notre cœur
et étaient toutes les deux pas pressées
de les quitter........

Chapitre V

Près des Pyrénées.

Donc nous quittâmes Palavini pour Luchon
Nous rencontrâmes maman à Toulouse
et de là nous partîmes tous les quatre
(maman, Jessie, Odile et moi) encore dans
un car pour Luchon . La j'en nous
avait réservé des places dans un hôtel
j'y passa 2 jours et puis maman et
j'en viendrait la chercher pour aller

19　à Biarritz (tout près de la frontière de l'Espagne) L'hôtel où jean avait réservé des places s'appelait "Le Royal" c'était un hôtel très bien et très confortable. Nous avions une très grande chambre avec une salle de bain. Dans cette chambre il y avait trois lits : Deux grands lits pour maman et moi et puis un petit lit pour Odile. ...... pour les deux ou trois jours qu'elle passerait avec nous avait une chambre à elle seule... Les deux premiers jours nous ne sortîmes pas beaucoup car nous passâmes presque tout notre temps à défaire les malles et examiner les alentours de la ville car nous ne voulions pas nous perdre !!!!! Enfin le troisième jour arriva et maman et jean arrivèrent aussi. Nous décidâmes que nous irions passer la journée de

19/2

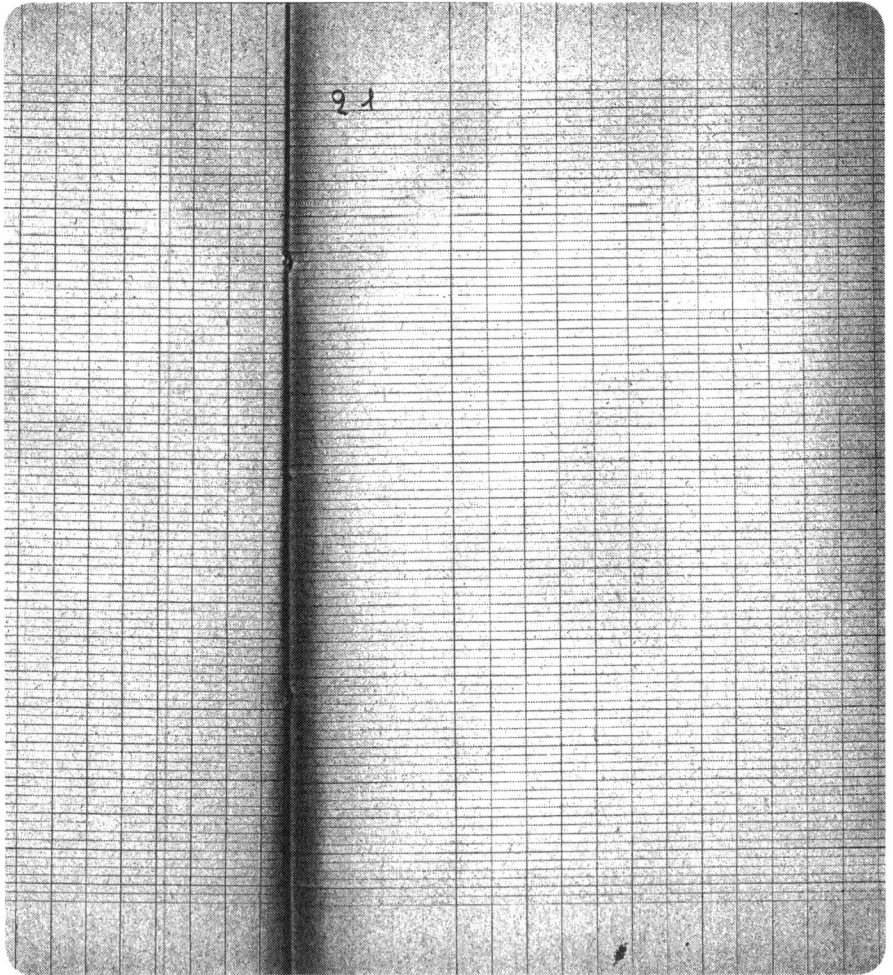

316

Mary Peatsil

My trip to America

the war troubles were beginning in
all France was excited. All the places
on the boat going to America were
reserved. My mother was at N.Y.
my grandmother in France
the first thing grandmother thought
about was to try to make me go
U.S... At the end she found a place
on an american boat the Mari...
and on I went for U.S. I was ...
sad leaving grandmother but on
the other side of the ocean it was
like if I would of see... mother...
for me..... I had to go with
-ne on that enormous boat. When
I did not know anyone. the Manha-
tan was use to carry two peoples
this time it was carrying two
like ladies and children. We could not...
cabins were sleeping all together in the the...
room there were 100 cats three w...

317

out any mattress and I knew it
was hard because I slept on one
of these. Some of the men who could
not have any cabin had to sleep too
in cots but they were sleeping in the
smoking room. I dont think they had
any mattress either. We stopped by
South Hampton the biggest part
in England and 600 passengers went
on the boat. After that we went on
to the way of Ireland where we
pick up 150 passengers, so we had
about 2750 passengers. After we left
Ireland the War declared. It was
very exciting and everybody was all
watching for submarines. We passed
an other way then the real way and
we were lucky because there were 5
submarines germans waiting for us to sink us
And at the end of 9 long days of an
-xiety we arrived at New york. Even
with the submarines I had lot of fun with
some other kids. And you
you see that they didnt sink the
Manhattan because if they did I would

ACKNOWLEDGMENTS

I want to give my thanks to Ron Holland for his editing and for his help and encouragement and to Clifford Oliver for the wonderful photographic work he did for this book and to Jeff Hecita of Xlibris.

My thanks also to my daughter Mary and to my son Marc, for the research they did.

And, last but not least, to my husband for being so patient with me these last two years—a patience that drove him almost to the point of exasperation until, in self-defense, he started writing his own memoirs.